Surviving White Island

Surviving White Island
Kelsey Waghorn

HarperCollins*Publishers*

A note on the history of names for Whakaari/White Island
The official name for the volcanic island was changed in 1997 to Whakaari/White Island. The full, original Māori name for the island is Te Puia o Whakaari ('The Dramatic Volcano'). It was later named White Island by Captain Cook when he sailed past in 1769, although he never set foot on the island. The author acknowledges the official name Whakaari/White Island but has referred to it as 'White Island' or 'the island' throughout the book as this is the name she was familiar with growing up.

Source: Bay of Plenty Regional Council and GeoNet. www.boprc.govt.nz/environment/geothermal/geothermal-systems/whakaari-white-island-group-1/ and www.geonet.org.nz/about/volcano/whiteisland

HarperCollins*Publishers*
Australia • Brazil • Canada • France • Germany • India • Italy • Japan
Mexico • Netherlands • New Zealand • Poland • Spain • Sweden
Switzerland • United Kingdom • United States of America

First published in 2026
by HarperCollins*Publishers* (New Zealand) Limited
Unit D1, 63 Apollo Drive, Rosedale, Auckland 0632, New Zealand
harpercollins.co.nz

Copyright © Kelsey Waghorn 2026

The right of Kelsey Waghorn to be identified as the author of this work has been asserted by her with the *Copyright Act 1994*.

All rights reserved. Apart from any use as permitted under the *Copyright Act 1994*, no part may be reproduced, copied, scanned, stored in a retrieval system, recorded, or transmitted, in any form or by any means, without the prior written permission of the publisher. Without limiting the exclusive rights of any author, contributor, or the publisher of this publication, any unauthorised use of this publication to train generative artificial intelligence (AI) technologies is expressly prohibited. HarperCollins also exercises its rights under Article 4(3) of the Digital Single Market Directive 2019/790 and expressly reserves this publication from the text and data-mining exception.

HarperCollins*Publishers*
Macken House, 39/40 Mayor Street Upper
Dublin 1, D01 C9W8, Ireland

A catalogue record for this book is available from the National Library of New Zealand
Kei te pātengi raraunga o Te Puna Mātauranga o Aotearoa te whakarārangi o tēnei pukapuka

ISBN 978 1 7755 4291 9 (paperback)
ISBN 978 1 7754 9322 8 (ebook)
ISBN 978 1 0381 0311 6 (audiobook)

Cover design by HarperCollins Design Studio
Front cover image © Eilish Burt Photography
Back cover image by NZME
Typeset in Bembo MT Pro by Kelli Lonergan

Printed and bound by CPI Group (UK) Ltd, Croydon, CR0 4YY

Contents

Preface   1

Part I
Chapter 1: Sea time   7
Chapter 2: The island   20
Chapter 3: River   31
Chapter 4: Unsurvivable   40
Chapter 5: Nothing   58

Part II
Critical care   63

Part III
Chapter 6: Mayday   215
Chapter 7: The teething period   225
Chapter 8: You thought that was bad?   244
Chapter 9: Ameliorate   261
Chapter 10: Taking off the training wheels   283
Chapter 11: Unfuckwithable   293

Acknowledgements   304
Where to get help   312

Preface

I am coming to you 'live' from the jungles of Borneo.

It took close to five years before I finally agreed to write this book, and then I opted to do it in a ridiculously tight six-month timeframe. I also had to inform my *very* patient publisher that, while I'd definitely get it done, I also happened to have a couple of trips planned at the same time: nine days in Borneo followed by, a month later, nine days in China. Then I went and crammed even more trips into that small window of time, because that is my current season of life: catching up on lost time, and saying yes to all the wild and incredible opportunities that come my way. So I lost about five weeks to travel, then I lost still more days and weeks to work (and life). Ya girl loves a tight deadline.

During this trip, I have been thinking about how I got here.

Here, as in Borneo.

Here, as in writing a book.

Here, as in life.

I never thought I would agree to put the story of my experience of the 2019 eruption of White Island in writing. I was terrified of what others might think, and that the other people involved in some of my stories might remember things differently or call me a liar.

Before the eruption, I rarely cared what others thought about me. I always marched to the beat of my own drum. Insecurity and fear were foreign beasts. But things change. *You* change, when you're in the trenches of a major trauma.

As time wore on – as I healed with the right help, and became stronger and more confident; as the constant, throbbing fear subsided and I began reclaiming my life – I started having more conversations about healing from the unhealable, about surviving the unsurvivable.

I want to preface this book by stating that I am not special.

I am not immune to pain.

I do not have an iron will.

Before all this happened, I would never have believed that I could have got through what I have been through. Hell, there have been *many* times where I've been sure that I wasn't going to make it, that *this was it*.

I also want to preface this book by stating the obvious: this book is written entirely from *my* point of view. These are *my* stories, from *me*, pulled from *my* memory, which is as wild and chaotic as the stories themselves.

I also want to acknowledge that there are parts of this story that are not mine alone. This was another factor that delayed the writing of this book – I was desperate not to upset anyone or reveal anything that others involved didn't know about in such a public way.

I am sure others will remember things differently, and that

some parts of this story could be told other ways, because there are many sides to every story. But this is *my* recollection.

I've been deemed a bad omen. Maybe I even need to have the curse on me lifted, but through this book I want to show you one important thing: life gets infinitely better if you keep trying.

Kelsey
April 2025

P.S. I hope you like footnotes.

Part I

Chapter 1

Sea time

I never intended to be on a volcano; that was not the end goal. It was always the ocean I loved.

I was born around 7.30pm on 12 April 1994, in Palmerston North Hospital. The horoscope app Co-Star reckons that makes me 'assertive, persistent, courageous, competitive, fiercely independent, deeply loyal', someone who will 'push things forward with energy and enthusiasm, and persevere through anything'. Pretty bang-on, honestly.

Growing up, I was never super-outdoorsy and I disliked being uncomfortable. PE was never my favourite subject, nor one I ever did very well in – mostly due to a lack of effort. I think I passed, but probably only by the skin of my teeth. I did do quite a bit of swimming when I was younger, but my coaches wanted me to start competing, and I never had the desire to do that. I enjoyed rowing in high school, but pulled out after our coaches became more competitive than the actual rowers in the boat.

Towards the end of my primary school years, my dad bought a business in Whakatāne, so the family was packed up and shipped up the country. I attended Whakatāne High School, and it took me until about the last two months of my time there to work out what I wanted to do with my life – and, even then, I only had the loosest grasp on it. In my later school years, I chose to take marine studies – better than maths or English in my opinion.[1] Not only did I get to learn how to scuba dive and dissect the otoliths (ear bones) of fish, but there was a Year 13 trip to the Great Barrier Reef. We had to leave our final-year school ball early, still all dolled up, to head to Auckland Airport in a minivan.

The trip itself was just over a week long, and on it I saw my first sharks while diving, my first manta ray, even my first humpback whales. Between the charismatic megafauna and the brilliance of the reef and all its weird (and sometimes aggressive) reef fish, that was enough to settle it: I wanted to do something in the marine field. A classic nineties-kid's dream.

My wonderful teacher, Fergie, helped me narrow down the tertiary marine science courses available in New Zealand, and I ended up picking the one that he said had the most practical work. Conveniently, it was based in Tauranga, which is only an hour west, meaning I could still be close to my family. So off I went to do my diploma in marine science.

I'll admit there was a lot more theory than I had envisioned, but all the diving and field trips and Dr Seuss readings (*The Lorax*, presumably for its conservation message) helped to even things out. Some of the diving was amazing, like when we got to enjoy the warm waters, ever-changing weather and delightful tropical marine species[2] of Lissenung and the islands surrounding

---

1 I first wrote 'Engligh' here, so perhaps I should have stuck with English after all.
2 Excluding those aggressive little bastard triggerfish that try to bite you all the time, making every dive rather edgy. You could tell one was near by the screaming of your classmates underwater.

it in Papua New Guinea. But some of the diving was ... colder. Such as beginning a dive on the bow of a boat on a grey, windy winter day and struggling into a cold, damp wetsuit, only to jump into 10°C waters to do a scallop survey somewhere off the Coromandel. (Picture hanging out on the seabed – stationary in the water, while your dive buddy circles you on the end of a rope, counting scallops. *Freezing*.)

After three years, at the end of 2014 I graduated with a Diploma in Marine Science and a Bachelor of Science majoring in biological sciences. I briefly weighed up the idea of doing my Master's, but my final year of study had been fraught with issues including a weird break-up and battles with online learning, so I opted to ditch study. I just wanted to be on the ocean, so I decided I'd get a job on a boat. Surely work experience would be beneficial alongside my paperwork, anyway.

I moved back to Whakatāne, and booked a trip to Perth in Western Australia for my cousin Ashleigh's twenty-first. *I'll mosey up to Ningaloo to ask for a job on their whale-shark boats*, I thought. So naive. Turned out that 'mosey' would have been a fifteen-hour drive north. That wasn't going to happen.

Then, a few days before I flew out to Perth, I got a call from Dad.

'There are jobs going on the White Island boats,' he said, 'taking tourists around the volcano.'

Showing tourists a bunch of rocks? Nah. I almost dismissed it ... but my only other option for local boat-work was commercial fishing, and that was not my jam. What did I have to lose? I sent through my CV, and within a few hours was on the phone to Paul, the Sea Operations Manager at White Island Tours. He asked me to come in for an interview, and we spent most of it comparing the places we'd been diving. At the end, he mentioned that there was a second part of the interview.

'Oh yeah, what's that?'

'You will head out for the day on one of the boats, as a passenger, just to watch the whole process from start to finish. You know – to see whether it's the job for you.'

Now that I have done over eight hundred trips to White Island, I don't specifically remember that one tour, but I do remember getting back to the wharf in Whakatāne because I was handed a contract. 'The job's yours if you want it,' Paul said. 'You can start when you're back from Aus.'

Well, how could a girl say no to spending her summer on the sea, when that was all she really wanted? I figured it was the perfect interim solution. It'd give me time on boats and help me get my sea hours up, then I could go off and get a 'real job'.

After a debaucherous week celebrating my cousin's twenty-first, I started coming down with some gross Australian lurgy. On the day I was due to fly home, I got an email from Paul: *Could you please start on the eighth of December?* That was … the next day. Which also happened to be my sister's birthday. I didn't want to turn down my new boss, so I said yes. *I'll just load up on cold and flu medicine*, I told myself. *All I have to do is make it through my first week.*

My new job was really a twofer: boat crew *and* tour guide. A job on a boat with a side helping of volcano.[3] That meant I had twice as much to learn. As boat crew, I had to know about the different boats we ran, the marine life we were likely (or unlikely) to encounter (no problem there), the talks to deliver to guests en route to the island, and just be generally seaworthy

---

[3] That's how I saw it, anyway – the company probably saw things the other way round.

(no problem there, either). To be a tour guide, I had to learn about the volcanology, geology and eruptive history of the island, as well as its sulphur-mining history and the small amount of wildlife that resided on and around it. Let's just say it's a bit hard to study when you're on a trip for a twenty-first. Harder still when you find half the content boring as *hellllllll*. But, thankfully, I survived that first week on the job – both the lurgy and the onslaught of information.

Then, just before Christmas, we were treated to an overnighter. We were scheduled to meet a cruise ship at the island early in the morning, and it was easier to make the hour-and-a-bit journey out there the night before and stay on the boats than to make an earlier-than-early trip out.

It was dark when we moored in south-east facing Crater Bay, so the deck lights were switched on and the crew began catching flying fish to use as bait for sailfish in the morning. I woke at four the next morning to discover we were already cruising along and, when I emerged on the deck, found that the fishing had already begun – they were doing it *before* the 8am tour. I went back to bed.

Over the next month, I well and truly got what I came for. Marine life en masse. Pods of long-finned pilot whales, bottlenose dolphins, sharks, many kinds of fish – you name it, I saw it.

This was going to be an epic summer.

Summer turned into winter, and I was still working there. Then summer rolled around again, and the idea of getting a 'real job' just seemed to keep getting pushed out. And that kept happening … for the next five years.

It was the ocean that had first drawn me to the job, and it's what held me there. My weird and unique position presented plenty of wicked opportunities. On a handful of occasions, I got to go on a ship survey trip – essentially the 'warrant of fitness' of the boating world. These trips usually happened in winter, which was our off season. Most of these trips took us just along the coast to Tauranga, and on one memorable occasion when it was just me and the skipper on board I got to see my first pod of orca. On another trip up to Warkworth, north of Auckland, Paul and I got to see blue whales in the Hauraki Gulf – and I am talking *many* blue whales, not just one or two.

White Island Tours had been running for about thirty years at this point and it had run thousands of incredibly successful tours – epic days at sea, clear main crater views, bucket lists ticked, social media photos snapped. It ran like a well-oiled machine, and there were scarcely any serious incidents – most were due to people tripping over or medical events. Working frequently in 'big nature', however, sometimes things do go wrong.

One dreary, grey, windy, rainy morning in January 2016 – during my second summer working for White Island Tours – the crew stood on the wharf and decided that the day's tour would probably be cancelled, even though we already had passengers waiting on *PeeJay V*. Then our skipper, David, bounded over the wall between the wharf and carpark and let us know that we were, in fact, still going. Several passengers had then decided that they weren't going to come, so our numbers dropped to fifty-three, but due to the conditions we were expecting on the way out to White Island, we kept all six crew onboard, rather than sending two home as we normally would.

As expected, the trip out was rough. We ploughed into, over and through the oncoming white-capped grey swell, and although our crew had been out in worse, most of the passengers certainly hadn't. Fortunately, the hour-long walking tour of the island's inner crater provided a much-needed break for those who weren't so sea-savvy.

Before we returned to the mainland, we pulled around to the southern side of the island, out of the wind and persistent rolling swell, so passengers and crew alike could eat their lunch in calmer waters. As we neared our anchoring point, I went onto the bow to speak to my colleague, Hayden.

'Hey,' I said, 'it's been a while since I've put down the anchor. Could you take me through it again?'

Always keen to teach others, Hayden jumped at the opportunity to give me a refresher. He'd been working for White Island Tours for years, and was the one who had originally trained me when I first started. Now he ran me through how to deploy and retrieve the anchor – an easy enough feat, but it was good to go over it again and remind myself of the process, despite the fact we preferred to use the three moorings in the bay to reduce our impact on the seabed.

The trip home was lumpy, as the wind hadn't let up much, but at least we were going with the swell now, and surfing towards home – a motion that more stomachs seemed to tolerate. At last, we neared the narrow, rocky Whakatāne River entrance, and a collective sigh of relief came from those who were well and truly over their day at sea.

Then I sniffed the air. Something smelt … hot. A couple of other crew members had clearly noticed the same thing. Where was it coming from? The oven that some of the crew had used at the island to cook some mussels, maybe? We went to investigate. No, not the oven – no noticeable heat or smell there. We walked around the cabin trying to pinpoint the source of the smell, getting strange looks from the passengers – still sniffing, still no success.

'I'm going up to the helm to let David know,' I said. When I informed our skipper that something smelt hot, he checked all of his gauges. Nothing. He turned to the Sea Operations Assistant who was in the helm with him. 'Mata, go back downstairs with Kelsey and have a look in the engine room.'

The moment we got to the bottom of the staircase, I could see the source of the smell. In the brief second before I shot back upstairs, I saw Hayden in the galley. Both of us stared at the dirty, dark-grey smoke billowing out from behind the fridge and freezer.

The following five minutes are rather patchy in my memory – as I would learn in the years to come, in these kinds of situations the brain drops into 'survival mode' and it doesn't bother to hold on to every minute detail of what happened – and rightly so. I do remember running back up the stairs yelling to David, then next thing I was outside.[4]

The lifejackets were easily accessible and plentiful in the main cabins, but those areas were filling with smoke so rapidly there was no time to grab enough of them for all the passengers. I shimmied through the crowd on the side decks to the helm.

---

4 I was later told I helped passengers get outside before going out myself, but I have no recollection of this.

'Where do you want me?' I asked David, an alarm on the dash now sounding. *No shit!*

'Put the anchor down so we don't drift.' The engines were now off.

A smile spread across my face. *Thanks, universe.*

I made my way to the starboard side, where a ladder ran down the outside of the boat from the top to the lower deck. Let's just say that if you and the ladder you're trying to descend are damp from rain and saltwater spray, and the boat you're on is bouncing around in wind-generated slop, you quickly discover that something that is ordinarily quite easy has become rather difficult. Thankfully, I made it to the lower deck, then went up to the bow.

All of the passengers from the lower deck had congregated here, out of the reach of the thick, black smoke rolling out of the back of the boat. I could see an occasional flame licking out of the darkness.

Just like I had done with Hayden an hour or so earlier, I grabbed the release bar from one of the front hatches, took off the safety rope and released the anchor winch. I don't know how many metres of chain I let out, but I let it run until David signalled me to stop.

Now that we were anchored about 1 kilometre off the river entrance and not free-floating with the current, my attention turned to the passengers. Some were calm, but most had their eyes wide with fear.

An inflatable boat was stowed in the rear of *PeeJay V*, and Hayden and Mata soon launched it and came up the side of the boat. From the inflatable, Hayden asked me and Josh, another crew member, to count the passengers on the lower deck, and the two crew upstairs to count the passengers on the upper deck. 'We need to make sure we've got everyone out,' he said. Fortunately, we had.

Flames were more visible now. Looking down the side of the boat, I could see them consistently rising from the aft deck. They were also starting to shoot out of the engine-room air vents.

I remember looking up and seeing our sister vessel, *PeeJay IV*, barrelling down the river and heading in our direction. It hit the swell on the river entrance in what seemed like slow motion, sending saltwater flying into the air before skating down the back side, ready to hit the next wave. *The cavalry was coming.* It was an impressive sight, and I laughed at the absurdity of the whole debacle.

Within a few minutes, several other local vessels had also appeared around our burning boat. Paul deployed *PeeJay IV*'s inflatable, so we had two little black boats shooting around us, ready for what was to come. It was becoming increasingly clear that there was no saving *PeeJay V*, and David gave the command to abandon ship.

I turned back to the passengers on the bow. 'All right, guys,' I said. 'Bad news is, we will be jumping off the boat. Good news is, we have two of the most experienced inflatable-boat drivers waiting down there to pick you up straight away. Who's first?'

Some passengers couldn't get off the boat fast enough, but others were clearly uneasy about having to jump into the ocean from the bow of a rolling boat, a couple of metres above the churning water. Some said they couldn't swim. 'Okay, who can float on their back?' I asked, my years of swim practice kicking in. Some said yes. The others? I made sure they got a lifejacket before they jumped in. A couple of passengers were literally sick with stress, and a few asked me to head back into the smoke-filled cabin to fetch items like their passports and car keys. *Yeah, not happening, doll.*

The crew on the upper deck began helping passengers to climb up over the rail and jump into the sea below. Once a passenger had hit the water and resurfaced, one of the inflatables would come in to pick them up, then reverse away again to create space for the next person to jump. Once there were several people in an inflatable, it would take off to one of the waiting vessels, drop off the passengers, then return to start over again.

A younger passenger who had jumped in with his father surfaced and started screaming. It was *blood-curdling*. I asked Josh to jump in and help them, and I was left alone with the remaining passengers on the bow.

Once the two crew on the upper deck had got all their passengers off, they then jumped into the water themselves. David managed to make it down the starboard ladder onto the lower deck to join me. Around this time, I started to notice that the deck was becoming warm and starting to flex under my bare feet. I could hear the cabin windows smashing as the flames grew hotter and closer, and the smoke billowing out the back of the boat was thick and black. *Time to go.*

The only passengers left were those who were the most reluctant to jump.

'I need some more lifejackets,' I called to Josh and Paul. After a quick trip to a waiting vessel, they came back with a stash of bright orange foam. Josh frisbeed a jacket up with all his might – and it went right over the top of the boat. I looked at Josh. He threw a second one. It went straight through a smashed window and into the fire. *Comical.* Finally, Josh got his eye in, and with a little encouragement and a lot of oomph, David and I helped the last of the lifejacketed passengers jump into the water below.

Only David and I remained, and there was just one lifejacket left. I told David to take it, knowing I was a confident and strong swimmer. After some back and forth about who would wear it, he forced the lifejacket onto me. 'The skipper leaves last,' he said as I climbed up onto the rail.

I jumped, without him.

It was the middle of summer, so the water was warm, and for a brief moment under the water it was peaceful. When I surfaced, Paul's inflatable came racing in to get me. Josh hauled me up and over the pontoons, into the bottom of the boat. Somewhere behind me, David swan-dived off the bow into the sea, and was collected by the other inflatable. I was dropped on the back of *PeeJay IV* and went straight into the cabin to help the passengers with sick bags and bottles of water.

I never looked back at *PeeJay V*.

After showering, fully clothed with a rum and coke in hand, I learnt that *PeeJay V* ended up burning to the waterline and disappearing into the Pacific Ocean. All fifty-three passengers and six crew plus our skipper made it safely back to shore, with only a handful requiring medical treatment for fairly minor injuries. There was an official investigation, but it didn't establish the precise cause of the fire because the boat wasn't ever recovered – other than the pieces that washed up on the beaches over the coming weeks thanks to that very same swell that had made everyone sick.

I had a couple of weeks off after the fire. My first day back was tough – I was shaky the whole day. I was grateful for the distraction of a super-pod of common dolphin that raced alongside our boat – trusty *PeeJay IV* – as we steamed towards home on that bright blue day.

I didn't realise until we'd made it back into the river entrance after our day at sea, but I had been holding my breath for most of the day on the boat, and only finally felt safe to breathe normally once we were within the river. It took a while for that feeling to leave, and I would still catch myself exhaling wholly once on the river after a day at sea, even three years later.

Chapter 2

The island

My favourite part of my job was (no surprise here) being on the boat. I learnt the bare minimum about White Island itself, swatting up on volcanology only when I had to. If a passenger asked a question I didn't know the answer to, I'd go and find out, and store the knowledge away for next time someone asked the same thing.

Sometimes we had scientists come out on the boats, either to study the island or just to see it,[5] and I'd pick their brains. Other times people who had personal connections to the island would turn up. One fairly drab day, while we were setting up, I got talking to an older gentleman who wanted to go out to the island but couldn't come on the boats due to his lack of mobility. He told me that one night back in 1914, his grandfather had been at the local pub when he was offered a job working in the sulphur mine that was running on the island at the time. He turned the job down, and a few days later – when all the new recruits were at work – a collapse in the crater wall caused a lahar to swallow the workers' camp. Ten miners died, and the sole survivor was a

5 Being relatively easy to access and rather lively, she drew quite the crowd.

cat called Peter, who earned the nickname Peter the Great. The man on the wharf wanted to see the island that could have taken his grandfather's life, and prevented his.

'Well, there's the option to fly out on a helicopter,' I told him. 'That way you can see everything, including the remains of the mine, without having to move a muscle.' I don't know if he ever made it out there.

It was a couple of years before I got my own opportunity to head out to the island in a helicopter. We were going out with a film crew, something that was always a combo of fun and boring: fun because you got to see the behind-the-scenes stuff of filming, get creative to find the best backdrops, and spend a lot of time on the island, really soaking it up; boring because, once the crew found their spot, you could be there a *very* long time. This particular trip was no different. The crew were using a drone to film around the crater, so they stayed in one spot for the whole day – ideal for them, given the amount of gear they had, but *horrifically* boring for me as their guide.

Once the day's filming was finally done, and loads of gear and the film crew were being shuttled off the island, I was left out there with the drone pilot to be collected in the last load. As the second-to-last trip back to the mainland left the island and the hum of the engine faded with distance, the drone pilot asked if we could go up to the main crater for a look.

'Absolutely!' My body desperately needed to move. After a quick power-walk, we were standing at the main crater's edge. He got a few shots, then we raced back to our pick-up spot and hopped in the chopper.

'This is my first time out here in a heli,' I told the pilot as he took off.

'Well, in that case, I'd better give you the full monty,' he said, and proceeded to fly us right round the island. It was *so* cool. The sun was setting and the colours were stunning, cast around the inner crater walls in a way I'd never seen before. Then, to top it all off, he spun the chopper into the crater and over the main crater lake. It was unreal. Seeing the island from the air like this gave me a much greater appreciation of its overall landscape.[6]

Being a live volcano, White Island is a place where things are always changing: the gas output, the colour of the crater lake, the colours of the island itself, and even the layout would change after eruptions or landslides. Seeing all these changes, I began to understand that the volcanic processes driving them were actually pretty interesting. I just needed to be able to see it all for myself, rather than read about it in books.

Oh, I realised, *maybe this isn't so lame.*

Taking tours out to White Island required a whole process. Before the guests arrived we'd set the boat up: washing the windows, making sure it was clean and tidy, checking we had all the stores we'd need, including cleaning products, face cloths and sickbags for passengers who might get seasick, lollies for the island,[7] and lunches for everyone. We had to check the inflatable boat stowed on the back, making sure it had fuel in it and that the pontoons were pumped up.

While we waited for everyone to turn up, the crew would have a meeting to talk about weather and sea conditions, and what the island was doing. Back then, the Crown Institute of

---

6 And incredible photos and bragging rights.
7 We'd give these out before reaching the steamiest parts of the islands – they helped with the tickle the steam could cause at the back of your throat.

Geological and Nuclear Sciences (GNS) (now Earth Sciences New Zealand) had three cameras set up on the island and one back on the mainland to monitor its volcanic activity, with images uploaded to the GNS website every ten minutes. There were also two sensors on the island that measured seismic activity, which were updated online every five minutes. We had access to all that information, and the staff and skippers would check the latest GNS updates before leaving Whakatāne. Sometimes another boat – whether one of ours or a local fishing vessel – would have headed out towards the island earlier in the morning, so we'd get updates from them too, but we always checked the sensors and the cameras on the island before leaving port. It was good to get a gauge on what you were going out to.

The trip out to the island usually took around an hour to an hour and a half, depending on which boat you were on and the sea state. On the way out I would talk about local landmarks, such as the statue of Wairaka at the Whakatāne River entrance and Moutohorā Whale Island – a whaling station turned sulphur venture, turned paddock, turned bird sanctuary.[8] From there, it was mostly keeping an eye out for marine life and chatting to the passengers.

On glassy-calm days, we would lounge and chat and have a splendid sunbathing cruise that no one wanted to end. The other end of the spectrum were the white-knuckle days. Our maximum sea state was a 3-metre swell – but the sea does whatever it likes, and sometimes we would find ourselves being thrown around by seas a bit bigger than that if conditions changed while we were already out there. But those were the days I loved. Moving

---

8 Apparently Sylvester Stallone tried to buy it at some point to build a fishing lodge or casino.

around the boat was kind of like being in a pinball machine – and I was the pinball. I'd go home worn out, covered in bruises, with my ginger hair full of salt. On these days, trying to help passengers move around was hard work – as they desperately tried to get wherever they were going, you could easily end up with a hand-shaped bruise on your arm. That was if they asked (or waited) for your assistance in the first place.

The skipper would try to make the trip as tolerable as possible by adjusting speed or course, but at the end of the day there was only so much we could do to combat the power of the open ocean. We took what we were given, or, if it was really bad, we turned around and went home.

As we approached White Island, I'd share some information about it with the passengers. It's commonly referred to as Whakaari/White Island, a combination of the abbreviated Māori name Te Puia o Whakaari (which is supposed to mean 'the dramatic volcano' – or a few other things, depending on who you ask) and the English name Captain James Cook gave it when he sailed past in 1769. It's currently New Zealand's most active volcano,[9] and lies at the northern end of the Taupō Volcanic Zone, an active area around 350 kilometres long and 100 kilometres wide. It's a *very* active area, with three of its volcanoes erupting frequently: White Island, Ruapehu and Tongariro/Ngauruhoe.

White Island is a cone volcano, meaning that over at least the last 150,000 years each eruption has left a layer of material that's continually built up, creating the cone-shaped structure you can see today. The bulk of White Island is actually underwater, and what you can see from a boat or a plane is only around a third of the whole volcano. A handful of attempts were made to mine

9 Prior to the 1980s, this title was held by Ngauruhoe, on the Central Plateau.

sulphur from White Island between 1885 and the 1920s, but all were fraught with bad luck, and the island was sold in 1933 to the family that still owns it today. In the 1950s, after it was placed in a family trust and declared a private scenic reserve, the island became the focus of tourism and ecological and geological research.

When we were around 9 kilometres from the island itself, it was time to go around and hand out inflatable lifejackets, helmets and gas masks to all of the passengers. The lifejackets were for getting to and from the island in the inflatables; once people were on the island, they could take the jackets off and do the tour with just their helmets and masks.

Once we were moored in the bay, getting everyone across to the island didn't typically take long, but it depended greatly on the swell coming into the bay, the size of the group, the mobility of the group, and the group's ability to follow instructions – sometimes this was hampered by a language barrier, sometimes it was just 'tourist brain'.

On the island, each group would go off with their guides for a safety briefing. The guide-to-passenger ratio depended on the Volcanic Activity Level, which was set by GNS – the higher the level, the lower the numbers of passengers per crew member. Alert Level 2 was riskier than Alert Level 1, for example, and I made sure our tourists knew that too, but, in my mind, it was a bit like driving to work every morning. You know that if you get in your car, you're putting yourself at risk of being in an accident, but you still get in the car. Or on the bike. Or on the plane. Knowing you're at risk and actually *believing* an accident will happen are two different things. Everyone has their own level of 'acceptable risk', and if you worried about all the ways you could get hurt you'd never leave your house.

Normally, I'd start by asking how everyone's English was – people from all over the world came to White Island, so it was important to make sure that at least the majority of the group understood what I was saying. Next came the reminder to keep their helmets on at all times, and instructions for the use of the gas masks – while the helmets had to be worn the entire time we were on the island, the gas masks could be taken on and off throughout the tour, depending on the comfort of the individual in the acidic steam.

Then I'd talk about the things that might become a safety issue. 'Right,' I'd say. 'Hazards. We've got three major ones out here. The first, and least likely, is an eruption. See where all that steam's coming from?' I'd direct everyone's gaze up towards the main crater. It was usually hard to miss the column of bright, off-white steam roaring up into the sky. 'If there *is* an eruption, that's where it's most likely going to come from. If that happens, put your gas mask on straight away so you don't breathe in any ash or gases. Then seek shelter behind anything you can find that's bigger than you are.' I'd point out the big mounds of rocks around the place, the stream beds, the walls of the old sulphur factory. 'Protect your head and neck. And as soon as we can, we will get you guys off the island and get out of here.'

The second hazard I covered was landslides, as there are a lot of sheer rock faces on the island. 'If a landslide happens, get out of the way. Go left or right of it. *Do not try to outrun it.* Once it's over, if it is safe to carry on, then we will. If it's not, we'll head back to the boat for lunch.'

The final hazard I'd mention was the track we would be using, which was rocky and uneven, and had a tendency to grab even the most sure-footed traveller. 'Watch where you're walking, stay between the guides and don't wander off.' It was important to keep groups close together, to ensure they were always on the track and, in case anything happened, to make sure everyone was safe.

Cellphone service was basically non-existent out on the island: you could get a patchy signal in some places, but for the most part phones were useless for communication. Instead, every guide on the island had a VHF radio, the skipper had the boat radio, and we'd all be on the same channel. Radio coverage was good all over the island, so you could contact the skipper from pretty much anywhere, plus the guides were always in sight of each other and communicating. That said, I had never had much issue communicating even without the radio ... there had been several mentions over the years that I would have made a good Sergeant Major: loud, firm, direct, bossy. The 'Foghorn Waghorn' trait had certainly found its way into my voice-box.

Along the tour, I'd make several stops to point out interesting features and give the guests plenty of photo opportunities. At one stop, I'd show them some of the seismic monitoring equipment on the island, and explain how the cameras, sensors and microphones worked and how the data from them was used. Another stop was at a big, sulphur-encrusted steam vent.

'This is what the GNS scientists call Fumarole Zero,' I'd say. 'The gases coming out of this fumarole have been recorded at temperatures between 100 and 300 degrees Celsius. As the sulphur in the gas begins to cool, it can crystallise, drop out of the gas and stack up on itself to form these sulphurous vents, or fumaroles.'

I'd stay there long enough for people to get some photos, then move on to the sulphur chimneys, which were smaller and skinnier. Just like Fumarole Zero, the sulphurous gases that came out of these chimneys smelt almost citrusy and felt acidic when they hit your nose. Your breath would catch in your throat, your eyes would water, and usually a few people would start coughing. This tended to be the area in which most of the gas masks would go on, or where people would ask for more lollies.

The centre of White Island is like a big amphitheatre, which we referred to as 'the crater'. The sheer rock walls of the crater, which dominate the island, reach a maximum height of 321 metres above sea level. There are three openings in these walls to the sea on the eastern and southeastern sides of the island: Sharks Bay, Wilsons Bay and the bay where we predominantly used to land, Crater Bay, which is the largest and most accessible. The rocky surface of the island varies in colour, depending on the chemical makeup of the magma that has been erupted, and how it has reacted with geothermal water and gases – a lot of the rocks are rich in iron, and therefore red in colour.

As groups of visitors walked around the inside of the crater, they could hear the dull rush of gases leaving the earth. On a rough sea day, we'd also be treated to the thrum of the waves breaking against the rocky exterior of the island. We could always smell the sulphurous gases being emitted from steam vents, and usually we took them home with us, too, as they seemed to weave themselves into the fibres of our clothes. On many occasions, this caused people to think something was on fire when I ventured into a shop after work.

The amazing sights never seemed to get old. It probably helped that the island changed regularly. Fissures would open and close. Fumaroles would collapse and new ones would begin forming in their place. Landslides would change the landscape and sometimes treat us to a new path. Water on the island would change colour with different mineral deposits. Sometimes the way gas would leave the earth created an almost heartbeat-like noise. It was a forever-changing environment that felt like it was alive.

As we walked up the small hill to the main crater, the grandeur of the main event would slowly reveal itself. There was nothing quite like it – there would be gasps and *wows* from behind you as passengers saw the 'guts' of White Island for the first time. Much to the horror of those who wanted to take lots of pictures, I'd make sure my group hung a couple of metres back from the edge of the main crater, to make sure it didn't collapse. At Alert Level 2, we were restricted to spending just five minutes up at the main crater, from when the first guide got up there until the tail-end guide left, so there wasn't time for mucking around.

The crater lake would change colour depending on its temperature and mineral composition, and any deposits coming from the vents under and around the area. The main vent, at the far end of the lake, would gush away in the background, sometimes treating us to a geyser – one time the violence of its emissions sounded like someone slamming a metal gate, and we could hear it from the wharf. Occasionally, if the wind was coming from the west, it would roll the steam back down across the back crater lip, blowing the steam straight in your face, and we would see nothing. The unpredictability was the beauty of it – unless you'd paid to see it, maybe.

When a lot of people think of volcanic eruptions, they think of flowing rivers of lava, like you see in Hawaii – but that's not the kind of eruption that White Island tends to have. Due to the level of silica in the magma (among other things), White Island is more explosive than the likes of the volcanoes in Hawaii – so, rather than producing beautiful rivers of lava that you usually have time to move away from, White Island tends to have sudden, violent eruptions. It'll throw lava bombs and blocks, generate massive columns of ash and gas, which rise above the island on calm days, and it's been known to have pyroclastic surges – fast-moving, ground-level flows of hot gas and volcanic debris. Lots of visitors found that fascinating, because they didn't know that there were different types of volcanoes and different kinds of eruptions. Some were disappointed, and just wanted to see lava.

'You *definitely* don't want to be here for an eruption,' I'd say. 'This volcano can throw balls of magma at you, and you're not going to be able to just step aside and watch them go past. You don't want to be here when that happens, 'cos you probably won't get off.'

Chapter 3

River

I've never liked birds,[10] and even though I appreciate trees and foliage and all the solid work they put into keeping us air-sucking species alive, for me, they have nothing on the ocean.[11] While working at White Island Tours, I wanted nothing to do with Whale Island, the pest-free sanctuary off Whakatāne to which the company also took visitors. Remember how I wanted to spend as much time on boats as possible? Well, compare White Island's one-and-a-half-ish-hour boat ride with Whale Island's twenty-minute trip, and I'm sure you can see why I wasn't interested. But once I reached my fourth year, I could no longer fight it. I *had to* learn how to take the tour, so, begrudgingly, I did.[12]

On one particularly nondescript day in early April 2019, I was assigned to take a party of around eighteen out to Whale

---

10 Unless you count birds of prey … which kill other birds. And parrots, for obvious reasons.

11 Both in terms of my general enjoyment, and oxygen production.

12 And I do have to say, one day when I was 'sentenced' to Whale Island duty, I saw a young humpback whale near the island, and got the most amazing photos of its tail flukes against the backdrop of White Island. So that time it was worth it.

Island with one other guide. Nine were over sixty years old, and the rest were over fifty – Whale Island was considerably more accommodating of older and younger guests than White Island, with more options of where to go and how long they could stay.

After the short cruise down the Whakatāne River, we headed out to the island itself, telling the passengers about the island's history and the conservation efforts that have made it the lush sanctuary it is today. After running the boat up onto the western beach, we disembarked onto the sand using the front steps.

Our plan was to make our way up to the western saddle, for the views out to sea – on a clear day, you get a great vista of White Island. Not everyone was up to making it all the way to the top with me, so some guests opted to hang out in the shade of the trees with the other guide, watching the birdlife flit about.

After meandering back down from the saddle, my group rejoined the others and we all made our way further down the track to a Department of Conservation (DOC) hut. There was a bit of a working bee on that day, and there were a few DOC staff floating around on the island.

Getting over to the next bay involved taking a narrow, winding goat track that ran along the edge of a steep drop-off, with waves breaking on the rocks below. If you looked down, you could occasionally spot a fur seal looking back up at you, or resting blissfully with its eyes shut. The track was only wide enough to walk single file, and there were roots and rocks jutting out of the surface, but as long as you watched where you put your feet and hugged the rock wall it was relatively safe. Many visitors to the island before us had travelled it without incident.

For this particular part of the tour, I was at the back of the group, acting as the sheepdog, making sure our group stayed together and that no one got left behind. From my position at the back of the group, I couldn't see most of the passengers in front of me, between me and the other guide, as we wound our way along the track.

About halfway to our destination, the other guide radioed me over the VHF radio: 'Someone has had a fall.'

I radioed back, asking if they were okay. *Maybe a sprained ankle or a grazed knee*, I thought.

Then the other guide replied: 'He's gone off the cliff.'

There was a split second when my blood ran cold, then I started telling the passengers ahead of me that they needed to move to the left and get against the rock wall. I needed to get past. *Now.* I managed to squeeze past the group and make it up to where the other guide was standing with a few passengers. They were all looking down, and that's when I saw the man lying on his back on the rocks below.

I took off along the track to find a place where I could get down to him. Nowhere was good or easy without massively overshooting and having to double back – taking up time I didn't think we had, so I decided fast was the best option. I crashed down through the trees and down a slightly lower part of the cliff, then ran back along the rocks to where he was lying. I paused a couple of metres away, I could see blood coming from his mouth, his eyes were closed and he wasn't moving. I was sure he was dead.

'*Fuck!*' I blurted out.

His eyes flicked open and locked onto mine.

'Help me,' he said.

I ran to his side, throwing my bag on the ground next to me.

'Hey, mate,' I said. 'What's your name? I'm Kelsey.' *He knows that, you idiot – you're his guide.* I winced at myself.

'Lionel,' he replied.

I scanned his body for anything obviously wrong, painfully aware that my first-aid course had not given my twenty-four-year-old brain enough knowledge to handle this particular situation. *We need help. Now.*

I can't remember if it was me or the other guide who radioed David, our skipper, or whether he'd just heard the earlier brief conversation, but he pulled up the anchor and came along the coastline to find us. He anchored just a few metres from where I sat on the rocks with Lionel. The boat was visible, but unable to help us.

'Where do you hurt the most, Lionel?'

'My back … my legs …'

I couldn't see any blood other than the little bit coming from his mouth. Perhaps he'd bitten the inside of his cheek or outside of his tongue when he fell? Multiple times he tried to move or writhe in pain and I did my best to keep him still. *Surely this is a spinal injury*, I thought, racking my brain, looking back up the cliff to where we'd not long ago been standing.

I examined what parts of his body I could without moving him. I lifted his shirt, expecting to see more than I found – just some scratches on his hip and stomach area from the fall. I couldn't see anything else obvious, and I wasn't confident enough to start poking around – not here, not on my own.

In an effort to keep him comfortable and still, I took off my jersey and tentatively placed it under his head, hoping it would offer him *some* relief. David was desperately trying to get a helicopter out to us, but the response was slow.

'It won't be long. Help is on the way,' I reassured Lionel *for over an hour*. We were 20 minutes from Whakatāne by boat, but no one was coming to help. I was on my own, begging Lionel to hold on.

'Just let me die' he said repeatedly. Tears began forming in my eyes and a lump caught in my throat as I began to break down.

Not now.

The voice in my head was calm, clear and firm. And boy, did it cut that shit out. Almost as if a switch was flicked, my emotions were curbed, and calm washed back over me. For an instant, I sat wide-eyed wondering what the hell had happened, then I heard a voice behind me that snapped me back to where I was. Another tour operator had been on the island, in the bay our group had been heading to, and hopped around the rocks to help me once the other guide had told him what had happened.

'How can I help?'

Relief washed over me instantly.

The autumn wind was bitterly cold, so we placed an emergency blanket over Lionel. We kept asking him questions – about his family, about his life – *anything* to try to distract him from what was actually happening in the moment. I made another desperate plea to David to hurry up that fucking helicopter.

One of the DOC workers turned up, and I relayed what little we had guessed about Lionel's injuries. As time wore on, his condition and his pain were worsening, and it was becoming harder and harder to console him.

He kept telling me to let him die. Every time he said it, it tore at me.

Finally, we heard the unmistakable thrum of an incoming helicopter. *This better fucking be for us.* Thankfully, it was. Paramedics were dropped off to us on the rocks, and a couple rushed in to stabilise and assess Lionel while another spoke to the three of us who had been trying to help him.

I began shaking. Was it the cold? Or was it shock setting in now that help had arrived?

It took another hour for the paramedics to make a plan, get Lionel loaded onto a stretcher, then get the helicopter back from the island's landing pad, and winch him up. After what felt like a lifetime staring into Lionel's icy-blue eyes, he was finally on his way to be helped. I was exhausted – emotionally and physically.

The other guide had got the rest of the group to our intended beach, where we would now be picked up by the boat – we weren't game enough to head back along the track to where we were supposed to reboard. Unwilling to leave the group, the other guide stayed on the beach, and I now had to make my way back up to the track and go back to the first beach, collect all of the belongings and the boarding steps for the boat, then carry it all back to the waiting group. I was broken.

With my finite medical knowledge, I had assumed that Lionel was going to be okay once he made it to hospital – a naive thought, in hindsight. I spent the next thirty-six hours in a daze, with his face and voice locked in my mind. Two days after this had all happened, I received a call. It was the police: Lionel had died from internal injuries.

I felt so hollow. Even though I *knew* there was nothing else I could have done for Lionel, I wished that I *had* done more, somehow.

On the Tuesday, I accompanied the police and WorkSafe out to Whale Island to retrace our steps, showing them where Lionel had fallen. Once again, I found myself sitting at the bottom of the cliff, faces looking down at me, wishing I was anywhere but there. The spot where Lionel had fallen from was measured to be twelve metres high. His voice echoed in my head – *just let me die* – and it did for months.

I never went back to that island.

Ever since I'd left home, I'd wanted to get my own dog. However, because I was working so much on the boats and bouncing between housesitting gigs (plus the age-old tale of not having enough money), I knew it wasn't fair to bring a dog into my life. Then, at the end of 2018, I'd started dating a dairy farmer called Tom, and things changed.

I'd been housesitting for my aunt Kath for a few months, and once she moved back to Whakatāne in early 2019, and I was spending most of my time at Tom's, I slowly, organically, just moved in with him. Tom already had a dog, a young shepherd-collie mix called Jess. He was also at home a lot (on the farm where he worked). I realised that the idea of getting my own dog had become somewhat more realistic, because it could spend the day on the farm with him, and it wouldn't have to be alone on the days I was at work.

I was still really struggling with trying to shake the awful feeling that the accident on Whale Island had left with me. I still saw Lionel's face and heard his voice every night, so I wasn't sleeping much. A couple of weeks after, I began looking at dogs on TradeMe, saying that it would be my 'emotional support dog' after what had happened – kind of as a joke, kind of not. Weirdly – and fortunately – Tom went along with it.

One day, at the end of April, I came across an ad for 'River – Collie X'. It had a picture of a dog lying on a table with his blurred wagging tail hanging off the side, big paws, and his head cocked and looking right at the camera. I clicked to read more:

With as kind a nature as his name suggests, this young fella is ready for his forever. He will melt your heart in as quick as one look at him. He has had a rough start but thanks to a couple of great fosterers, he is ready for that next step. Found under a bridge next to a river, he was very afraid, but there is not a shred of aggression in this boy's body, he just wants to be loved. He may take a few moments to warm up but once he does, he is going to make someone a fantastic companion. Ideally we believe a house with kids is the place for him. He has a great time with other dogs and is certainly being well socialised currently.

I don't recall asking Tom whether we could go and meet River, but next thing I was on the phone, wanting to know more about him. A day or so later, I was heading off to see him, with Tom and Jess in tow.

I first met my best mate in the reception of a dog daycare in Tauranga. I sat down on the floor and River ran onto my lap. The connection was instant. I knew he was mine.

We took him to a field to meet Jess on neutral territory, to make sure they would get along. They hit it off instantly, so I assumed we'd move on to the next step – maybe a home visit and answering a million questions to make sure we were the right fit for River.

'Well,' said the man from the Western Bay District Council who was in charge of rehoming River, 'I see no reason to say no. If you want to take him, you can. We'll just need you to sign off some papers back at the office.'

Totally unprepared for a second dog – no collar, no extra bowls,[13] no bed – I signed the papers and paid the $250 adoption

---

13 He ate out of an old frying pan for about a week before I got him a bowl!

fee. As I took River's leash, the man casually mentioned, 'If you bring him back within seven days, you'll get a full refund.' I held the leash closer to my body.

After a bit of snooping, I discovered that River had in fact been adopted out a couple of times previously, and brought back. This was *not* mentioned to me, only that he'd been there longer than any other dog the rescue had in their care. They were all really attached to him, so they said, yet, after the seven-day return period, my email updates went unanswered. I have never been able to understand this. As I type this, he is asleep on the floor next to me, barking in his dream, probably at whoever abandoned him in the first place. *Good boy, River.*

River was meant to be a house dog, but it turned out that the collie in him was strong. After learning about electric fences (the hard way) and gaining some confidence in the wide-open spaces of the farm, he taught himself to round up the cows. He proved to be better – in both keenness to work and intensity – than any of the other farm dogs at getting the cows in, and certainly at moving stubborn bulls.

True to his collie nature, the boy is whip-smart and cunning – don't let his sweet face fool you. I took him to a scent course recently, and when I asked him to 'find it' – thinking I would save some time by using our command for hunting rats on morning walks rather than teach him the 'search' command – he trotted past all of the food and 'distraction scents' on the floor and began pawing at the corner of the room. I turned to the lady running the course and said, 'I think you have rats.'

Good boy, River.

Chapter 4

Unsurvivable

On my fifth anniversary of working for White Island Tours — 8 December 2019, I was heading into town for my sister's birthday when River, who was sitting in the front passenger-seat footwell, started whining. Because the main road had been blocked by a crash, we were taking the back way, bumping along a narrow, winding dirt road. River is not a big fan of the car at the best of times, but the whining on this day was new. And he wouldn't stop. His black-ginger ears were pinned back and he was getting more and more restless by the second.

He'd never done this before and I had no idea what was going on. I pulled over.

I'd only just come to a stop on what little verge there was when a lifted white Hilux ute came flying around the corner, taking up every other centimetre of the narrow gravel road. If I hadn't just pulled over, we would have been in a head-on collision.

The ute zoomed past, engulfing my car in a cloud of dust, and disappeared. Shaken, I glanced over at my dog, who was now totally still and quiet. I sat there for a moment, catching my breath.

'Fuck this.' I said.

We could head into town later, once the main road reopened. I drove up the road a little way to find a safer place to turn around, then we headed back to the farm. River settled into the footwell and didn't make another peep for the rest of the drive home.

The next morning, I was helping shift calves when I got a call from work. A cruise ship was coming over from Tauranga, and Paul wanted to know if I could come in to work to help take a boatload of tourists out to the island. I'd injured my left thumb a few days earlier and was meant to be taking time off while it healed, but I said, 'Yeah, I'll come in – as long as someone can be my left hand and do the heavy lifting.'

When I got to work around 10.30am, the rest of the crew was already on the boat – *Te Puia Whakaari*. After the skippers and staff had run through the usual pre-tour prep, including sea conditions and what the latest information on the island was, Hayden and I spent some time going over it all with our two younger crew members, Jake and Tipene. The island had been at Alert Level 2 for a few weeks, since 18 November, which meant there was moderate to heightened volcanic unrest. 'It means there has been a change in the volcano, including gas composition and output, and it's a fairly good indication that the magma is moving around a bit more,' I explained. But I wasn't overly concerned – I'd been out to the island at Level 2 several times without anything happening, and even just after a Level 3. Level 2 didn't always mean an eruption was imminent. Level 1 didn't always mean that an eruption *wasn't* imminent. The beauty of big nature.

Hayden and I started to discuss the layout of the day, and I asked him which group he wanted to be in: one or two?

'I'll take group two,' he replied, 'so I can push you around the island if you're too slow.'

'Whatever,' I retorted. 'You won't be able to keep up with me. You're out of practice, skipper.'[14]

'Pfft!' he laughed. 'You'll need elbowing around the island.'

'Just try to keep up, slowpoke,' I said, writing his name on the sheet next to group two and my own next to group one. Then, knowing how much he loved teaching the new guides, I turned to him and said, 'Do you want to take Tipene with your group today? I know you haven't been out with him yet.'

'Yeah, I'll take him – I can un-teach him all the bad habits you've taught him,' Hayden said, laughing his infectious laugh.

Since it was Jake's birthday, I offered to lead our group's whole tour. That way, Jake could have the easier task of hanging out at the back chatting, making sure the group didn't get too spread out.

'And make sure Kelsey keeps moving too, eh,' said Hayden, grinning.

We were just heading out to continue getting the boats ready when he stopped me. 'How's your thumb?' he asked.

'It's still a bit sore, but it's okay.'

'Do you want to wrap it?'

'No, I think it'll be all right.'

'I'll wrap it,' he said, and when I told him again that it was fine, he insisted: 'No. I'll wrap it for you – it'll help protect it if you need to use it.' He was very particular about wrapping it up in a medical crepe bandage, taking ages, making sure it was done just right. But at last, he was happy and let me go.

14 Hayden had been driving the boats more frequently after gaining his skipper's ticket, so he was on the island guiding a lot less.

'Finally,' I said, grinning and rolling my eyes.

Our tourists for the day arrived, boarded, and it was time to leave. The trip out was pretty good – a little lumpy, but certainly not rough. Because we were on *Te Puia Whakaari*, there was plenty of nausea.[15]

While taking care of our various duties, Hayden and I were still bantering about which of us was going to make it around the island faster, and Tipene and Jake were covering all of the 'two-thumb' tasks. Nothing special stands out in my memory about the start of that trip. It really was just another day at work: business as usual.

Two of the other boats in the White Island Tour's fleet – *PeeJay IV* and *Phoenix* – had headed out to the island before us, so the wharf was all set up when we got there. These boats were moored in the bay – *PeeJay IV*'s passengers were preparing to leave the island, and *Phoenix*'s passengers were halfway through their tour, with Paul leading one of their tour groups. A couple of helicopters from other tour companies were on the island, and one would land with five on board a bit later while we were on the island, after the other two had left.

We got our inflatable into the water and had it lined up next to the boat, ready to start loading passengers – and pretty much every one of them decided that this was the time to go to the bathroom. We were already on a tight schedule to get them back to their cruise ship in time, and this was chipping into their island time, so Bozzy, the skipper of *Phoenix*, came over with his inflatable to help us speed things up. He ferried some of our

---

15 Earlier in the year, we had started using this boat built specifically for White Island Tours. It had all the bells and whistles to help make the 50-kilometre ride as smooth as possible – yet, for some reason, it seemed to make a lot of passengers sick. The crew, too.

passengers over to use the toilets on his boat, then took them over to the wharf.

Once we were finally on the island, Jake and I took our group down to the beach for the normal introduction and safety briefing, then set off ahead of Hayden and Tipene's group. At one of the first stops, I talked about the alert level. I explained what the level meant, how that affected our guide-to-visitor ratio and our timing around the island, and then I checked that everyone was happy to continue with the tour. I remember asking this multiple times: 'Is everyone happy to carry on?' And every time they nodded their heads: *Yes*.

Knowing we only had under an hour to get our groups round the island due to the cruise ship's tight schedule, we condensed some of the general-interest information, but kept in all of the safety stuff. We made sure everyone got all their photo ops, but there weren't so many talking stops. We led the way through the gas and steam and bubbling water that was always there. It was all as normal as ever — nothing to raise any alarm bells.

At the main crater, too, everything was as normal as ever. It looked fine — steamy, but then, it was always steamy. When our allocated time was up, Jake and I moved our group on and started heading down the middle of the island. Behind us, Hayden and Tipene started leading their group up for their turn at the main crater.

In the middle of the island, there are a couple of streams that wind their way down to Crater Bay. We'd always pause here because it was a good place to make sure the groups were close together after a bit of a walk, and also to discuss the taste of the water. The two streams tasted very different, as they came from different sources — one very iron-y, one sharp and acidic. I was busy explaining to everyone that they could dip their finger in the water to taste it, and telling them why it tasted the way it did, when suddenly everyone started talking and pointing all at once.

I heard someone say, 'Wow!'

And someone else exclaimed, 'Look at that!'

Then my radio started screaming.

I had my back to the crater.

I turned around.

The moment I saw it, I knew what was happening. The island was erupting.

From about this point, for the next two minutes, time slowed down. What I thought happened in the space of about ten to twenty minutes was actually over in 120 seconds.

An enormous black-and-grey plume was rising rapidly above the island – already higher than the peak. It was beautiful, actually, set against the bright blue sky. Beautiful and awful. And *silent*. There was no sonic boom. No earth-rumbling heads-up. No hiss or roar or bang. The only noise now was the radios blaring something along the lines of 'ERUPTION! TAKE COVER!' and me yelling, *'Everyone, with me! Run!'*

My reaction was immediate. My safety training kicked in, and I headed for shelter, running along the track about 10 metres, up through some mounds of boulders, and ducking around to the right to hide behind one. The absurdity of the whole situation bubbled through like a tiny laugh in my head: *This feels just like our drills. This is insane.* Most of the tour group came my way, while some went to the left and hid behind another mound of rocks, still within sight. We were 300 or 400 metres from the main crater. My thinking was that, once we'd taken shelter, I'd assess the situation and decide our next move. That was the best-case scenario.

Worst-case scenario? A pyroclastic surge.

There are a few ways pyroclastic surges can happen, but one is when an eruption column collapses. The column goes shooting up with a huge amount of force – a massive ejection of acid, gases, ash, rock, all that business. That's what the black-and-grey cloud now looming above us and the island was made up of. But all that heavy stuff just can't keep going up, because gravity. It begins to collapse, and a massive wave of hot gas and volcanic debris bursts out of the bottom of the column and rolls along the ground – it's denser than air, which causes it to drop and flow rapidly along the ground. If you've watched a video of this type of eruption, the pyroclastic surge is that huge wave that comes out at the bottom of the plume. I knew enough about pyroclastic surges to know that, if you saw one coming for you, it was a white-flag moment. The stats were terrible: people usually don't survive being engulfed by one.

Jake came running in and joined me behind the mound of rocks. I remember him crouching down right next to me and just saying my name, his voice wavering. I remember saying, 'It's going to be okay.' Less than a minute had passed, and some people were still running to find shelter, but to me every second stretched out like a lifetime.

I turned and looked at the northern wall, as the main crater was obscured by the mounds of rocks now sheltering my group.

And that's when I saw the pyroclastic surge – our worst-case scenario – rolling along that wall towards us.

*

Years earlier, I'd read *Surviving Galeras*, in which volcanologist Stanley Williams tells the story of being caught in the crater of a volcano – Galeras, in Colombia – when it erupted in 1993, killing six of his colleagues and three tourists. Williams was gravely injured, and lucky to get out alive. As well as the horrifying account of the eruption, the book also includes a wealth of more general volcanological information. There is a *lot* on the deadliness of pyroclastic density currents.[16]

As I watched this pyroclastic surge sweep down and over White Island's crater walls towards me, enveloping everything in its path, a quote from Williams popped into my head, clear as day:

> [If] we were ever caught [in a pyroclastic flow] in the open, we should find a depression in the ground, cover ourselves with whatever was available, and try to hold our breath until the flow passed. Those who panic or exert themselves are more likely to gulp great drafts of ash and gaseous air, quickly clogging their airways and rendering them unconscious after a few breaths. Those who completely cover their mouths until the worst of the pyroclastic flow passes have a better prognosis.

A pyroclastic surge is not a slow-moving beast, but as this one bore down on us my mind was in overdrive, and that made it seem to be moving a lot more slowly than it actually was.

16 There are four types (according to Google) – flows and surges being the two at opposite ends of the scale. Flows (like the one experienced on Galeras) are more dense than surges. Surges (like the one on White Island) can move rapidly and aren't confined to the topography, meaning they tend to travel faster, farther and with less predictability.

In that moment, I felt as though we may as well have still been standing on the main crater's edge, completely exposed. A brief thought crossed my mind, *Maybe we can make it farther down the island – somewhere more sheltered.* But, besides Jake, I'd only known the people I was with for a few measly hours. I had no idea of their fitness or agility levels, and as I've mentioned, it's not smooth terrain out there. It's all rocky and unstable underfoot – not an easy run – and hell, I'm not even a good runner on flat ground. So I stuck with Williams's words. Ignoring every fibre in my body telling me to run, I stayed still. I kept the group where it was.

Seek shelter. Cover yourself. Hold your breath.

That voice echoed in my mind with the same clear, calm firmness it had back when it told me *Not now* when I was with Lionel on Whale Island. I understand why people believe in god in these moments.

Fear had filled my body as soon as I saw that ashen cloud barrelling down the island. My breathing increased ten-fold. My body shook. I knew our odds of survival were basically zero. In an effort to do *something*, I put my gas mask and sunglasses on. If there was to be *any* hope – and it was minimal – I knew I needed to be able to see and to breathe. I pressed that mask and those glasses as hard as I could against my face.

There was no way I could hold my breath. Despite trying to slow my breathing, I couldn't. I was panic-breathing. Hyperventilating. My body and brain knew what was coming. *This is how you die.*

I thought of my family. Mum was going to be so mad. She had been right: this was dangerous and I should have quit. I thought of Tom. I thought of River, and how I was never again going to pat his soft head while he looked up at me with his big brown eyes. I thought of my dad and my sister.

David knows we're in the streams. At least they'll find our bodies …

And then the pyroclastic surge hit us.

Everything went dark.

Initially, it felt like standing on the beach on a really hot, windy day – loose sand and little sticks swirling around. Hiding behind the mound would hopefully block anything bigger from hitting us, but even though I was squatting behind the rock, curled into a foetal position, the rush of air and gases wrapped around the mound and a deluge of tiny rock fragments kept hitting me. Quickly, the temperature rose. It got hotter, and hotter, and *hotter.*

This is how you die …

I knew from history, and the kind of volcano White Island is, that these eruptions tend to be short but sharp. I knew the last one had lasted about 90 seconds, and I held onto that:

90 seconds … 90 seconds … you can hold on for 90 seconds …

I want to say it was quiet, but it wasn't. People around me began screaming as their – *our* – skin began to burn.

This is how you die …

It felt like being in an oven, and the temperature just kept rising.

90 seconds …

My exposed arms started to feel like they were on fire. I fought the urge to start trying to brush it out.

90 seconds … keep your hands on your face.

My body began vibrating. Everything in me was screaming at me to drop my hands, swat at my arms, run.

90 secon—

I couldn't bear it any longer. I dropped my left hand from my face and began frantically brushing at the burning of my right forearm. Then I dropped my right hand to start brushing my left forearm. My screams now joining those around me.

This is how you fucking die …

90 sec—

And then everything went still.

And everything went quiet.

The air around me stopped moving, and everything was silent. Even the screams from my group were now reduced to whimpers and quiet crying. I couldn't hear the swell on the rocks. I couldn't hear the rush of steam escaping the vents. Just the sounds being made by my group, and my own breath heaving through my clogged gas mask.

I didn't move for a moment. Waiting. My eyes were still slammed shut, I was still crouched behind the boulder, and for a couple of seconds I just listened. Was there more to come? My breathing slowly reduced from whole-torso pumping to more air-grabbing gasps. Tentatively, I pulled down my sunglasses and opened my eyes.

The island was coated in a dull, grey-green ash, and my group – the people I could see around me – were slowly moving, covered with the same ash. I couldn't tell who was who, but I knew that Jake was no longer next to me.

I caught a glimpse of my arms and hands as I lowered my sunglasses, and realised that the burning sensation had been my skin starting to … *melt*? Almost like cooling candle wax, my skin was whitening, blistering and falling off. It's not lava or fire that makes a pyroclastic surge so lethal: it's the extreme heat of the steam and gas, and the combination of toxic gases and acid fluids, and the projectiles that come with it. I didn't know this at the time.

My hands dropped to my thighs and felt for my pockets, where my radio should have been. It wasn't there. Maybe it had fallen out while I was running for cover, or it may even have been directly underneath me. But there was no way I was sifting around in the ash with *these* hands.

I had no idea if White Island had a Round Two up its shifty little sleeve, but I wasn't planning on sticking around to find out. The fact that we were still alive after passing through a pyroclastic surge was a fucking miracle, and I wasn't about to waste whatever time we had left tempting fate.

Move. Now.

Decision made, my fight kicked in. I stood up abruptly.

'Get up! We've got to go! Get up!' I shouted at my group.

No one was moving.

'GET UP! WE HAVE TO GO *NOW!*'

'We can't … we're really hurt …' someone in the ash replied.

'SO AM I. GET UP.'

Things weren't moving fast enough for me. I glanced back towards the main crater. It was still sending up a huge column of ash and gas, but it looked like we were in the clear. For now, at least.

I needed to get my group moving. By any means necessary.

'No one is coming for you,' I barked. 'You need to get up.'

I'm going to get in so much trouble for saying this, I remember thinking. *Of course they're coming …* I didn't know it then, but what I'd said would turn out to be true – there would be no official rescue party.

Slowly, the surface of the ashy landscape began to move as people tried to get to their feet with whatever little energy they had left. Once enough of the group was attempting to get up, I told them to follow me. *We need to get back to the boat. We need to get off this fucking island.*

I started walking – not along one of our tracks, but in a straight line from where we were to the wharf. I knew the ground was solid and safe – or at least, it had been before the eruption – and I also knew time was not on our side. We were taking the shortcut.

As I made my way towards the wharf, my focus shifted to the helicopter that had been parked not far from us – it had been shunted off its landing platform by the force of the pyroclastic surge. Two of the rotor blades had snapped, and were hanging down.

What the fuck …?

The sight of the exposed and damaged helicopter sparked another thought: *Group two …* They'd been heading away from the crater, their backs to the silent eruption, heading for where we had been at the streams. The walk from the main crater to those streams is across incredibly open ground.

My head whipped around in the direction of the main crater, scanning the monochromatic landscape for Hayden's group. *I can't see them …* There was no movement on the ground, and my eyes kept wandering up to the dark column still rolling up into the sky, the air within the crater walls still snowing ash. *I need to get my group off first*, I thought, *then I'll come back and find Hayden.* Adrenaline is no joke.

As I walked, I started throwing off my gear. I wanted everything off me. Off my melting skin. My helmet hit the ash first, followed by my gas mask and then my guide bag. I threw off my sunglasses.[17] I marched on, and I didn't look back at the crater. I could hear small noises from my group behind me – quiet talk, whimpers, heavy breathing – as they followed my footsteps.

It took less than five minutes to reach the wharf.

Just before the eruption happened, *Phoenix*, with Paul, Bozzy and their group, had left Crater Bay to do a lap around the island. The boat had been on the northern side of the island when the eruption column had appeared, stretching up into the blue sky. By the time we made it back to the wharf, Bozzy was already pulling back into the bay. Paul deployed the boat's inflatable, and dropped one of *Phoenix*'s crew members onto *Te Puia Whakaari* to help the skipper David get it up and running again.

Our flash new boat that made everyone seasick was no longer white. Now, she was the same drab grey-green as the island, caked in ash. To get her going again, that ash needed to be removed from the air vents so it didn't get sucked into the engines.

I could see a couple of people in the water near the beach – it didn't register at the time, but it was the group from the helicopter. Paul turned his attention to them next, hauling them up into the inflatable and getting them to the safety of *Phoenix*. Gathering slowly on the wharf, my group began asking why he wasn't coming to help us first.

'I don't know,' I said. 'I'm here with you guys.' But they just kept saying it: 'We need help. Why isn't he coming to get us?' Over and over again. My eyes watched as the little black inflatable boat roared around the bay between *Te Puia Whakaari*

---

17 Or so I thought. They were on one of those cords that prevented me from losing them over the side of the boat (I had lost a couple of pairs before). The cord must have got tangled in my hair, because a guide who wasn't working that day found them in the bottom of the inflatable boat a day or so later. I still have them, covered in ash, in a bag.

and *Phoenix*, Paul organising everything and everyone for what was about to happen.

And then I heard Jake's voice. I turned around as he sat down next to me on the wharf. 'Help me,' he said.

'I can't touch you, mate. I'm sorry,' I replied. 'We'll stick together.' His exposed skin looked like mine – everyone's skin did. It was whitening, and beginning to slough off.

I started yelling – wailing, if you ask him – at Paul to come and help us. I remember thinking, *This is going to haunt him* (and it did) but my adrenaline was dropping fast now, and the pain – an unbearable throbbing and heat I didn't know my body was capable of producing – was beginning to rush in, and it was the only thing I could think to do.

Paul pulled the inflatable up alongside the wharf at speed and, without touching anything with my melting hands, I stepped onto the top rung of the ladder, onto the side of the inflatable boat and sat next to Paul. 'I can't find Hayden. I can't see him,' I said, the realisation that I wasn't going to be able to make it back onto the island to look for him starting to sink in.

'I'll find him,' Paul replied, as Jake and the other passengers gingerly got into the inflatable.

It took a couple of trips for Paul to ferry all of us across to *Phoenix*. In a daze, I walked off down the port side of the boat, as though I'd just come back from any normal tour and was setting off to drop my gear in the helm.

Halfway along the side of the boat, my burning arms held out in front of me, I woke up to what I was doing, and turned around. At the back of the boat, I sat on the port lifejacket hatch, facing out towards the east coast of the mainland – not that that's where my gaze was. Rarely did I lift my eyes off my hands.

I didn't know it yet, but all the exposed skin on my body had been burnt. I knew my hands and arms were melting, but I don't remember noticing my legs were in the same state. I'd been wearing my work T-shirt, shorts and hiking boots with socks, so my feet and ankles, torso and upper thighs had been protected. But my shirt must have ridden up while I was crouched down behind the boulder, because I was burnt across my lower back, and this wrapped around onto my stomach on the side that was away from the mound of rocks.

Phoenix's passengers had been sent inside the cabin as they had raced around the eastern end of the island – outpacing the end of the pyroclastic surge as it slowed and dissipated once it reached the sea. Now, they stayed inside to make way for us in the cockpit. Several of them were standing in the back doorway, looking out at us with expressions of pure horror. But despite what they were seeing, despite their fear, despite their lack of training or qualifications to deal with this kind of fallout (and let's be honest, who the fuck is actually trained for this kind of situation?), slowly, one by one, two by two, they came out to us.

A few had basic first-aid knowledge, and we were lucky to have a couple of doctors onboard who were on holiday. Most didn't have any knowledge of what to do here. With their own bottles of water, with the literal shirts off their backs, they came out to help us. They held up their bottles and tipped fresh water into our mouths, they rinsed our melting skin and tried to remove as much ash and debris as they could, they used their shirts as covers for our wounds. They spoke to us, sang to us, asked us questions, trying to distract us, to reassure us – all with fear in their eyes.[18]

[18] I need it to be known that these actions saved our limbs and our lives. All of the medical staff over the time I was in hospital said so – multiple times.

My limbs were beginning to swell, and I became keenly aware that the crepe bandage that Hayden had wrapped around my left hand to protect my thumb at the beginning of the day was now becoming tighter – the pain in that joint that I had had for the last few days now non-existent. Suddenly frantic to get it off, I unsuccessfully tried to tear the bandaging off with my teeth – not wanting to touch anything with my right hand. Seeing my inability to remove it myself, Bozzy unwrapped it for me.

Even once everyone who'd made it to the wharf was loaded on board, *Phoenix* didn't depart immediately. We sat there for a while with the engines running, free-floating in the bay, eyes locked on the crater floor. Waiting for Hayden, for Tipene, for *anyone* from group two.

Seconds felt like minutes, but it was soon clear that we couldn't wait any longer. Some of the injured passengers were lapsing in and out of consciousness, and we couldn't see any movement on the island. No one else coming down towards the wharf. We had to go.

The impossible call was made for *Phoenix* to leave, in the hopes of saving the lives on board.

The jet engines of *Phoenix* roared as we left White Island at full speed for Whakatāne. For help.

The trip took around an hour, and I could hear that *Phoenix*'s engines were being pushed to their limit. Unbeknownst to me, while I was out the back quietly praying to the boat that it could do it – specifically, *'Don't fuck this up'* – Bozzy was doing the same at the helm.

Paul stayed on White Island with the extra inflatable and David and two other crew members from *Phoenix*, who were cleaning the air vents on *Te Puia Whakaari*. He had strategically left our colleague Arnika on board *Phoenix* for our mercy dash to shore. She was training to be a doctor, and if I could have written her a letter of recommendation so she could have skipped the last part of her studies, I would have. That girl was overseeing *every single person* on that boat.

When we were about halfway back, a Coastguard boat met us and dropped off two paramedics. I didn't find this out for another year, but there had been some wicked breakdown in communications within the emergency services – including, but not limited to, someone on the receiving end of the 111 call thinking it was a prank. In fairness, it's not like this was a normal or common emergency.[19] The paramedics who got sent out to us had been told there'd been an eruption and that people had been injured, but they were thinking they would be dealing with injuries like broken legs and grazes from falling over. You can only imagine the look on their faces when they realised what they were *actually* dealing with: about twenty severely burnt people requiring urgent medical attention for burns, with nowhere near the right gear to care for them all. They did an absolutely incredible job at looking after us with what they had.

At no point on that trip back to Whakatāne did it ever cross my mind that we weren't out of the woods yet. I never imagined that I might still die.

We had just survived the unsurvivable. We shouldn't have been alive, but we were.

So that, in my mind, was that.

We'll get back to the mainland, they'll fix whatever this is, and we'll be okay …

I had no idea.

---

19 Thank god.

Chapter 5

Nothing

We finally roared across the Whakatāne River bar and pulled alongside the wharf. It seemed as though every first-responder in the Bay of Plenty was there – and, in fact, most of them were. Fire engines, ambulances, police cars, anyone of importance – all waiting for us within a makeshift cordon.

As we'd pulled into the wharf, against the odds, in the sea of people and uniforms I saw my mum, my sister and my nana.[20] I looked down at my hands again: swollen, my skin white and falling off. *They cannot see me like this.*

Once the boat was tied up, we weren't let off immediately. To me, it felt like there was no sense of urgency about getting

---

[20] Mum and Holly had been in the supermarket when Holly got a call from her friend asking whether I was working today and to call me because the island had just erupted. Holly tried calling me, and I didn't answer. She texted me, but knew the signal at the island was sketchy, and that if I was in the middle of a tour, I wouldn't reply. She checked the cameras out at the island and couldn't see anything on them – they were coated in ash. She showed Mum, and relayed the message from her phone call – they threw all of their groceries in the car after quickly paying, and raced down to the tour company's office. As they arrived, they saw police cars outside and knew it was true. After waiting for more information from work, they decided to just head down to the wharf to try and find me when I came in on *Phoenix*.

us off the boat and to the hospital, although I like to think that feeling was not shared by anyone on that wharf. There seemed to be a lot of faffing about – I don't know why this was, whether it was to do with name-checking those of us on board, or because there was some designated order for us to get off, or some other bureaucratic bullshit. I was having none of it. Not wasting time had got me here in the first place, and now that I'd been sitting around for about an hour, my limbs were starting to seize as the burnt tissue started to restrict. *Bugger this*, I thought.

I stood as well as I could, although I couldn't straighten my arms or legs, and my lower torso felt strangely tight.[21] On the trip back, my body had started convulsing – whether because of shock or cold or both, I didn't know – so I'd made my way inside to get out of the wind. Now, I felt like I couldn't get off the back of the boat because my family would be watching like hawks, looking for me. More than anything in the world, I didn't want them to see me like this – in pure agony and melting.

'What are you doing?' Arnika asked when she saw me heading towards the helm.

'Getting off this fucking boat,' I said.

I made it up the couple of steps to the helm, turned left and Arnika helped me over the almost knee-high threshold out onto the port side-deck. The only way onto the wharf from here was up and over the handrail. I remember stifling a scream as I was helped off, the hands on my body pushing me up and off, twisting and pulling at my burnt skin with every movement.

---

21 I didn't know my lower back had been burnt at this stage – or not to the extent it was, anyway.

Once on the wharf, Arnika tried to get me loaded into an ambulance.

'We're getting the worst first. We're getting the dead,' someone told her.

She looked at me, and then back at this 'someone'.

'Well, she's not breathing,' Arnika said, and pushed me onto a stretcher. If it wasn't for her, I probably would have been left waiting longer than I was.

Everything starts to get a bit hazy from here. Like one of those horror films that cut in and out between total chaos and black nothingness.

I vaguely remember being in the ambulance on the way to Whakatāne Hospital.

Nothing.

I remember being on a bed in the hospital, people around me, and one of them telling me my family was there and wanted to see me. Some police friends at the wharf had told them I was being taken to the hospital, and they'd raced there expecting to see me straight away. 'Don't you let them in until you get my pain under control,' I told the medical staff. I was on enough medication to put down a horse, and it was barely touching the sides.[22]

Nothing.

My memory of Whakatāne Hospital ends here. I don't remember seeing my family. I don't remember my limbs being

---

[22] I'm not kidding. About a year later, when I met some staff from Whakatāne Hospital, one told me that one syringe of one of the medications they were using would normally kill a person if they were given the whole thing – and we averaged three syringes *each*.

wrapped in plastic,[23] the skin beneath blistering and tightening – restricting movement and blood flow.

I don't remember getting taken by ambulance to Whakatāne Airport with Mum. I don't remember getting transferred by military helicopter to Trentham Military Camp in Upper Hutt,[24] heavily sedated and with earplugs that kept falling out because I had so much ash in my ears. (Though I *do* remember Mum drip-feeding me water off a gauze bandage in the dark of the helicopter. I remember being *desperately* thirsty.)

I don't remember arriving at Hutt Hospital Emergency Department to a sea of medical staff and being whisked away from Mum.

I don't remember being put on a ventilator, or being wheeled into the operating theatre around two in the morning to have my burns assessed and cleaned and dressed.

I don't remember being transferred to the ICU a few hours later, still sedated and heavily medicated.

I don't remember being taken for a head scan around ten the next morning, or being seen by doctors, nurses, physiotherapists, plastic surgeons, dieticians and social workers.

I don't remember being kept sedated and stuck with tubes to deliver me food and medication and everything else.

Nothing.

---

23 Hospital staff were sent out to the local supermarkets to get as much plastic food wrap as they could, to cover our burns. Apparently, they'd filled trolleys and just run out without paying.

24 Patients were triaged at Whakatāne Hospital over the course of approximately twenty-one hours. Patients were sent to different regional burns units, and it took a few days to figure out who was who and where they'd been sent. I was flown by helicopter to Trentham and then moved by ambulance to Hutt Hospital.

Part II
Critical care

My family had a couple of group chats running to keep everyone updated, and for obvious reasons I haven't included everything here – just the important bits.

I've also combined the different group chats into one thread.

Monday, 9 December 2019
Family Messenger Chats

6.34pm, Mum [Shelley]

She's in a lot of pain so we can't see her until they get it under control.

9.59pm, Dad [Graham]

Kelsey flown to Hutt Hospital, burns to arms, legs and back.

Shelley's gone with her. We're lucky to still have her.

Tuesday, 10 December 2019
Family Messenger Chats

1.36am, Mum

Kels and I have just arrived at the burns unit in Hutt. She has full-thickness burns to her arms and legs and is being taken straight to surgery. I will let you know more as I have information.

1.55am, Mum

Hi, guys. I'm guessing you won't be sleeping much so thought I would update you. We didn't take off until 10.30pm because Kels needed her pain managed. Whakatāne Airport had about 8–10 choppers there! Ride went okay. She slept most of the way. Landed at Trentham Military Base and then ambulanced to hospital. Huge group to meet us and Kels has been whisked away for surgery. They said it may be a couple of hours or so. We will know more about the extent after surgery. She's being great when she can xx

Holly [sister]

Thank you for the update, Mumma. I'm so happy you were able to go with her and that she's getting such good care. I love you both so, so much! Let me know if there's anything I can do.
Where are you? Have you slept? xx

Mum

Not really able to sleep haha …

3.48am, Mum

A nurse just came to give me a pillow and said she'll still be another couple of hours.

Jenny [Nanna, Mum's mum]

No not sleeping, just thinking of you ... Thank you for the update. Wish we were there, my darling. You shouldn't be on your own.

Mum

I'm okay. Please look after Graham and Holly though. It's awful knowing how hard this is for them too xx

Jenny

That goes without saying. You just concentrate on you and Kels, and we will be here for them.

5.45am, Mum

Still in surgery.

Jenny

[Your] Dad is going out to see Tom, and I will check on Holly XX

Mum

Thank you all so much. Please check on Graham too. He got a bit of a rough, detailed call from me this morning. I think he's trying to be too brave.

Peter [Grandad, Mum's dad]

I will go see him now, then head out to Tom.

7.59am, Mum

I'm about to go and see her. She's on a ventilator and asleep. I have to turn my phone off when in there but will message you all again a bit later xx

Holly

Okay, Mumma. Tell her we love her! ♡

8.15am, Mum

Kels is in critical condition in ICU. She's in an induced coma and will be having multiple surgeries and ongoing rehab. I can't tell you any more at this stage. Will meet with the doctors soon. Have to turn my phone off in ICU so contact will be difficult. X

9.58am, Mum

They're taking her for a CT brain scan now.

Donna [aunt]

Oh, Shelley. How are you holding up? Thank you for letting us know. We are all so worried for you all.

Mum

I'm okay. Digging deep. Xx

Carol [aunt]

I am so sorry to hear she's in an induced coma. Is that because they don't want her to move after her surgery? A brain scan as well. Oh, Shelley. I hope you are holding up on your own.

Vicky [aunt]

Just devastated this has happened to your beautiful girl. I wish one of us could be there with you to hold your hand and offer some comfort. Sending love and wishing for the best outcome for Kels ♡

Mum

Thank you so much. I have a friend who's been here all morning, plus Graham and Holly will be here later today too. Hospital is sorting us accommodation and if not them then White Island Tours will step in.

The coma is to keep her calm and ventilator to keep her breathing regular. She can breathe on her own but she hyperventilates. The medics on the scene were concerned that she was oddly disoriented so that's why the CT. Getting the best care. They're even looking after me pretty well too.

Donna

Leigh [cousin] heard about it in the USA and messaged me hoping Kelsey wasn't there … Big disaster for NZ, just watched the Australian Prime Minister give a brief on what's happening. While he was giving a brief, helicopters were flying overhead to the bushfires – we are smoked out again!![25]

3.32pm, Maree [aunt]

Any updates? All awaiting. Doug [cousin] just called, and wondering did you want us to come across earlier? Xx

Mum

She will be here for months. Will have at least ten more surgeries in the next couple of weeks. Will be kept in a coma for several more days.

---

25 While I was in hospital, parts of Australia were literally burning down. It was wild to come out of a coma and find out about the magnitude of the eruption, let alone the wildfires in Australia. Not to mention the United States possibly starting a war with Korea, and this new bug called Covid. How long was I asleep?!?

3.47pm, Mum

Been sent to doctors' room for sleep and shower but can't sleep. Head is pounding, heart is broken. But at least I'm clean? This feels like a nightmare.

8.38pm, Donna

Thinking about you and wondering if any news on Kelsey? We are worried about you xxx

Carol

They'll be in ICU, Donna. No phones allowed xxx

9.34pm, Mum

Just got to our motel. It's so hard leaving our girl behind. She's hanging in there and will have her second operation tomorrow. It's going to be a hellish few months ahead. Just trying to pull it together for our beautiful, brave, amazing girl.

Donna

Second op already, poor baby.

Mum

She'll have one every 2–3 days for the next few weeks. She faces multiple skin grafts and blood transfusions.

Donna

Thank god she is still with us. Wish we could magic-wand it away ♡

Mum

Me too. We're all just doing what we can and looking out for each other. We are just so scared and so broken. Your love and support is such a big help. Thank you all xx

I'm adding the rest of the family to this chat as it's getting so hard to keep track of all the messages and updates

Donna

Hope you all get some sleep tonight. We won't bother you all the time, but we are worried sick. Just put messages on here when you can xxx

10pm, Donna

Wendy [family friend] just messaged to ask if Kelsey okay. Her work colleague's son is a tour guide and they lost him yesterday.[26] He would have been Kelsey's work colleague.

Mum

Was his name Jake??

Donna

Wendy didn't seem to know his name, just said he was a tour guide and the son of a man she works with. Terrible.

Donna

Inman was his surname, Shelley, from Whakatāne.

Donna

Hayden I think is his first name.

---

26 Mum later told me how hard it was, hearing on the news when another person from the island had passed. They would then be inundated by messages from family and friends, panicking that it was me.

Mum

Yes, we know about Hayden. He was a close friend. Kels doesn't know yet.

Donna

Oh no ... how devastating, sorry to hear they lost their son 😞

Mum

Two have so far.

Wednesday, 11 December 2019
Family Messenger Chat

6.16am, Mum

Good morning, everyone. It's so good having Graham and Holly here too. Kels goes in for surgery at 10am. Each surgery will take her two steps back, but it's a means to an end. They are concentrating on her hands and elbows as they have been so badly affected. Over the next few months, infection will be her biggest challenge.

Family support right now is getting us through. We love you all so much and are so grateful to have you on our girl's side. We will send another update later after surgery. Love to you all xxx

7.52am, Mum

I'm sure it will come as no surprise but obviously we won't be in Hawke's Bay for Christmas now. We will have to try and cancel our AirBnB as we will need the money here.

Red Book[27]

9am, medical notes

Taken to operating theatre for cleaning of burns, skin grafts to hands and forearms, and new dressings put on. Given lots of pain relief during operation.

Family Messenger Chat

Group call started; no answer.

---

27 The Red Book was the idea of one of the ICU nurses. It is a lined 'red book' that they encouraged everyone to use to keep a running diary as to what was going on so that I could look back at it and fill in some blanks. It also helped my family keep track of what had happened while they were in the trenches.

9.34am, Mum

Sorry, guys, but we're really not up to talking on the phone right now.[28] Please just continue to send your messages as they really help. Sorry xx

Do you guys all mind being really careful about what you put on social media as it leaves a trail straight to us. We have been hounded by media and they are tracking us in the most devious ways.[29] Kels is really private and would not want to be splashed all over the place xx

Red Book

6pm

Transferred back to ICU. Looked after overnight, still sedated and on breathing machine. Carrying on pain relief and other medication, mouth cleaned regularly with little sponge scrubs, eyes checked regularly and ointment applied to stop them getting dry.

Family Messenger Chat

9.08pm, Mum

Kels came out of surgery at 6pm and they have done blanket grafts on her arms and hands. She's taken a couple of steps backwards but we're hopeful she will settle and be ready for next surgery on Friday on her legs and back.

---

28 Mum said her phone was going nuts, but she didn't want to actually talk to anyone. She especially wouldn't answer any calls from unknown numbers, because they were most often (and alarmingly frequently) media.

29 The reporters were relentless: dressing up in lab coats to try to slip into the burns ward and ICU, pretending to be family and/or friends to gain access to me, turning up at our family home in Whakatāne, messaging and phoning Mum day and night from all over the world. We even heard of one burning themself on purpose to try to get into the burns wards. For anyone wondering why I never spoke to mainstream media, *this is why*.

Soraya [cousin]

Gosh! What a full-on day ... and they will keep her in the coma until after the brunt of these surgeries are done? May I ask what do you mean she's taken a few steps backwards? And what blanket grafting entails? Xxx

Mum

After each surgery her body basically goes into shock from the trauma. Heart rate, etc, becomes high ...

Dad

They will keep her in a coma for around six days. Blanket graft means full sheet of skin as opposed to the skin being mesh-like, apparently gives a better finish.[30]

---

[30] As Dad says, blanket or sheet graft means they shave off a whole sheet of skin from an undamaged area on the body – usually a layer and a bit for a split thickness sheet graft, which is what I mostly had. This sheet is then placed straight down on the receiving site. Once healed, this kind of graft tends to be smooth. Mesh grafting is where they take that same sheet and punch loads of tiny holes in it so they can stretch it out and cover a larger area – a great method when you have a lot of real estate to cover, but not a lot of viable donor site to use. Once healed, this kind of graft has an almost 'fish scale' look to it, as the holes heal over.

Thursday, 12 December 2019
Family Messenger Chat

7.30am, Mum

Op from 9–6 on hands and arms yesterday. Legs on Friday when skin arrives from US. There are news reports that two more have passed away overnight. Kels is still with us. She's doing okay. We will be with her in an hour or so and let you know how she's doing today after her big day yesterday. Xx

Kirsten [Soraya's fiancé]

Hey fam, I cannot begin to imagine what you're all going through over there but one thing I do know is Kels is super strong and will fight hard to get through this. Stay close and hold on to one another, remember to look after yourselves too. It's a horrible tragedy what's happened, but Kels loves that job and that island so stay strong for her and soon she will be sitting up with that big smile telling you all about it. Big ♡

Red Book

Morning, medical notes

Being cared for in ICU, all interventions ongoing, still sedated and on breathing machine, monitored closely.

9.30am

New feeding tube inserted, given extra medication beforehand so not unsettled by this, continuing to be given fluids and liquid food as using up lots of energy.[31]

---

[31] If a person suffers severe burns, of over 40 per cent of their total body area, this usually causes their body to go into 'hypermetabolism' – meaning their metabolism starts working extremely fast to provide the energy their body needs to heal. As a result, severe burn patients require extra nutrition so they have enough energy to heal and maintain their body weight.

During the day
Seen by lots of different teams, providing support to family also. Sometimes needing blood transfusions.

Mum
Good morning, my gorgeous girl ♡ This is your 'Recovery Diary' and we will try to keep a record for you to read when you are ready.

Last Monday (9/12/19) – it's all a bit of a blur to be honest and I don't know how much you will remember either. Holly and I were at the supermarket when we started getting texts and messages asking if you were okay. We then saw all the posts about the eruption.

We came straight to your work to find out what was going on, and from there things just escalated. Waiting for you to come in on the boat was horrendous. We knew you were on the first boat because we got a bit of inside info from cop friends.

Do you remember talking to us in Whakatāne Hospital? You were pretty drugged up, but very feisty. Typical!

You were helicoptered to Hutt Hospital at about 10pm. I flew with you, my darling girl. The next 24 hours are a lot blurrier. Being by your side and making sure everyone was looking after you is all I care about.

You have had two big operations now. I know you hate this sort of stuff, so I'm not going to write any of the details down for you. But you are fighting hard and we love you so so much. We will be with you every single step of the way and beyond. You can totally beat this – just because you are you! There is so much love and support for you, honey.

Keep being you, baby. You got this. And we got you!
Mumma xx

Family Messenger Chat

11.01am, Mum

We have just seen Kels this morning. She looks peaceful. No other news. If any of you want to send her little video messages, we will play them for her. She's in a coma but can hear them.[32]

Carol

Oo I think that might be a bit high-tech for me. So pleased she is looking peaceful. You are in our thoughts. A round of big hugs to you all xxx

Tori [cousin]

That's a wonderful idea. Will send one after work xx

Mum

Don't feel pressured to do a video. Just write a message and we will read it to her and also write it in the book the ICU have going for her. Photos will be great too. The ICU staff want to get to know her xxx[33]

Red Book

3pm, Tom

Approx. 30°C outside. Approx. too hot in here.[34]

---

32 Several family members sent beautiful video and voice messages in response to this.

33 Cue the arrival of a big barrage of literally all the worst photos my family had of me – looking at you, Tori and Ash! The ICU and burns nurses encouraged my family to fill my room with as many photos of me and my life as possible, so they could get to know me while I was unable to tell them about myself.

34 My room was kept extra-warm to help the skin grafts take, and because my body's ability to regulate its own temperature was severely impacted.

5.15pm, Tom

The nurse tells us you're doing really well and even us dumb-dumbs can tell the difference from this morning. Shelley said she's going to paint your toenails while she has the chance.[35] You've got a huge day tomorrow, so we're going to let you have a nice big sleep tonight without us prodding you.

Family Messenger Chat

4pm, Leigh [cousin]

Thanks for posting the link to the donation page for supporting you all.[36] Are we okay to share the link on our Facebook profiles too? Just want to make sure xx

Mum

Absolutely. We are aware that it's going to open us up to media but at least it's the facts told by us xxx

Leigh

Great! Thank you 😊

Mum

We are keeping her location private. There is a guard on ICU, as media and weirdos are a problem.

Leigh

It's so terrible that you have to deal with that! As if you don't have enough going on.

---

35 I hate people touching my feet!
36 My Aunt Rach set this up to help my family out, but it became rather overwhelming for all of us. More on this later.

Mum

The hospital are onto it. They've sheltered us from most of it. We are just concentrating on Kels x

Leigh

As you should! Will be careful not to post any additional info xx

Mum

Thanks, sweetheart. Facts are fine. Just not personal details of her condition or location xxx

Leigh

And you can tell her from me that I miss my daily River dog Instagram story content!

Mum

Me too!

4.34pm, Soraya

Just at work but you can let her know that we will be bringing Orlando down to see her when we get there … She's not going to miss out on meeting 'lentil' xxx

She will understand the lentil comment. When she came to visit last year, Orlando was only the size of a lentil in my belly. Now he's the size of a small elephant. Hehe. Love you all xx

Red Book

7.16pm, Holly

Monday 9th December will forever be the worst day of my life. From the second I heard what happened I feel like my body shut down and I became numb. That feeling still hasn't changed today.

You have been an absolute trooper right from that horrific moment. When I saw you at the hospital Monday night in Whakatāne, you still managed to keep me calm by being your stubborn and witty self. You were in so much pain but you talked to us. I miss your voice.

On Tuesday 10th Dad and I arrived down here to be with you too. Before we came down, we went to the Kiwi Burrow,[37] where all of the crew and everyone from White Island Tours came together to support each other, give hugs and love, and they all send their love and wish you well.

I am trying to stay the strongest I have ever been so I can be there for Mum, Dad, Tom and of course YOU!

You are doing so well and I am so incredibly proud of you. You were already one of the people I admired and looked up to most. But now you have shown me true strength, fight, patience and unbearable pain. But I thank you for that.

I love you so much I can't begin to explain. Keep fighting, Kezzels.[38] You are going to get past this. The universe still isn't strong enough to get you down.

I will be right here with you every step of the way, and we will take on this new path of yours together.

I can't wait for our first sister date after all of this.

Love you more than the moon. See you in the morning.

Goodnight, my best friend xx

---

37 A meeting place work had on the wharf. Basically an empty room with seats and information on White and Whale Islands for passengers to wait in when the weather was shit.

38 A nickname I picked up in intermediate school, when 'Kesley Woghorn' was called up for an award. It was shortened to Kez, then somehow extended to Kezzels.

Friday, 13 December 2019
Red Book

4am, nurse

I'm one of the team looking after you, and met you early on 10/12/19. Your gorgeous mum thanked me for looking after her 'baby' 😊 Pardon me for reading previous entries from your whānau, but it's nice to get a picture of you while you can't speak for yourself. It sounds like you're a bit stubborn, which is great because determination helps healing.

It will be a long journey for you all, and we're here to support you. As are many people far and wide. It's humbling seeing the support that you have. I look forward to hearing about your reflection on this journey and know that *great* things will come from your experience.

Morning, medical notes

All interventions ongoing, still sedated and on breathing machine, hair washed with shampoo cap.

Family Messenger Chat

6.52am, Mum

Kels has about 45 per cent full-thickness burns with superficial in other patches. They have done the grafts on her arms and hands to be able to concentrate on getting movement ASAP. She goes in for third surgery this morning to put cadaver grafts on legs.[39] So

---

[39] Cadaver skin (skin off a dead donor) is used temporarily, like a dressing, on major burns to give the donor sites on your own body time to heal. Since it is skin from another person, it cannot be used for permanent grafts – your body will always reject it. Many family and friends went to their doctors to see if they could donate skin, but the only person who could have donated skin to me would have had to be my identical twin. Which I do not have.

far they have used her own undamaged skin from her upper back, but now they have to wait for that to regenerate before they can take more. Her upper arms, shoulders and lower back are still to be addressed.

7.39am, Leigh
So great to wake up this morning and see all the messages of support on Kelsey's donation page. I hope when she's awake and feeling up to it, she'll be able to read the messages and see all the people who have been thinking of her and sending her love and support xx

Red Book

8.37am, Mum
Good morning, sweetheart.

Another big day for you today. You are looking stronger today and the swelling in your gorgeous wee face and feet has gone down quite a bit. As I write this, your physio is here and helping you to move your arms and legs to keep your joints nice and supple. You're doing great, sweetheart!

It's so hard seeing you like this, and I know you can hear us and must want to talk to us.[40] You are in really good hands, honey. Everyone taking care of you is so caring and genuine. Plus, we are keeping a close eye on you every single day – making sure you know you are loved, safe and not alone.

---

40 While I don't remember hearing anything while I was sedated, there were several occasions where I responded to prompts. At one point while I was in the coma, I started getting restless and visibly uncomfortable, and my family asked whether I was in pain. Apparently, I nodded. When they asked where it hurt, I lifted my arms – swathed heavily in bandages – out in front of me like a zombie lying down. It freaked everyone out. I was given more pain relief, and put under deeper.

Keep strong, sweety, and fight hard. We love you and this world is so black and white without you.

Love you, baby girl. Mumma x

9.05am, physiotherapist

Hi, Kelsey. I'm one of the physios working with you. I've just done some work with your breathing, helping to clear sputum off your chest,[41] and done some exercises with your legs to keep them moving. You are off to theatre today, but we'll see you again after. The journey with physio is only just beginning – you'll hate us soon enough haha.

I am so privileged to be able to care for you.

9.17am, Holly

Good morning, little Kezzels ♡

You are looking so good this morning, and everyone is happy with how you are progressing. That's because you're stubborn, and don't give up 😋

There is one of those white birds with the yellow mohawk, a cockatoo or something, at the motel we're staying at. It's giving us a good laugh every time we come and go because it always says 'Hello' or 'Hello, Pickles' (his name), and the newest one, 'Hello, cookie', when we come in, and 'Bye-bye!' and laughs every time we leave!

Stay strong for another big day ahead of you, big sister. I'm right here in your corner the whole way.

See you in a few hours ♡

---

41 A mixture of saliva and mucus that forms in the respiratory tract, which you would usually cough up, but when you're in a coma, you can't. It can cause infection if it builds up in the lungs. Ew.

9.26am, Holly

Your nurses are washing your hair right now. You seem a bit frustrated by them moving your head around and your cute little face is frowning a bit. It will feel so much nicer for you when it's back to its big curly crazy Kezzel curls ♡

It's cool how they do it. They have a cap which has shampoo and water in it and they put that on your head and give it a good massage and scrub. Tom is right next to you talking to you while you get pampered. They're going to brush your hair!!! Good luck to them haha!

9.35am, Tom

You've been fighting away for the past three days now and it's really showing. I'm so glad you're here with this team. They really are doing everything they absolutely can. Even though you fight back at them brushing your teeth and cleaning your hair ... you really know how to test people, don't you? But the best thing is your stubbornness is finally coming in useful haha!

We're all really excited to see you when you're awake, and there's so many people wanting to see you and just do anything they can for you. I'm extra excited just for you to see your lil River-child again and hear all of his shenanigans since you've been on 'holiday'.

9.52am Holly

Didn't break the comb! But, as usual, everyone is covered in your hair now.

Nurse

Hi Kelsey, I'm one of the ICU nurses who has been looking after you for the past few days. I was here on the unit when you arrived to Hutt ICU, and everyone was busy making sure you were okay after the transfer. It looks like you're already progressing in the right direction – testament to how strong you are and to the support of your lovely family. Good thoughts are coming your way from everyone here and around the world. I hope you don't mind me adding to this and having a look at previous entries. As my friend said, it's great to get to know you a bit better while you're asleep just now.

11.30am, medical notes

Taken to operating theatre for cleaning of burns and skin-graft-type dressings to back and legs, etc. New dressings put over the top.

Family Messenger Chat

3.55pm, Mum

Kels in third surgery now. Should be coming out soon hopefully.

4.39pm, Holly

The girl is out! ♡

Tori

That's wonderful. All went well??

Mum

Just waiting to see her ... They were hoping to take the breathing tube out but have decided she's not quite ready.

Tori

Did they say why she isn't quite ready? (Only if you are up to talking about it x) Everything else went to plan?

Mum

Tube only comes out when she's ready, but her pathways must be swollen and a bit compromised. Will know more when we talk to the surgeon this evening.

It's okay to ask questions, guys. We don't mind. It's a scary time so lots of questions are normal. We'll do our best to answer them and keep you all informed x

Tori

Thanks, Aunty Shelley. It's really appreciated xx

Maree

What a champion!! Well done, Kelsey. They would be needing a lot of skin to go around with so many operations.[42] Do they have enough to go around?

Soraya

Great news that she's out. Can I ask: what was the surgery for today?? And also, which part of Kelsey's body is the most concerning and difficult for them to treat? Xx

---

[42] They did. It was reported that New Zealand ordered 1.2 *million* cm^2 of cadaver skin from the US to treat the survivors of the eruption – and 464cm^2 was used on me. They had to import skin from out of the country.

Holly

Surgery today was to graft her leggies and they said that all went to plan. As for the most concerning and difficult to treat, I think it's her arms and hands, because they are quite bad, and to graft hands is a long and tricky process.[43] They checked them today during her surgery and said so far they look like they're doing good ♡

Vicky

So relieved. What a little trooper Kelsey is, and how amazing are the surgeons ♡

Red Book

5.07pm, Holly

We're breaking hospital rules! But don't tell anyone. All four of us are in here with you (Mum, Dad, Tom and me). You have just come out of surgery and they said you did so well and everything went well. At this point, we are all at the delirious stupid laughing stage. Pickles has made us look crazy to everyone else around us.[44] Bananas are also taking over our motel room. We'll save some for you[45] 😊

---

43 Hands are fiddly, complicated, intricate to work with; there's a lot of moving parts, and maintaining sensitivity is important. My whole right hand was burnt, so that ended up being the one that required the most surgery, physio, hand therapy, etc. Thanks to the bandage Hayden had put on my left hand, my fingers were burnt only down to my 'punching knuckles', and then my arms from the wrist up to my T-shirt line. Funnily enough, I forgot about the bandage for a good month; as I said earlier, it had been removed on the boat back to the mainland, so everyone was pretty baffled by the weird way my hand was burnt!

44 They kept talking to the bird!

45 A bottom-rung 'gingers are orangutans' joke. Funny.

5.12pm, Mum

Well, you are amazing, aren't you! You are fresh from your third surgery and everything went to plan. You look great and your stats are so much better than last time (not that I have a clue what I'm looking at). Nurses say all is really good right now – so please keep it up.

Your grafts are all done.[46] Yay! Now you just have to heal, sweetheart.

While I write this, Dad is rubbing your beautiful (somewhat greasy) head – it's got a bit of paraffin in it, but it is clean haha. Holly is watching me write this, and Tom is chatting ~~up~~ to the nurse. Just kidding – we all like to get as much info from the carers as we can, so we always ask them heaps of questions. They're so good at giving us all the info and making sure we are completely comfortable with everything they are doing. The love in this room for you is HUGE!! Keep on healing, sweetheart. We want you back with us so we can hear your voice and hug you tight! Love, Mumma xxx

7pm, Tom

You just keep impressing everyone here – not just us, but all the team here are so stoked with how well you are doing. It's so, so good seeing you like this, babe, and just another step closer to you seeing River soon. In fact, your little doggo is potentially going to be the poster boy for a vet raffle. The vets are setting up some sort of dog-toy raffle for River to get you home. It's just overwhelming how much support you are getting from all around the world. You've had another big day today, so we're letting you have an early night to rest up. Plus, you're getting physio soon, so they'll be kicking us out.

---

46 Grafts to my arms, hands and lower back were complete, but I still had leg grafts and touch-ups to go.

9.30pm, nurse

Hi Kelsey, I am looking after you tonight. You came back from the operating room at 4pm. It all went really well.

Your face looks much better than a few days ago. I have met your amazing family and your lovely boyfriend, Tom. I am sure that they will all be a great support for you for your recovery, as that will take a little while. But I am sure that you will do well!

It was a pleasure to look after you.

11pm, nurse

Hi, Kelsey. I was here with you yesterday as well. You look a lot better today. When we said your name, you slightly opened your eyes, too. I'll tell you one thing – you are so blessed because you have got a lovely family and a partner. For me it's time to go home. I have got a baby girl and she is waiting for me. But it was a pleasure to look after you today and yesterday. You are doing really great. You take care and our wonderful ICU staff will look after you well.

Saturday, 14 December 2019
Red Book

8.35am, Tom

Holly and I are lucky, we got to see you first this morning. Just as you were getting your teeth cleaned and frowning away. But as soon as you knew we were here you seemed to settle down a little bit. You've been a good girl overnight, and they're just topping up your blood this morning[47] to get you ready to wake up. I am so excited and scared for it, but it's such a good step forward.

9.30am, medical notes

Sedation turned off to allow time to wake up. Reviewed by ICU doctor and monitored closely.

Me

The first thing I remember is not being able to see, and not being able to breathe.

Something is down my throat?!

I tried to move my hands to my mouth to free whatever was there, but I couldn't lift them. I couldn't move *at all*. I started panicking.

I was on a lot of medication. My eyes had been closed for five days, and they were full of the paraffin wax that had been smeared on my face to hydrate the superficial burns on my forehead, around my eyes, and down my cheeks and throat. I had *some* vision, but everything looked double, and had an orange glow.[48] *Why am I in a tent?* I thought. *A tent is not very sanitary.*

Then I heard a familiar voice say, 'Kels, it's all right.'

---

47 A very normal sentence.
48 Mum said my eyes were basically rolling around in my head. I picture a chameleon's crazy eyes when I imagine this.

Dad.

Measured. Steady.

'Just calm down. They're going to pull the tube out. You just need to calm down.'

I don't remember Mum's voice – just Dad's. Mum had been there, but she stepped out of the room because watching me 'come to' was too much. Thanks to the media being assholes, ICU was in lockdown, and once the door into ICU closed behind Mum, she couldn't get back in. No one could. Apparently, it was a while before anyone was able to let her (and Holly and Tom) back in.

It was supposed to take a while for me to wake up, so the doctor had left to see other patients. The nurses weren't allowed to remove my ventilator tube without him being there (in case anything went wrong and/or I needed to be reintubated), but they were there in the room, trying to get me to move my toes. I don't remember hearing their voices, either – I was hyper-focused on Dad's.

Thankfully, I don't remember the feeling of the nurses pulling out the ventilator tube once the doctor returned.

Red Book

9.30am, Tom

Holly and I were outside while your mum and dad were with you and the doctor decided to wake you. It was tough for me seeing you with the tube in and just as tough seeing you wake. But holy fuck I am glad you are. It feels like months have just flown by. We're all staying by your side as much as allowed, and you're doing so, so, so good.

Family Messenger Chat

9.53am, Donna

Hi all, just wondering how you are and if any more news on Kelsey. You are in our thoughts constantly. There are such lovely messages to Kelsey and you all on her donation page, people all pulling for her. She is so loved and respected by friends and tourists she has taken to White Island. She is very precious. Love and hugs to you, Graham, Shelley and Holly. Tori and I will come to visit when it is the right time. Love you ♡ xxx

Red Book

10am, medical notes

Breathing tube removed and ventilator stopped. Now breathing completely independently!

Over next few hours ...

Needing a small amount of oxygen via nose/nasal tubes.

    Moving head and arms, and opening eyes, listening for family's voices.

11.55am, Mum

Tom is talking to you now, while I write this. You have had a huge morning, darling girl. You're no longer on the ventilator, so that pesky tube has gone from your chops. You look so peaceful and calm. I am overwhelmingly proud of you, honey. I can only imagine what is going through your mind,[49] but we are all here for you and not about to leave your side. We are so looking forward to giving you big hugs and telling you to your beautiful 'awake' face how much we love you.

---

49 Pure delusion and insanity.

Dad and Holly are out in the waiting room, waiting for their turn to come and see you. We're only allowed in here two at a time, so we have to share you with each other. We are forming a tag-team to make sure we are always with you. You are not alone, sweetheart.

I keep looking at your perfect little feet. (I know! Me, looking at feet!)[50] I want to tickle them so much haha. You keep screwing up your nose. It's cute. You're so gorgeous. Mumma xx

12.22pm, Holly
Hey, beautiful big sister! You were woken up this morning and the tubes taken out. It was a very distressing time for you, but you are doing so well now! I love you so much, and I am so proud of you xxx

Family Messenger Chat

1.14pm, Mum
They've taken her off the ventilator and woken her up. She's in so much pain, so is heavily sedated. She tries to talk. We've just been told she has an infection.[51] It's been one hell of a traumatic day so far.

Douglas [cousin]
That's no good 😔 She's a bloody tough one though! What an absolute trooper.

---

50 Mother hates feet. But other than my head, they were the only part of my body not swathed in bandages. Desperate times.
51 A very common complication in burn survivors – sometimes the infection can crop up in the donor site, the grafted site, or even in the blood.

Tori

Worried and thinking about you all. Wish there was something I could do to help. Sounds like an awful day 😔 Have they done the right thing waking her up when she is still in so much pain?

Mum

Her medical team are all incredible and super experienced, so we have every confidence in them. It's not uncommon to get infections but obviously not ideal. They're working hard to sort the right antibiotic.

Donna

Good to hear medical team are the best. Be strong, Kelsey. Such a hard time right now ♡♡

Red Book

2pm, medical notes

Starting to say a few words, voice a bit raspy.

3.52pm, Holly

It is so good to see you smile! You look so beautiful and we missed it so much! You are still struggling to talk, but we are figuring it out. You said you were hot, so I got the nurse to get you a fan, and she did. All four of us are here in the room with you. We love you more than we can express and are so proud of you. Xxx

3.58pm, Mum

You are smiling! It's the most beautiful thing I have ever seen. The mention of Tom's name is all it takes! It's *so* good to have you awake, honey. We know you want to talk to us and must have so much to say. But there will be plenty of time for that, sweetheart.

I love you to the moon and back, Kels, and will be here for you right throughout this journey. You are the strongest, most determined (some might say stroppy and stubborn) girl I know. So you can do this! No more writing for me today, because I just want to sit and look at your beautiful face. Mumma xxx

4.30pm, Tom
The best day of this year just seeing you smile again. You look so comfy now that there's a fan in here too. Holly and I both said we wish we could just snuggle up with you.

I know there's so much going on in your head right now and so many questions. We are going to be here every step you take, and there are so many people here to help you. We're all so lucky to have you, and so lucky you're a tough and stubborn girl who just keeps fighting. We are sticking by your side. We all love you so much.

Evening, medical notes
New line in right foot through which to monitor blood pressure and also take blood samples. Another new line in left subclavian vein to give pain relief and antibiotics. Voice still a little weak,[52] but will improve daily. Speech comprehensible. Only a tiny bit of oxygen. Continuing with intravenous antibiotics.

6.50pm, Tom
Today was supposed to be a nice rest day for you after your surgery yesterday. Damn, what a day! No complaints from us because you're awake. Even got you to say, 'Hi, baby,' and, 'Hi,

---

52 This has literally *never* been said about me, before or since.

Mumma.' Graham has been giving you his stumpy-handed[53] massage for almost an hour. You're well and truly fast asleep now, and you even said 'goodbye' – even though we weren't leaving. Where did these manners come from? It's been what feels like a month but just a really long week.

Hopefully you can finally get some well-deserved rest tonight and tomorrow.

We love you so much, Kels.

Family Messenger Chat

9.30pm, Dad
Hi all, hectic day but ended okay. We got a smile out of Kelsey. Cheered us all up. They seem to be getting her pain under control, and trying to get on top of temp/infection. So far so good.
Thanks heaps, guys, for all the support.

Vicky
Brilliant news. Big sigh of relief all around. She's a little beauty 🫶💕

---

53 Dad is missing half of one of his thumbs – he's a sheetmetal engineer, and when we still lived in Palmy, his glove got caught in a pipe roller and crushed his thumb off. He loved freaking out Holly's and my friends by jamming it in his eye or ear, making it look like he was in up past his knuckle.

Sunday, 15 December 2019
Family Messenger Chat

9.03am, Maree

Hello, another day closer to healing and recovery for Kelsey today. Wondering if there's any indication as to how many more surgeries will follow? 💕

Mum

One more big one – possibly several smaller ones.

Red Book

10.15am, Tom

Pretty slack that no one else has been writing since me! I guess everyone is just super excited to chat with you now. Your first worry when I came in was, 'Who's looking after the dogs?' Just in case you forgot, they are in safe hands with [my] Mum and Dad. River slept inside once and chewed a whole bunch of stuff. So now he sleeps on the deck.[54] Haha. They are being very good, and Riv only did his howly bark for one night.

You said you thought you'd been here for five weeks. Which is what it feels like to me too, but luckily only six days now and you're doing so well.

Family Messenger Chat

10.20am, Mum

Just seen our girl briefly. She's trying to talk. She's asking about the

---

[54] River was a little menace as a pup, once even managing to de-pot my cactus without knocking over the pot, and placing it in the shagpile rug, where Tom stepped on it barefooted as he was leaving for work.

others.[55] She thinks she's been in hospital for five weeks and she says the doctors are mean and ignore her,[56] but that the nurses are nice. They're turning her now and she told us that we don't want to be there for that.[57] Her eyes are really blurry so she can't see us. They're getting her looked at by an optician next week.[58] She's had a bit of physio too and scoffed a lemonade ice-block 🙏

Tori

How did the physio go? What kind of physio is it? Aww, poor Kelsey asking about the others 😢 I hope her blurry vision is only temporary – good the optician is coming next week.

---

55 I was so heavily medicated that I kept hallucinating, and forgetting where I was (despite being told almost hourly) or what was going on, despite remembering the eruption itself. The nurses told my family that due to the level of medication I was on, I would struggle to retain a lot of information, so they kept the details to the necessities, and dodged questions that they didn't want to have to repeat the answers to – especially what had happened to Hayden and the others on the island. I sometimes knew I was in hospital thanks to the eruption, but I had no idea how severe things were – not for me, not for everyone else. The aftermath was something I had yet to discover.

56 They just couldn't hear my tiny voice! Also, I was hallucinating, so they couldn't exactly help me other than reassure me that everything was okay.

57 Arguably, being turned or 'flipped' in the bed was worse than actually being burnt. Every two-ish hours, I would be moved from lying on one side to the other, in an effort to prevent bedsores. The nurses would tentatively enter the room, knowing they were about to cause me extreme pain, in order to prevent further stress on my already overtaxed body.

58 I remember not being able to focus. I could kind of tell who was next to me, but I couldn't see them clearly. Everyone was hoping it would come right as my medication was decreased over the coming days and weeks. My ACC forms (filled out by medical staff) said I had been hit on the head on the island, so there was a lot of concern about that – hence the early head scan. I am *certain* I wasn't hit on the head, though: I remember that my helmet was intact when I took it off, and I had no external head injury, which you would expect with the force with which that shit was being thrown around on the island.

Mum

She's still fighting the infection but *so* good to hear her whispery, raspy voice and see the odd smile. Physio is just having her legs moved and feet flexed a few times and three big breaths.[59]

Leigh

So glad she's up for ice-blocks! It must be so hard to know what to tell her about the others.

Mum

Nothing at the moment. When she asks, we just tell her that we have been only focusing on her.[60]

Leigh

It must all be very disorienting for her, and I'm sure she's on mighty strong painkillers to boot!

Mum

Yes, she has said she's so confused, but then she seems to come out with things that really surprise us.[61]

---

59 An attempt to help keep my lungs clear of sputum. Ew.

60 Despite how hard it was for my family to keep hearing me ask about what had happened to people like Hayden, and for them to keep avoiding having to answer, I believe they did the right thing not telling me for as long as they did. By this time, 15 December 2019, sixteen out of the forty-seven of us who had been on the island when it erupted had been confirmed dead, and two were missing (one of those being Hayden).

61 Mum said she doesn't remember now what these things were, but apparently from very early on I would remember the names of the medications I was being given, and I always wanted to know who was in the room and what their purpose was.

Carol

Oh, Shelley, it must be such a relief to be able to communicate with her at last. Good she's responding to you and medical staff. Our love and thoughts are with you all xxxx

Soraya

Just saw Kels on the news. Brought tears to my eyes!! They said she said she felt the eruption and got her group to get behind rocks??[62] So is she recalling things, or perhaps that's come from someone who was in her group?? I can imagine Kelsey would have been so incredibly brave in the moments this all unfolded! ♡♡♡♡

Mum

Must be from someone in her group. They're also saying that she is the one who got her group back down to the jetty.

Maree

She's a fighter, so strong. Will they need to induce a coma again? ♡

Mum

That's our girl. Hopefully not. But she will have to go back to surgery and have the breathing tube in every time they change her dressings. We have also been told that she and Jake went back and helped others down too – but we haven't had it confirmed.[63] We have been living in our little Kelsey-focused bubble and trying to shut out most of the media stuff.

62 Classic media. Fifty per cent accurate.
63 Again, I don't know where this information was coming from, and given the chaos that unfolded in the days and weeks after the eruption, a lot of things were said about what happened by people who weren't there. But you've read what I did on the island now. You know.

Donna

You should be so proud of her, Graham and Shelley. She is amazing. Credit to her parents. Even the people who were on the boat with the fire in 2016 are praising her. She is a hero 😍

Mum

I know. The messages are beautiful. She's a pretty cool chick. 💕

Donna

Douglas found the link to the news bit. *[Posts link.]* For all those asking. Hope that's okay, Shelley?

Mum

It's all bullshit!

Holly

Brad Inman?!

Donna

Kelsey told them?????

Mum

No. She's been in a f-ing coma!!!

Donna

Unbelievable. They must just make up things.

Holly

Makes me so mad 😣😖 Kels doesn't need this.

Mum

They didn't even get *Hayden* Inman's name right![64] They are disgusting morons!

Leigh

Must be so frustrating that they are just pulling stuff out of nowhere. Good thing you're staying away from the media if you can. They are just desperate to say anything, I think.[65] Try not to let it get to you. Unlikely anyone will take note of such a short, inaccurate report 🤜

Red Book

During the day, medical notes

Eating a little bit of fruit and drinking some juice (by mouth), and continuing liquid food via nasal feeding tube (for energy and protein). Carrying on strong pain-relief infusion and small amounts of oxygen via nasal tubes. Continuing intravenous antibiotics.

Chatting to staff about family and Tom.

---

64 This article also butchered Tipene's name, and the reporter claimed to have spoken with me. It said *I'd* told them, among other things, that I was in Wellington Hospital and that I had called my mum from the island (despite the lack of cellphone service – and lack of cellphone) to tell her we were halfway to the summit (we were in the crater – no one went to the 'summit'). I am aware that tensions were running high, that things were happening behind closed doors and that people who knew the facts weren't talking about what had happened, because the important thing in those early days was getting us help – but that is no excuse. This entire story was a fabrication. And getting Hayden's name wrong was awful. My family was *livid*. People were still looking for his body, and the reporter couldn't even get his name right.

65 Unfortunately, it wasn't just the media riding the wave of interest that the eruption had generated. Strangers, ex-colleagues, ex-friends and people who had been shit to me in uni were all trying to attach themselves to the story. Suddenly, everyone was my best friend.

Staff helping to reposition on alternate sides. Dressings redone to lower back as a bit oozy – doctors came to check it, given extra pain relief for this as a bit sore.

Drinking water through a straw.

10.38am, Holly
You were chomping on a lemonade ice-block when I came in today. I've never seen something disappear so fast in my life! You didn't quite finish the whole thing, and when you were done with it you said, 'Ice-block over.' That made me laugh.

It's been so nice being able to talk to you and see your smile. I'm going to go talk to you now 😊

I love you. Keep doing what you're doing.

2.13pm, Mum
Well, you are awake and making sure we all know it. Apparently you don't like the doctor 'Peter'.[66] According to you, he ignores you. But you like all of your nurses except one that you just said was a 'bitch'.[67] Haha.

Tom has just fed you lunch – again, according to you, 'gelatinous goop'. You are such a stroppy wee thing.

We are all so proud of your attitude so far. It's not going to be an easy road at all, but if you try hard to keep this strong attitude going, you will go a long way a lot quicker. And we will be with you every step of the way. Mumma xx

---

66 There was no Peter.
67 This makes me laugh – none of them were bitches. But, looking back, medicated Kelsey was a hoot!

3.06pm, Mum

While Tom was just feeding you ice cubes, the nurse had a quick look up your gown just to check all was well.[68] You very indignantly looked up and, in a bit of a posh voice, said, 'Excuse me! Announce yourself!' You are so funny!! But fair enough.

Lots of good long peaceful sleeps, baby. We are just sitting beside you. We'll be here for you when you wake up. Love you so, so much. You amaze me every day. Mumma xx

6.48pm, Mum

You crack me up – and everyone in the room! A lovely nurse just came in and asked you 'Are you sleeping?', and you went mad at her because you thought she asked Tom if he was single!![69]

---

68 She was checking my catheter tube.
69 Hahahahaha!

Monday, 16 December 2019
Red Book

Overnight, medical notes

Sleeping for a few hours at a time overnight.

4.30am

Woke up from a dream about being in a bar. Reassured by staff and settled back to sleep.[70]

4.50am, nurse

Hi Kelsey, I've been looking after you in ICU overnight. You're doing great at the moment, drinking lots of water which us nurses are always happy with!! You've slept for a good few hours overnight. (I have tried my best not to disturb you too much – just checking on you a lot from the doorway to make sure you are okay.) You are able to move your arms and legs a little, although you remind us that they feel very heavy! You were cracking jokes earlier and making us all laugh – you have a great sense of humour. It's lovely to be able to talk to you a little bit. I introduced myself earlier and you said, 'Mum said you're really nice,' which was so kind. Off to finish my other paperwork now. (You are fast asleep 😳)

Family Messenger Chat

8.05am, Carol

Morning, Shelley, Graham and Holly. How is our Kelsey today? We are hoping they have her pain under control, her infection is on its

---

[70] Funnily enough, I vaguely remember this! Not enough details to put in here, but enough to know I didn't feel safe. Someone was after me because I didn't do enough on the island during the eruption.

way out and that she is comfortable. Biggest hugs and kisses from us. You are always in our thoughts.

Red Book

10am, Tom

They finally let us in to see you again. We are pretty naughty – we just show up whenever and expect to see you. It's nice and cool in here this morning, and peaceful. Hopefully you're allowed to relax for a while. I miss your banter so much, but it's also great to see you finally relax a bit.

You are heading back into theatre today to get your dressings changed and get you all nice and clean. You've done really well every time you go in. So proud of you for staying tough, baby.

[Your] Mum and I are here, and [your] Uncle Scott is waiting outside but he might come in later today when you're a bit more awake. The support from back home just never stops, ever. Arnika has volunteered to help me milk!

So much love is rolling in every day. I don't want to go for two days, but the admin has to be done. Then I can be back here for as long as you and I want. Love you so much, baby. Keep doing it xx

Family Messenger Chat

7pm, Kath [aunt]

Hi, everyone. How's Kelsey today? 😢

Red Book

7.40pm, Scott [uncle]

My first visit with Kelsey. First sight was her asleep and her big pie-hole wide open! Poor girl – we had a wee conversation. You asked how the kids are and some other small talk. I was blocking the fan, so I was asked to leave ... funny. Then told to stand in the corner! That's when I wrote this![71]

Family Messenger Chat

9pm, Mum

Hey, lovelies. Sorry, but I had to make the decision to have a phone-free day. The weekend was really rough. But today was great! Even after a surgery. I am totally shattered tonight. Scott is cooking dinner and Tom poured the wine. I reckon I will be asleep in about ten minutes. Thank you all for your love and ongoing support. It's honestly a huge help in coping with what each day brings. Xxxx

Rach [aunt]

Sleep well ... good luck with Scott's dinner. Do the letters KFC or McD feature? 😄 Loved seeing Graham and Holly today xxoo

Vicky

Keep up the great work Shelley and co. You are all doing an amazing job. Kelsey will definitely be responding to all your love and support. Big hugs to you all ♡♡♡

---

[71] Apparently 'me on loads of drugs' has no filter! There was another time where Dad was speaking to me about something in ICU, and I told him to shut up, because there were a couple of nurses talking in hushed voices in the corner of my room and I desperately wanted to know what was going on with me all the time.

Tuesday, 17 December 2019
Family Messenger Chat

7.48am, Mum

Yesterday was a good day. Chatty and cheeky. Less delusional and pain slightly more under control. Infection identified and appropriate antibiotics prescribed. We were so incredibly shattered last night.
Not a great sleep, but have moved motels to a much nicer one within walking distance. Holly flies back tomorrow, and Kels has her fifth trip to theatre. Xx

Holly

♡♡♡ I love you guys xxx

Soraya

Sounds like things are starting to become a little more calm. Sending you all lots of love! Xxxx

Donna

Thank you for the update, Shelley. Keep strong all of you. You're doing wonderfully under circumstances that we can't even begin to imagine. Does Kelsey have surgery again today? Give Kelsey our love. We are proud of her, and she is doing so well and being incredibly strong. Love to you all ♡♡

Red Book

10.07am, Mum

You had a really good day yesterday – despite having a three-hour trip to theatre to change your dressings.

Your thoughts are a lot more lucid and your vision has slightly improved, although it still takes a lot of your energy to try to focus.

You have such an incredible strength within you, honey. Sometimes I think you're being strong for all of us. That's just who you are, isn't it.

You're very sleepy – mainly due to all of the happy juice in your system – but you want to see and hear everything that's going on around you. Not much to see or hear today though. It's going to be a day of well-deserved and needed rest.

On Sunday, which was a pretty tough day for you,[72] we came in as the nurse told you she needed to give you an injection in your tummy to ensure you didn't develop any blood clots. You were a bit distressed and annoyed, saying that no one ever consults you – they just come in and stab you. So I sat with you and we had a 'consultation', where you finally agreed it was in your best interest and were satisfied that there had been an official sit-down consultation! Talk about standing up for yourself! Very impressive and also quite amusing. Go, you!!

You are eating puréed food now too. Along with your feeding tube in your nose. One of your nurses made the mistake of trying to make your protein/carb tube food sound appetising by telling you it was bacon! Your face said it all. I had to very quickly tell her you are a vegetarian and she had to do a very quick back-track and say it was kale-flavoured instead!!

You don't like a lot of the puréed food they give you. But you did enjoy the carrots last night. Plus a kind nurse found you a strawberry smoothie drink that you polished off in seconds.

We have started bringing in some of the many, many cards and gifts you have been getting. There are literally *hundreds* of people all over the world sending you love and support and

---

72 The day after I'd been woken up from the coma.

messages of encouragement. You have clearly touched many lives, my amazingly wonderful girl.

You are sleeping more soundly the last two days. A wee bit of snoring even. You look so peaceful and more free from pain too. But we know you are digging deep and are so proud of you, honey. Mumma x

1.15pm, Tom
Apparently your head fell off the bed while they were washing your hair. Bit of an adventure getting your head back on haha![73]

Gave you some more puréed peach, which is possibly your favourite here so far. You were offered more but said you were satisfied. Even though you're in and out of sleep you seem to remember each day really well now. Plus your vision is slowly getting better, so it looks like you'll still have better vision than me! They are also thinking of shifting you to the 'valley view' room! Talk about special treatment! But at least you'll have a window and a lot more light, mostly to keep you up during the day hehe.

I don't want to go home, but you have approved my leave so I guess I'd better do it. Gotta make sure [my dad] Jim is looking after the kids [dogs] and not lying to me. Plus the cows probably need a break from his shouting. I can't bring any plants back sadly, but I will make sure they're all alive and that someone is checking them. Wish I could bring Jess and Riv back with me but they would just pull your dressings apart.

---

73 In my brain, I was in an old, green-tiled bathroom, which was round, on a rickety, wrought-iron bed, and my head was hanging off the edge of it so my hair could be washed. I don't think that's what was actually happening!

I'll bring the next best thing though: Graham! I'm glad you're snoring away now, resting up.

Keep on being a tough bitch, bebe.

Family Messenger Chat

8.59pm, Scott

Hope it was a good day.

Mum

Unfortunately not. She seemed so sad all day.

Kath

Sadly this is par for the course. She needs physical and emotional healing. I'm sure counselling will come for you all most probably. Unfortunately, as much as you want to, you can't shield her from this. Just be there and listen. Words aren't always called for 🥲

Mum

Thanks, Kath. I know ... Counsellors and victim support etc are coming out of the woodwork for all of us. We're all still processing, I guess. Xx

Wednesday, 18 December 2019
Red Book

Time unknown, Mum

#5 – Theatre – dressing changes, 5 hours.[74]

Family Messenger Chat

12.07pm, Mum

She goes in soon. She's struggling today. It's a lot for her to come to terms with. Will try to update later after surgery x

Carol

It must be dreadful for her, the poor darling. We are all sending her brave thoughts, to you as well, Shelley. You are amazing too xxx

1.42pm, Donna

Do you have someone with you, Shelley?

Dad

Holly just arrived back, and Shelley's parents.

Tori

Big hugs and love, Aunty Shelley. Can only imagine what you are all going through. Is the pain medication she's on still really strong/affecting whether she is disoriented?

4.08pm, Mum

Kels back in theatre. Plenty of pain meds on board. A bit in and out of sleep/La La Land xx

---

74 The only Red Book entry on this day. Must have been a *bad* day.

Vicky

Where are they operating on Kels today, Shelley?

Mum

Her back and also checking all other grafts and re-dressing. About four hours.

Rachael [cousin]

So after this op she'll have had her back, arms/hands and legs grafted? How many more ops do they think she'll need? Xx

Mum

I've been really terrible at updating, sorry. Running on empty.

Her first major op was eight hours the night we arrived (1.30am). That was to 'scrub' off as much burnt skin as possible and clean everything. Second op also about eight hours was to graft arms and hands with skin taken from her back. Third op was about six hours to do grafts on her legs with donated cadaver skin.

What we hope will be her final big op will be to replace all of the cadaver skin with her own skin, plus grafts on lower back and upper arms. But her back got infected where they had taken her skin from, so the regeneration has taken longer. So it may be delayed, as they are hoping to use that new skin.

In between all of this, she goes back to theatre every two days to have dressings changed, grafts checked and fixed up as required, and cleaned. This is about two to four hours each.

She has also had a chest infection. Infection and blood clots are very common in burns patients, as they are so at risk without skin acting as a barrier, plus the patients can't regulate their own temperatures.

I hope that helps fill in some questions. Xx

She's on a cocktail of pretty much all the pain meds you can imagine. They up the dose whenever they turn her (or 'flip' her, as she puts it). She gets turned every three hours, and it's really painful.

Rachael
Thanks so much for the detailed update, Aunty Shelley. Sounds like Kels is nearing the last of her major operations if all goes according to plan. Hopefully they can get on top of her infections soon and keep that horrible pain under control. Lots of love 💕

Leigh
Gosh she is going through so much! She is a legend. No need to apologise – we all know you have your hands full taking care of Kelsey! She is priority number one. Hope you are also managing to take care of yourself. Is there any update on her vision? I think last you mentioned it was blurry and someone was going to assess. She is our hero right now, that's for sure! ♡

Mum
Oh sorry. Yes her vision is still double and blurry. She will see a neurologist soon. Not sure when yet as surgery today.

Leigh
Hope today's surgery goes well and you get good news from the doctors going forward ♡

5.12pm, Mum
She's out but still in recovery. Apparently all went to plan xx

Thursday, 19 December 2019
Red Book

11.05am, Holly

Kezzels! I made it back *just in time* to see you quickly before you went in for another surgery. I was so happy I got to see you.

Wow! You're a new woman! You are talking so well, and moving around so much more too! You're shocking all the nurses with how well you are improving.

Mum is brushing your hair right now and you are almost purring, you're enjoying it so much.

So many people send their love and are thinking of you on the daily. You have made an impact on so many lives. Keep being exactly who you are, Kezzels! You couldn't be more perfect!

11.31am, Mum

Well, you are a very bright little button today! Very chatty and so much more movement!! Not only does this make your nurses' life easier, but it's amazing progress for you that will help so much in your recovery! Great attitude too, honey. You want to 'get out of bed' so you can make it more comfortable to get back in. We love you so much, sweetheart. Your smile is the most amazing gift each day. Your soft-toy collection is growing. I wonder if, when you get home, River and Jess are going to inherit some new chew toys!

Keep on being you, honey. You're doing so incredibly well and, like we all keep saying, we will all be with you every step of the way. Mumma xx

P.S. We love that you refer to your catheter bag as your 'bag of gold'.[75]

75 Who the hell am I?!

1.37pm, Holly

WOW!! You just sat up for the very first time in ten days!! You had a bit[76] of assistance, but you did so well and you are so happy about it! We all are! You had such a big smile on your goofy little face.[77] OMG, and right now we just got the news that they're moving you to the ward at 4pm *today*!! You are making the most amazing improvements and your attitude is incredible!! Keep this up and you'll be out of here in no time! I am so proud of you, and we all love you so much xxx

Red Book

Nurse

Hi! I'm one of your nurses in Hutt ICU. I'm the clumsy one who keeps dropping stuff and tripping on things. Last night I was trying to unblock your 'fish tube', as you call it,[78] and I ended up squirting water on your face! I know you got really annoyed with me 'cos who wouldn't?! I feel really bad, but I'm hoping you'll look back on it with a bit of a chuckle![79] Geez, the kind of nurses you have to deal with, hey? You deserve a medal just for putting up with us!

Anyway, I've looked after you for three days now. And I know you've been hearing this so often that it might feel like people are just

---

76 A lot.

77 I remember this so very differently. I remember it being incredibly painful. I remember not wanting to do it at all. Moving me only about 45 degrees hurt like hell, so you can imagine what trying to sit up was like.

78 My feeding tube! I don't know why I called it my fish tube. Maybe because every time they tried to move it, it seemed to get caught on something, and my body went one way while my head went the other as I tried to avoid putting tension on the stitch in my septum that kept the tube in place – kinda like a hooked fish. I'd usually yell, 'MY NOSE!' I remember this incident well – I trusted this nurse so much, despite the water in my face!

79 I do! At the time I was deep in a hallucination in which monkeys and men were trying to come through the skylight in my room, so I was less inclined to laugh.

saying it, but you really have been getting better every day! It might not feel like it – especially after the afternoon we had yesterday – but it's true. Yesterday you went back to theatre, and they gave you some 'good stuff' and you came back with psychedelic dreams. Our pain team has been trialling you on different pain meds to see what works for you as we get you ready for the ward. You said you just want to sleep but your brain won't shut down. We have been playing this game where, when you see my face, you tell me what's going on in your head and I tell you if it's true or false.

I'm so sorry our afternoon didn't feel like you are well on your way to better days. It's a long journey and sometimes it'll feel like that. There might even be times when you take a step back, but that doesn't mean it won't get better. It's all just a part of the process. Just know that every day you wake up, no matter how hard the day will be, is one day you're getting closer to beach walks and boat rides! I'm sure you'll get there, you beautiful, strong, vibrant woman! You have endured so much and yet you still find it in you to throw a few jokes here and there! I feel bad we met this way, but it's been a pleasure looking after you! Keep on shining, Kels! The great outdoors is waiting! You got this!

Me

I never got to see this nurse again, but I am so grateful to her. This was my most hallucinatory period, and she would 'true or false' me to help me to determine whether what I was seeing and thinking was real or not.

The beauty/horror of hallucinations is they are *so real* when you're experiencing them. I was seeing, feeling, tasting and hearing everything – and it was bloody hard to wrap my head around being told that what I was going through so vividly wasn't, in fact, 'real'.

What were my hallucinations, I hear you ask? Well, you already know the being-in-a-tent one. In another, the band Slipknot was playing outside my room, and the 'fake blood' – which was part of this very exclusive show and was pouring through the bottom of my hospital curtain – looked very real. They were very good live.

One time, on the way to surgery, I went through a cheese waterfall. It remains unconfirmed whether or not it was real cheese – it looked very yellow. Can't have been good New Zealand cheese.

Several hallucinations featured the medical staff – like when I had twin doctors and one was evil. Or when medical personnel from around the world were coming to the boss's office (which I was parked outside, in my hospital bed) to offer gifts in a bid to win the rights to fix me. I remember a plate of boiled potatoes was one of the offerings.

There was the one where the nurses in ICU were sick of me being so dependent, so they kidnapped me. I was 'too much' and taking up too much time and resources for someone who'd done this to themselves 'voluntarily'. Initially they hid me in a small house, which I remember was near the sea. My hospital bed was far too big for wherever they had placed me, and things were digging into me and becoming painful.[80] I was moved into kitchens, back rooms and between cabinets. Then I was moved to someone's dingy living room, and there was a dead body in a recliner near my bed. I remember calling out for help, but my tiny voice reached no one. I wanted to get up and move, but I felt *sooo* heavy. My limbs were wrapped so big and tight. And now I had the crookest guts.[81]

---

80 This part was probably true. My bandages bothered the hell out of me, so some truth would leak into my delusions.

81 I assumed from the stress, in my delusion, but it turns out the high-fibre meal going in my nose was too much for my system in real life.

I didn't want to be even more of a burden than they'd said I was, but I called for help. When someone finally came back, they yelled at me: 'This is why we're getting rid of you! You're so much fucking work!' I was crying and tried to tell them about the dead body in the chair, but when I looked up, they were *pulling the arms off the body and shoving them into a bag.*

Eventually they moved me to some creepy, tiled cellar – it was a blue-green hue. I was tied to the bed, a fire-extinguisher pin was put through my foot to hold me in place, and they decided they would kill me and dispose of the body. I remember their shadows outside my windows, and how they lurked around outside while I desperately tried to escape. In fear, my stools loosened and my bowels let go – which only irked the nurses further.

Rather than kill me then dispose of the body, they decided to just do both at the same time: they brought in a pig to eat me alive. The pig was very small, though, and I was too full of medication, so it wouldn't eat me. Thankfully, Mum found me (and she was very calm about the whole situation?!)

After I got moved out of ICU, on my first night on the burns/plastics ward, I was hallucinating something chronic. In my mind, gangs were taking over New Zealand. They had taken over Parliament. They were turning over cars, and they had turned their attention to the hospitals. They'd surrounded us and were breaking in. I was terrified. I couldn't move, but I could see and hear them getting in. People were being killed in front of me.

At some stage I believed that I managed to get up and started leading some people out of the hospital and across the hospital grounds. There was a road that was blocked with cars and gang members, and we were creeping through the bushes trying not to be seen or heard, just trying to get to safety ...

Don't do drugs, kids.

Red Book

Nurse

Kelsey, you are making great moves forward. I have enjoyed getting a glimpse of your fun side and character. Be loud and proud – remind us when we jibber acronyms at you – call us out. Kelsey, it has been humbling being able to be part of your recovery.

Me

Every day that I was in ICU, Mum would ask the doctors and nurses if I was going to make it, and they would skirt around the question. 'She's very sick,' they'd say. 'She has a long way to go.' But this day, the head of ICU came to tell her they were moving me to the plastics and burns unit, and said, 'You know you've got her, right? She's going to be okay.'

Mum bawled her eyes out. So did the head of ICU. This was the first time my family was given confirmation that I was going to make it – ten long days after the eruption.

I remember waking up during the night on my first few nights on the burns ward (to be fair, it could have all been the same night), and there was always someone sitting in the dark in the corner of the room, with a dim night-light on, doing some kind of paperwork.

Initially, I didn't say anything, but I eventually asked one of the nurses what she was doing lurking in the darkness. She said something about me being on 24/7 surveillance. I guess this was because I was so fresh from ICU. For some reason, I thought I was on suicide watch.

Family Messenger Chat

8.30pm, Mum

So, *a huge* day today. Kels was pretty good this morning and, despite having some interesting delusional moments, asked to sit up on the side of her bed! It took a lot of effort and assistance but she did it!!!! Most of her lines were removed today too, which is massive progress for one day. Then they moved her out of ICU and up to the plastics and burns unit.[82] She's still in isolation and still has multiple surgeries ahead of her, but things are looking up.

    A rough afternoon due to exhaustion and discomfort. It's a bit old and ugly in her new surroundings, but it's *epic* progress and we are beyond happy.

    I hope you all sleep better tonight, because I reckon I will!!! Love you all so much xxx

Vicky

Woohoooooo!! This is amazing news! What a huge relief. Kels is a little champion!! Great Xmas gift for us all 🫣💕💕💕

Mum

Please keep all of this a little hush-hush. Because she is the only surviving Kiwi/guide who can talk,[83] media will be even more of a pain in the butt than they have already been. Kels is currently unaware of the magnitude of the event or the loss of life. She needs to be much more stable first.

---

82 The burns ward is part of the plastics ward, and we used 'burns ward' and 'plastics ward' interchangeably.
83 Jake was still in a coma.

Friday, 20 December 2019
Family Messenger Chat

9.12am, Mum

Holly and I just went and saw Kels off to theatre this morning. She was in a good mindset – some interesting delusional conversation, but that's just a part of the recovery. She'll be in for about three hours, then up to an hour in recovery. Body temp down a bit too now which is wonderful.[84]

Red Book

2.41pm, Holly

You have had such a big day again. You were in theatre from about 8.45am and they have only just finished up working with you now! From your elbows right down to your fingers are all uncovered now, for the first time. The colouring will settle over time, so even though it's a bit shocking at the moment, this will become more settled.[85]

While you were in surgery, Mum and I went and got a couple more things to brighten and decorate your room. I think you'll like the cow yoga calendar. As always, you're doing amazing. Keep positive, my crazy sister. I love you more than the moon. Holly xxx

---

84 My body did some funky stuff while trying to get through this intense period. It was unable to control its own internal temperature, under major stress, and had the unwanted input of infections, so on multiple occasions my temperature and heart rate spiked.

85 I did *not* react well to seeing my arms and hands – they looked like something that belonged to a zombie or decomposing body: black, bloody, swollen. I barely looked at them, which was quite a feat given they were stretched out alongside my body while I lay in bed, propped up on pillows.

3.03pm, Mum

Another big day for you today, sweetheart. The trips to theatre really take it out of you. You are currently sleeping soundly after an exhausting day.

It's so good to see your hands and lower arms freed from all those layers of bandages. They must have been so uncomfortable. Your grafts look amazing and will only get better with time, honey.

It amazes me what you have been through and how you have rarely complained. Your manners are impeccable – even when you must surely want to tell everyone where to go! Our pride for you just grows every day.

Being up in plastics is a big move, but it is a really positive one, honey.[86] It was sad for all of us saying goodbye to the wonderful team in ICU. They saved your life, sweetheart. For that we will be forever grateful.

Now your job is to recover fully and live that precious life of yours to the absolute fullest. When the going gets tough – and it will – just remember how loved you are, and know that we are here for you always! Love you so, so much, sweetheart. Mumma xxx

---

[86] I also did not react well to being moved out of ICU. I was so scared about any sort of change – despite recently thinking that my nurses were trying to kill me. I begged to stay, I cried, but as with all things in life, progress is only made by going forward – and you can do it scared.

Saturday, 21 December 2019
Family Messenger Chat

6.24am, Dad

I arrived last night. What a difference from when I left on Sunday. Kelsey looks awesome. Talking well, occasionally a little confused, and plenty of smiles. I know that might be different today, but great to see that Kelsey spark returning.

Donna

That is wonderful. Did surgery go well yesterday? Kelsey feeling all right after it? Love and hugs to you all ♡

Dad

Surgery is just to change dressings and a few touch-ups until next Friday – a big one to graft her legs. She's in good spirits again this morning, so good to see. Sight now good.[87]

Donna

Thank you for the update and I hope things keep improving. Wonderful news about Kelsey's eyesight. Phew! ♡

Maree

Good to hear, Graham. Gives her a week's recup time before the next big surgery. We're all believing in the best possible outcome for her. Are there more mini surgeries before the big surgery? Is she still in isolation with minimal visitors?

---

87 Reduced meds and a bit of time were all my eyeballs needed.

Dad

If they see anything that needs touching up while changing dressings, they do it then. That's why in surgery. Yes, still in own room, but now in burns unit not ICU.

9.16am, Mum

She's talking way more today and has recounted the whole event. She is having kidneys and heart monitored closely though, because there are some concerns there.

Red Book

9.48am, Mum

Day three up in plastics and you are coming ahead in leaps and bounds. To see your hands finally released from your giant mitten-like bandages is so good. It must feel so much better.

One of your nurses is taking out the Luers in your collarbone area. It's a bit of a tricky process, as the tubes go right down to the top of your heart. You will need to breathe slowly and lie flat for half an hour to ensure there are no 'air embolisms'.[88] But you're amazing and doing so well, so I reckon it's going to be a breeze.

---

[88] I'd been lying flat and still for over a week now, so not exactly a change for me here. Embolisms occur when an air or gas bubble forms in a vein or artery. This can block the flow of blood, which is obviously life-threatening.

Sunday, 22 December 2019
Family Messenger Chat

7.06am, Dad

Another good day yesterday for Kelsey. Chatty in morning, tired in afternoon. Rest day today, surgery for dressing changes and touch-ups tomorrow.

Donna

Good to hear, Graham. Great to hear she is chatty and getting a rest today. Is she in much pain?

Dad

Pain level varies 5–7. She doesn't want any more meds on board than need be.

Vicky

So happy to hear Kelsey is having some good days. She really is an incredible young lady.

Dad

Takes after her dad 😊

3.56pm, Soraya

Hi, all. Just spent the last few hours at the motel with everyone. A very quick trip up to the hospital for a cuddle and hello with Kels, and now we are heading back to our accommodation. She's doing so great. Her sense of humour is still just as witty as ever and she's joking away with the nurses and us. Very proud of the courage and strength our gorgeous Kelsey is showing! What a gal! It was a relief to see her in such good spirits, considering everything.

9.36pm, Carol

Kelsey is an inspiration to us all. A gorgeous, witty, loveable, brave, warm-hearted darling. I came away from the hospital after seeing her smiling face and [her] telling the nurse to take enough blood so that she didn't need to come back for more! It was so good to see how Orlando took a liking to her immediately. She's one special girl.

Me

The doctors needed regular (almost daily) blood tests, but my body was so swollen and most of my veins had 'disappeared'. One arm had a vein visible in a gap between grafts – but that had been used for 'medication in', meaning it couldn't be used for 'blood out'. The lines in my neck were also used for 'ins', which meant no 'outs' there either. So they started trying to get blood from the veins in the tops of my feet.

This was even more painful than it sounds. My feet were swollen too, so they needed a vein finder – which was a bit like an ultrasound machine for finding veins as far as I could tell – and the veins were so deep and constricted that they were almost impossible to get to. Even the most experienced phlebotomists struggled. They would make multiple attempts, and I would be bawling my eyes out while my family tried to distract me (fat luck) and hold me still.

At the end of it, they'd be lucky if they got the bare minimum amount of blood needed for the most important tests that I needed pre-surgery.

Monday, 23 December 2019
Red Book

7.59am, Holly

Good morning, little Kezzel. You are bright and bubbly again this morning. Dad is helping you bend all your fingers and he's loving it![89] It's good that it's not hurting you, and you said they feel much better bending today than even just yesterday!

You have another theatre visit today for your bandage changes and any graft touch-ups. I love seeing you happy and chatty. Keep up the amazing attitude. That's what's helping you heal so quickly. I love you so much!! See you after theatre xxx

Family Messenger Chat

9.47pm, Mum

Kels's theatre visit today went really well. She's a bit sleepy but currently enjoying looking through all of the Givealittle messages with Tom. She was super shocked and surprised to learn the actual sum raised, as she thought what she read was $9500.[90]

Graham, Holly, Tom and I all went to donate blood earlier but only Tom was viable haha.[91] At least we tried though, right? Tom gave generously and is very much Kels's hero xx

---

89 Dad earned himself the nickname 'physio-terrorist' because he'd come into my room and, before even saying 'hello', sanitise his hands, glove up and start bending all my fingers to stretch my new skin and get my joints moving. Awful for me but he loved it.

90 It was, in fact, $95,000!!! *Unbelievable*. The final total would end up at $120,120, given by 1980 very generous donors.

91 All of my family were blacklisted due to having recently travelled to places you're not allowed to donate blood after visiting (for a while, anyway)!

Dad

Kelsey good this morning. After surgery not so good, in a bit of pain and very tired. Hopefully a good night and she'll feel better in the morning.

Me

This was a massive day.

Arnika came to visit on her way to the South Island for a well-deserved break from the chaos of home, which I still had no idea about. Apparently before she came into my room, Mum pulled her aside and warned her that I still didn't know about everything that had happened after I left White Island, but that if it came up Mum would address it then and there. My medication had been reduced enough that I was lucid and my memory was reliable again.

Sure enough, almost as if Mum had known,[92] I asked Arnika about Hayden. 'How is he doing?'

Her eyes immediately shot to my mum.

Despite having an inkling ever since *Phoenix* had sped away from Crater Bay, I'd held onto the hope that I was wrong – that not seeing Hayden after the eruption meant nothing. But I think I knew.

Mum moved closer, tears in her eyes, voice wavering. 'He didn't make it.'

The rest of the morning was spent answering my questions and filling in the gaps.

About the loss of life: 'Nineteen have been confirmed dead.'[93]

About Hayden: 'They haven't found his body.'

---

92 Mum *always* knows.
93 At that stage. The final death toll from the eruption would be twenty-two.

About those of us still fighting for our lives in hospitals across New Zealand and abroad – to which I responded, 'Oh, is *that* why you guys have been so dramatic about being "so lucky to *still* have me"?' The reply was a resounding: 'YES!'

About the media frenzy: 'The hospital is in lockdown, and there is security *everywhere* to protect us and you from the media.' They'd been calling and messaging Mum *relentlessly* since within the first twenty-four hours after the eruption, showed up at my parents' house more than once, and tried to break into hospitals to talk to survivors. My family had security escorting them to and from their hotel room for the first week.

During my midday rest, I had two hours alone, but I didn't sleep a wink. My eyes were glued to the door to my room. *What happens if the media comes in? What if they barge in and have cameras? I can't even cover my face with my hands, let alone press the call button for help or yell loud enough for security. I can't protect myself … I am alone for the next two hours with no protection …*

Within those four walls of my room – which had, until this moment, felt so safe – suddenly I felt like I was in the most exposed place on earth.

Tuesday, 24 December 2019
Red Book

8.45am, Tom

It's Christmas Eve already! Sorry I haven't written in here for ages. It's just been too exciting getting to hang out with you again.

[Your dad] Ham is back at stretching your fingers again. I think he's addicted.[94]

Last night was a bit rough for you, when we tried to move you, so I'm glad you're back to happy Kels this morning. We're gonna try and get you up out of bed today, which is huge but it will be tough.

You're pretty lucky you've got such an incredible family here to help you (and me) through every step of the way.

The longer you can keep up this positive attitude, the sooner you'll be back with River. I actually can't believe how fast you're healing all round. I mean, I'm stoked, but just wow.

I got a bit carried away with Christmas for you and what I've got so far isn't even everything! I am here to spoil you and give you everything. Xx

8.56am, Holly

Happy Christmas Eve, Kezzels! Probably not where we thought we were going to be this year, but we are still all together and we'll make it super special anyway.

It's been so exciting seeing you each day and watching your amazing progress!

Hopefully you'll feel like some tasty Christmas treats tomorrow! We'll bring you some extra-good fruits.

Keep that smile and continue to shine, little Kezzel. Xx

---

94 He was.

12.36pm, Mum

You are having so many 'milestone' days now, sweetheart! This morning you managed to move from your bed to your chair!![95] It was a *huge* effort, and even though you were in pain and felt so hot and nauseous, you never once gave up! We are so, so proud of you. Now that you're in the chair, you are completely exhausted and taking a very well-deserved nap. Holly and I are quietly sitting with you, while Dad and Tom pop back to the motel for lunch.

Your 'special self-adjusting airbed' has been taken away and swapped for a better 'normal' mattress that we hope will make life easier for you when turning or getting in/out of bed.

You have been disconnected from your feeding tube all morning too. You even managed to eat a few mouthfuls of falafel.

I can see you having deep thoughts as you stare into space sometimes. I know there must be so much going on in that beautiful head of yours. But I hope with all my heart that you know that you are loved and supported beyond imagination and that you are absolutely strong enough to get through all of the physical and mental hurdles laid in front of you. Your mind is going to be your best weapon in your recovery, and we are there for you all the way. Mumma xxx

Me

I have no memory of the first time I spoke about what had happened to me. There was no single flashback moment where it all came flooding back, either; it was just there. Like any other vivid memory. Like it had always been there.

Apparently, in Whakatāne Hospital, I had very animatedly described to my parents what had happened on the island –

---

95 *Massively* assisted.

once I finally let them see me. Even after I was out of the coma, I kept repeating the same stories. I never forgot what happened, despite everything.

Once I'd been told that people had died – and were still dying, from the injuries they suffered during the eruption, I would get stuck thinking about it. About the 'lucky dip' of that morning, deciding who would lead which group, and how easily it could have been me and Jake in the place of Hayden and Tipene. The what-ifs – a vicious little loop of survivor's guilt – would swallow me up whenever it was quiet.

Family Messenger Chat

4.35pm, Mum
Kels doing well. Has been sleeping all afternoon after an exhausting morning of physio. The physios have been so lovely. They got her into a chair this morning but it took over an hour with lots of wet cloths on her forehead, oxygen and pain. She never once asked to quit though. But she's slept ever since. Theatre tomorrow morning xxx

Rach
Tell Kelsey that physios are called physical terrorists for a reason! We are so pleased with how well she is doing. I will have a gin for you all tonight 😘

Wednesday, 25 December 2019
Family Messenger Chat

7.03am, Dad

Merry Christmas, everyone. Thanks again for all your support. Kelsey got out of bed onto a chair yesterday. Took its toll and tired after. Big step forward though. Today another dressing change, and get her onto the chair again. Everyone have a great day.

12.10pm, Dad

Kelsey already out of dressing change and a lot brighter than yesterday, have opened presents with her, and fed her fruit 😄

Ashleigh [cousin]

Merry Christmas, family! I had a wonderful dream last night – Kels and I were having dinner at a restaurant, drinking wine, catching up, and we were both so pleased with the scars and grafts and how they all healed! Woke up smiling 😊 Can't wait for that to be a reality ♡

Red Book

3.02pm, Mum

Merry Christmas, you gorgeous girl! You are quite simply the best Christmas gift we could possibly ever get.

You had a trip to theatre at 8.30 this morning, so we all went for a drive into Wellington. It was kind of nice to go for a ride and see some of the outside world for the first time in two and a half weeks.[96]

---

[96] Mum only ever left the hospital to go to the motel to sleep and eat – or when she was forced out by the amazing nurses to go and take a break – then she would come back to my room in the morning. Other than that, she never left my side until I was discharged.

Your theatre trip this morning hasn't fazed you. You came out of the anaesthetic without any issues for the first time, which is great!

Dad, Holly and Tom went back to the motel for lunch earlier, and I got to stay here with you. It was so nice. We enjoyed (or at least I did) a nice long chat about your recovery, the media circus, how close we came to losing you and just how incredibly loved you are. Love you, precious girl xxx

3.18pm, Holly

Merry Christmas, little Kezzel! Today has been such a good day, and seeing you being the smiley and funny ginger you are makes me feel so good and happy. I got to help you do some bendy, stretchy physio on your hands this morning. It was scary at first because I didn't want to hurt you, but I got used to it, and you didn't seem to mind 😄 I loved being able to touch your skin and hold your hand. I got a couple of photos, and I think they are a couple of my favourite photos ever! They're so special ♡

Enjoy the rest of your Christmas Day with us four right by your side talking shit, brushing your hair and constantly yelling 'WIGGLE!' at you.[97] Cheers to you, Kezzels xxx

3.32pm, Holly

Tom just brushed and tied up your hair. He needed some guidance with the tying up, but he brushed it very well. Now you kinda look like a Troll doll with that very high ponytail!

---

[97] This was, indeed, almost constant. I had to wiggle my fingers to try to stretch the skin and keep the joints moving. I had to wiggle my feet and pull them up towards my shins to try to prevent 'drop-foot' – a general term for difficulty lifting the foot, which could have happened to me due to muscle wastage and damage.

Me

I didn't have the strength to hold my head up for long enough for my hair to be brushed and, since I was always lying on it (and it wasn't top of the priority list), it got badly matted at the back. Once it finally did get brushed properly, Holly taught Tom to put it in a top-knot.

It was incredibly entertaining, always, spending time with those two. One time, Mum and Dad had gone out for lunch and it was just the three of us in my room. My feeding tube had been bothering me – the paraffin they put on my face to moisturise the burns made it so slick that the tape holding the tube in place would come off, and it was always getting caught when I turned my head, which pulled on the stitch in my septum, so my nose was always really sore. After mentioning it to Tom and Holly, they decided this was something they could help me with.

They sanitised their hands and gloved up, and found scissors, tape, alcohol wipes and whatever else they thought they might need. Then they pulled the moveable light over my head and set it to the 'rugby stadium' setting, right in my face. I was giggling away as they both leaned over me, planning, then removed the useless tape from the tube, wiped it down with alcohol, and alcohol-wiped my face to clear away the paraffin, before discussing – at length – the best place to put the new tape.

Once they'd decided, they started chopping off the length of tape and began sticking it on, when all of a sudden the room fell deathly quiet. We all turned towards the door to see both of my parents standing there, frozen, eyes wide and locked on the three of us. It must have looked *incredibly* concerning – I can only imagine what was running through their minds when they walked in to see what looked like a full surgical procedure happening. Holly and Tom fixed that tape problem, though!

My time in bed was spent with many pillows to prop up my body. I am *sure* that I had the whole ward's worth of pillows. A couple under each leg, sometimes with bonus ones on the outside or inside, depending on the need. One or two under each arm. One or two at the end of my bed to flex my feet to ninety degrees.[98] And if they had to flip me onto one side or the other to prevent bedsores, they'd throw another couple under my back for good measure. Keep in mind that I was in a single hospital bed, so there was not a lot of room.

One basic personal grooming thing that scared me was my fingernails. They started to get quite long, but I was too scared to have them cut while I was awake – I was *sure* it was just another thing that would cause me pain. My blackened fingertips did *not* look like they would handle my fingernails being cut with clippers or scissors. So, before I went into the operating room one day I asked the nurse if she could trim them for me while I was unconscious. She was so sweet and obliging, and shared her own burns scars with me. As far as I can remember, that was the only time I needed that service done under anaesthetic.

---

[98] Preventing drop-foot again. Gotta keep those shin muscles workin'.

Thursday, 26 December 2019
Red Book

12.17pm, Holly

Another day up and into the chair! This time was so much better for you than last time. You had less pain and managed to do it all in one go! Only a little bit of light-headedness but otherwise fairly smooth sailing.

You've said you're feeling like you really don't want to be here today and you're feeling quite down. You're scared for your (hopefully) last *big* surgery tomorrow, which is understandable, but you got this!! You've done it before and we'll help you through it again. You are stronger this time around, and you are doing amazing. You continue to impress me every day, Kezzels. I love you so much xxx

Family Messenger Chat

12.41pm, Donna

Morning, thinking of you and wondering how Kelsey is today ♡

Mum

She's very tired and a bit uncomfortable today. Went from bed to chair again a bit more successfully than last time, but still a huge effort for her. She's currently having a well-needed sleep. X

Donna

Aww, poor Kelsey. So hard for you all. How are you guys?

Mum

Tired.

Me

I kept being told I had to get skin grafted onto my legs. It was the last bit of grafting and it 'had to be done', but I really didn't want them to do it. I knew post-grafting in ICU had been a massive ordeal – it's one thing I *do* remember correctly. It was hideously painful and uncomfortable. And if it had been that bad on that much medication, how the hell was I going to cope on the ward, lucid, on way less medication?

Friday, 27 December 2019
Family Messenger Chat

8.32am, Dad

Kelsey just going into surgery. She will be about five hours. Poor girl, she's nervous.

Mum

It's actually a seven- to eight-hour op.

Vicky

Will it be her last long operation?

Dad

This should be her last big op. Hopefully just dressing changes and touch-ups from now on.

Mum

She's had three big trips to theatre, plus every second day goes back for dressing changes and touch-ups. So all up this will be her tenth.

Vicky

Wow, it's so hard to comprehend. Poor little darling. So hard on all of you ♡♡♡

Mum

Her attitude is amazing! Understandably she has had her moments, but she is trying so hard to be grateful and focused, despite the pain and psychological effects it's having on her. We are managing. It's a huge help knowing you're all there. The love and support we have all been getting – even from complete strangers – is phenomenal and so humbling 🥺💕

Me

Going into that surgery was the scariest thing I've ever done. Hands down. I didn't want to go through with it, but it was the next necessary step in my shitty little journey.[99] So off I was wheeled into theatre again, to have skin on my back, butt and thighs shaved off, and to have that skin placed on my legs.

Family Messenger Chat

5.12pm, Mum

Kels is out of surgery and everything went to plan except her blood pressure dropped and she had to have blood transfusions, so is still being monitored in recovery for another hour or two. They may send her back to ICU for 24 hours. Will let you know when we know. Xx

Maree

Is that drop in blood pressure standard?

Mum

Yes, it can be.

Tori

Is Kelsey awake after the surgery or do they keep her sedated a while after? Glad to hear the procedure went to plan. Poor Kelsey with more blood transfusions. What a huge day for you all.

---

99 I hated the word 'journey'. Still do.

Mum

She was still sedated when the surgeon phoned me before. I think they were still sorting her in recovery before pulling the breathing tube out.

Maree

Are you okay? So stressful.

Mum

We're all very tired and worried about our girl. It's extremely tough to see her going through this. But she's doing the best she can and so are we xx

8pm, Donna

Any news? Sorry, but we are worried xx

10.01pm, Dad

Just left Kelsey, surgery went according to plan. She's a bit groggy but talking away, will be in a bit of pain from her donor sites for a while (back, bum and thighs). Huge day, but so far so good. Holly is staying with her tonight.

Saturday, 28 December 2019
Red Book

6am, Holly

Good morning, sleepy head ♡

Yesterday was your last BIG surgery. Yay! It was about eight hours long, and then you had to spend about two and a half hours in recovery. We didn't get to see you until just after 7pm last night, so it was a big day for all of us. I stayed the night with you at the hospital last night. I was so happy I was able to. It felt good sleeping next to you and being able to help you with anything during the night that you needed.[100] It was also so good waking up with you and having some time alone with just you and me. Keep healing, Kezzels, and keep that amazing, strong fighter attitude up, because that is going to get you through. I'm right here for you always for whatever you need. I love you and you are so special to me. Follow the turtle.[101]

11.30am, Tom

Oh, babe, what a hell of a morning you have had. Just when you're starting to settle down a bit, you have to get moved to keep you fresh.

I feel so useless having to just stand back, but the nurses here really don't hold back on looking after you. There were six of them

---

[100] I regularly had hot flushes, due to the shock my body was going through and my lack of functional skin. This was worse after I had my legs grafted, so it was amazing having someone on hand to race down to the ward's fridge/freezer, grab *all* the ice and start trying to cool me down.

[101] I'm not sure who started this saying, but it was an attempt to get me to slow my breathing when I was getting stressed or whenever the nurses needed to readjust me in bed. It needed to be said so often that it became like nails down a chalkboard to me.

in here at one point just to make things as quick and easy as they could.

It's really rough for you but, just so you know, they do absolutely everything they can for you. Lucky for them you're one hell of a lady and you just keep on fighting your way through. You might not realise it at the moment, but your attitude is really keeping me going, and I'm sure your family would all say the same thing. That's one of the best things for us, seeing you strong and motivated. It's also what you need for yourself, and it'll keep your body healing hard and fast. It's only been three weeks (feels like three months) but you're just speeding along. Everyone, including the doctors, is so thrilled with your progress. Every day I come back in and see you is mind-blowing! I think it won't be long and you'll be snuggled back with River in our super-comfy bed, which is gonna feel a million times better after being in this 'flash airbed'.[102]

I'm still getting so many messages every day, and every time I give friends and family an update they just give you more love. It's gonna take a while for you to read through everything that has been coming in. Just another thing for us to get through together. It really is one hell of a battle you're fighting. I wouldn't be anywhere else. Just gotta help you get through these next few days and, like the doctor said, you'll be 'on the home straight'. Straight back to our little fluffy kids.

Jess never got too excited when I went back, but I reckon she will lose it when you show up. River is either going to flop over in a heap or try to pile on you with all his love. I know he's doing lots, just being on your mind to keep you going. These last two

---

102 I hated that bed so much! I could never get comfortable. Although, maybe it wasn't the bed ...

days may have been your hardest yet and hopefully tomorrow you'll actually get some decent rest. It's still gonna be bumpy but you've made it through the worst and it's gonna get easier now. Plus you've got me stuck here annoying you for the long haul.

Family Messenger Chat

1.30pm, Donna
Hi there, how is Kelsey after such a big day yesterday? Xx

2.08pm, Mum
Kels not doing so well today. Spent two and a half hours in recovery last night. In agony today after nine hours in theatre yesterday. She's all splinted up for the next five days, so unable to move.[103] She's trying so hard to muster a positive attitude but it's a huge struggle right now. She'll go back to theatre on Monday and Friday for dressing changes. Had about five nurses in here earlier to change her linen. It was hell. Had to give her gas, morphine, anti-nausea, plus a couple other ones and she still screamed in pain. She's asleep now.

At least it's the last big surgery out of the way. We just have to get her through these next few painful days …

Vicky
Words just don't express how upset we are to hear this news. I'm so sorry Kelsey and you all are going through such a horrendous time. You are constantly in our thoughts and prayers. ♡♡

---

103 Heavily bandaged and splinted to protect my new skin, I was discouraged, and unable, to move my legs, in order to give my grafts time to take.

Mum

They're talking about moving her back to ICU for a few days. They'll be able to sedate her there to turn her every two hours. They exhausted every drug they're allowed to administer up here and it wasn't enough. Apparently even the nurses were traumatised by it this morning.[104]

Kath

Actively promote that move because that's cruel and I totally get how it would've traumatised all. She will need plenty of rest between turns but at least she will be able to tolerate it better. This is where you speak up, Shel xx

6.32pm, Kath

How did you get on, Shel?

Mum

Still doing battle.[105]

---

104 The nurses were leaving my room crying because of how much pain they'd inadvertently inflicted while helping me. Without a doubt, this pain was *significantly* worse than being burnt. According to Mum, my pain nurse at the time began dropping my pain medication before this big surgery. My family questioned it, knowing what was coming, but they were assured that everything was under control. However, the surgery ended up going for much longer than anticipated. My body was so stressed from the day in theatre that it took over two hours to stabilise me enough in recovery before I could be moved. I was having hot flushes, where my temperature would spike dangerously. I couldn't move, and I was never comfortable. The two-hour 'rests' between the nurses moving me seemed to be getting closer and closer together.

105 After my first twenty-four hours on the ward after my legs had been grafted – by which time almost all the nurses were traumatised – Mum was ropeable. She hunted down an anaesthetist (who'd never met me), the head of the burns unit, and a couple of our most loved and trusted nurses, and she begged them to put me back in ICU so I could be sedated for the next week or so until things calmed down. I don't remember this conversation, but it happened at the

Kath

You stand strong and firm.

7.36pm, Mum

Okay, so not going to ICU but have had anaesthetist chart more meds. I was a bit mean to him – but, to be fair, he was a bit of a dick.[106] More methadone and fentanyl on top of everything else.

Kath

At least she got more analgesic charted. Both of those are pretty effective.

Mum

Yeah, she's had them before. I hope they help because I don't think she can handle much more.

Red Book

3.17pm, Mum

Hello, my gorgeous girl. Today is one of the rough ones. It breaks my heart to see you in so much pain and distress. But you continually amaze me with your understanding and cooperation. Know that all of this has to happen as part of your recovery.

---

end of my bed. In the end I *wasn't* moved, but I did get more medication and the A-Team – a bunch of nurses who'd been at Hutt when it was the National Burns Unit, so had experience dealing with patients with burns over more than 20 per cent of their body. (Since anyone with over 20 per cent coverage tended to go to the National Burns Unit, which is now at Middlemore in Auckland.) A lot of the Hutt nurses had never dealt with burns as extensive as mine.

106 Tensions were *very* high. I don't remember him being a dick – I think he just had his hands tied in terms of what he could do. And Mum regrets being 'mean' to him – she was stressed and tired and over seeing her girl in pain, understandably. But she doesn't regret storming the hospital to get me help.

As always, we are all here with you, trying our best to reassure and comfort you. We would all change places with you in a heartbeat if we could.

I love you so much, honey. Your smile and the way you stare straight into my eyes just makes my heart melt. Kissing your clammy forehead and inhaling your special Kelsey smell is just the best. Mumma xx

Sunday, 29 December 2019
Family Messenger Chat

5.36pm, Mum

A rough couple of days since the last surgery. Now that Kels has either graft sites or donor sites on pretty much all of her body except her feet and head, there is literally nowhere to touch her that isn't incredibly painful. They need to turn her every two to three hours, check wounds and change sheets and pads using four or five nurses. It's hell.

She goes back to theatre in the morning for full dressing changes again. They almost took her tonight because there are patches of green forming[107] but have decided to wait. Kels's mood is very low. Understandably. So is ours.

Hoping tomorrow brings some relief xx

7.17pm, Dad

Pain team finally got meds sorted-ish for manoeuvring Kelsey, so not so traumatic for everyone today. Surgery tomorrow for new dressings. We knew Friday was going to be a step backwards. That's now a couple of days behind us, so now hopefully it's just time to heal.

8.14pm, Mum

She's a bit more settled now, thank goodness. She's still up in the burns ward. She has her own isolation room at the end of a corridor so it's nice and quiet.

---

107 Infection strikes again.

Me

The splints put in behind my legs after grafting dug into the back of my legs something chronic – especially when my legs were elevated, which was ninety-nine per cent of the time. In fairness, though, almost everything hurt me in those early days. I came to expect pain so much so that I would panic even when little things were going to be done or tested – things that I *knew* weren't going to cause me any pain or discomfort. That fear lingered for months.

The night before the first check of my newly grafted legs, Tom was helping get me settled when one of the nurses came in, looking a tad puzzled, and said, 'Your brother is here to see you ...'

I stared at her a moment, looked at Tom, then back at her. 'I don't have a brother.'

'That's what we thought. But someone is trying to get up here to see you, saying they're your brother. I'll get rid of them.'

I didn't sleep much that night, worried that somehow this 'brother' would get in and find me. We all assumed it was another deranged journalist. Ever since I'd found out what the media had been up to, every odd sound or unfamiliar face that appeared in my room spiked my heart rate. I felt incredibly vulnerable, and it terrified me.

Monday, 30 December 2019
Family Messenger Chat

7.43am, Donna

Good morning, we hope it goes well for Kelsey today. Thinking of you 🙏

12.09pm, Mum

Thank you. She went in about 9am and is due out after 1pm. Poor thing keeps getting sweats due to her body not being able to regulate its temperature. Hoping for staples and some bandages to be removed today and possibly even the leg splints, which should help her be cooler and more comfortable. She was quite tearful heading in this time as they needed to put a line in to monitor her blood pressure while she's awake. They have such a hard job finding a vein now that she's pretty much traumatised by it.

Donna

Will they remove the splints? Really hoping she will be more comfortable and the pain is less for her. Three weeks today xx

Mum

Not too sure. Everything depends on what they find when they remove the dressings.

Me

That day, Paul came to the hospital and somehow slipped up to the burns unit in time to watch my bed being wheeled off to theatre, which I would only find out later. He caught up with my parents, and last night's mystery 'brother' revealed himself. When Paul had said through the intercom 'Kelsey's my *assistant*', the receptionist had heard 'Kelsey's my *sister*'. Paul is very, *very* clearly not related to me, being a solid Māori dude and I a pale ginger lass.

After my surgery, as I was being wheeled back into my room, he followed me in. He only stayed for about thirty seconds, and I don't really remember the conversation we had, but there was a lot of apologising on both sides. We both cried, and then he was gone. I can't begin to imagine the weight he'd been carrying.

Family Messenger Chat

3.28pm, Mum
Not a great day. Grafts on legs not taken due to infection. This means last Friday's surgery was not her last major one. Will now have to wait until her back and thigh donor sites heal enough to take a third graft and try her legs again. It probably adds a couple of weeks to her recovery. She doesn't know yet, but will be so upset. It also means that her legs will now be patchy, as it won't be a constant sheet graft but combinations of old and new grafts. We are all gutted. Many tears today.

Peter
A few tears here too, Shelley, I can assure you.

Tuesday, 31 December 2019
Red Book

7.49am, Holly

Happy last day of the year! I don't know about you, but I am happy to see this year be gone. I am super excited about what 2020 has in store for the both of us. Surely it's going to be an amazing year, because 2019 has been a shitshow. I think we both (especially you!) deserve some goodness, positivity and luck!

You've really been put to the test this year, Kels, but you have pushed through and made it out the other side every time. This is just another test that you *will* get past. You are going to continue to do great things in this life. If your past is anything to go by, you are very special and here for an important reason. I admire you so much. I hope I am even half the person you are, because even being half is still way above the rest.

I love you so much, Kezzels. Continue to smile that happy smile and keep your head in a positive space. We are here to help with all of that.

Goodbye, 2019, and bring on the new adventures and new chapters of 2020!

Family Messenger Chat

3.39pm, Dad

Hi all, yesterday's dressing change did not reveal what we were hoping for. The grafts on legs look very fragile. Docs not sure how much is going to take. Another dressing change tomorrow, then Friday, and by then they will have a better idea. Arms and hands continue to do well. All the meds cause their own issues, which we're trying to get on top of.[108] Another couple of tough days but still slowly moving forward.[109]

Tori

Oh, poor Kelsey. Obviously only answer if you want to, but what are Kelsey's options if they don't take? Such a stressful time for you. Sending lots of love and our hearts go out to you ♡♡♡

Dad

By the sound of things, if these grafts don't take they will have to regraft until they do.[110]

---

108 Constipation, nausea … you name it.

109 My rational positive dad ♡

110 It wasn't clear to my family how long this was an option, if infection kept occurring. If no donor sites were ready when new skin was needed, how long would my body be okay with temporary cadaver skin? How much skin could my donor sites give? At what point does amputation become the only option? *Was* that an option …?

Wednesday, 1 January 2020
Red Book

2.48pm, Mum

Happy New Year, sweetheart! Even though you slept through, I was with you and it was pretty darn special. I could see the fireworks on the Wellington waterfront from your window and really enjoyed knowing you were sleeping soundly.

You have just come back from theatre after another dressing change. You're sleepy, but so adorable. Dad and Holly are fussing over you – Holly is moisturising you[111] and Dad is on ice and cool-cloth duty. Tom is holding your hand.

You have some really incredible nurses up here too. I am amused by the fact that you have a Mary-Anne and an Anne-Marie, and a Lyn and a Lynley, two Rebeccas and two Emilys! It's like Noah's ark up here – they come in twos!

So here we are in 2020. It's true that it's off to a less than ideal start – but if anyone can turn it around, we can. And will. This year, you have been given the gift of life and new beginnings. Keep being your amazing self, Kels. You are one beautiful human and the world is a better and brighter place because of you and all you have to offer. Welcome to 2020, gorgeous girl. May this year be all that you dream xx

Family Messenger Chat

5.44pm, Mum

I stayed with Kels last night. Her temp etc spiked at 3am so was a rough time. Went to theatre at 8am and out at about 2pm. Very sore and very upset. She's starting to really struggle with the constant pain and whole situation. Can't blame her. Nurses are amazing! They're

---

111 A seemingly never-ending task to this day.

all pretty emotional about Kels too, and even pop in after their shifts when they're not her nurse that day. A massive blow last Monday, learning that the grafts were not looking so good, but today's verdict was that they weren't any worse. So we'll take that as a win.

Maree
I don't fully understand why these operations have to happen so quickly and put Kelsey through so much physical and mental trauma. Is it possible to be postponed until she is stronger?

Mum
No, because the risk of infection is way too high. Plus it's crucial to get on with it or she loses mobility too.

Soraya
I honestly get lost for words with how much you are all going through. You're all doing such an incredible job of navigating your way through each step. Hang in there. Xx

Thursday, 2 January 2020
Family Messenger Chat

7.02am, Mum

Thanks to you all for your kind words of love and support. Sometimes it's just so hard to muster the energy to reply and relay all of the stuff that's happened in a day. It's tough.

We are exhausted and so heartbroken seeing our beautiful girl having to endure so much pain, knowing she still has so many days like this ahead. Like all of you, we feel helpless too. But we have to keep reminding her – and ourselves – that this situation is temporary. It's hell now, for sure, but eventually she will get to go home.

In the meantime, it's just one foot in front of the other. Deep breaths and lots of love and encouragement. This is our new reality. A lot of it we don't like. But we love her and we treasure the fact we still have her every single day. We got this!

Red Book

11.15am, Tom

Damn it's hot in here! You must be getting better if you're warming the whole room up 😊

I just came back after having a bit of R&R at the motel. I sleep so much better being here with you overnight. Just a shame the chair is a bit rough, but I can't really complain.

You've had a busy morning: flipping, toothbrushing, cleaning, physio with Dad, and then physio again with the physio. We all wish you could just sleep for at least a day and catch up a bit. But the harsh reality is you just have to push yourself, and we may even have to push you a bit too. I don't think you'll have any problems though. Just keep up your usual and you'll be fine.

I can't wait to be taking you back home to the fluffy kids! Keep up the good hard work and maybe I'll even make you a cake!

Family Messenger Chat

7.05pm, Dad

Kelsey had a rough start early this morning, but then came right and the rest of the day has been pretty good so far. A bit buggered at present. We have just snuck out for dinner.

9.01pm, Mum

It's quite the emotional roller-coaster ride. Her last grafts didn't go so well and they have struggled to get on top of her pain. Now she also has a blood infection. Despite all of that, she had a relatively good day today mood-wise. Theatre again tomorrow, where we will be waiting anxiously to hear how the grafts are taking. We are all taking it day by day but it's rough. Moteliers have just decided to upgrade us to an even bigger room on Saturday that has seven beds and two bathrooms, plus bigger kitchen, etc., so we have plenty of room for family and friends to come and go over the next couple of months, which is so nice. Just me and Tom here from Saturday.

Me

That week was especially rough – for all of us. We'd all been holding so tightly onto the idea that once my legs had been grafted it was all smooth sailing after that, that we never considered the possibility of something going wrong. After that first check-up revealed that it looked like the grafts weren't going to take, we were broken. I didn't know if I could go through that level of unbearable pain again, and my family weren't sure they could watch me go through it either. I don't think I will ever be able to do justice in describing how devastating that news was to us.

Friday, 3 January 2020
Family Messenger Chat

8.18am, Donna

Good luck for today ♡

Mum

Thanks, Donna. I have passed that on to her. Will go to theatre mid-morning-ish ...

2.50pm, Mum

Better results from today's trip to theatre. She's still in recovery but surgeon has just been and talked to us. Grafts are looking better. Will wait at least two more weeks before taking her for final graft repairs but they are really happy with where she's at today. They want her to start moving from tomorrow. Get her into a chair and eventually walking. We are stoked. Still working on blood infection strain but she's on a preliminary antibiotic until they know exactly what one to treat xx

Red Book

5.51pm, Holly

Today has been such an amazing day! You were smooth sailing this morning before going into theatre for your dressing change, and then once you were out – before you got back to your room – your surgeon came to tell us how happy and positive they are about how your grafts are healing! From the news we got on Monday that they were a bit concerned and not happy with how the grafts were looking, and talk of another big surgery, today was a massive relief for all of us!! We are so happy and can't wipe the smiles off our faces. You were so happy too! And you have every right to be. See!! There is always some good news and something good to happen. So focus on that on your low days, because goodness, happiness and progress will always be right there to remind you that you have a lot to be grateful for.

I love when you smile and love the sound of your laugh more than ever right now. So keep that going. So proud of you, Kels. You *will* get past all of this.

Saturday, 4 January 2020
Family Messenger Chat

10.44am, Mum

Kels says this morning has been a mix of highs and lows. Lows include vomiting and crying. Highs include sitting on the edge of the bed and bending knees almost to forty-five degrees![112] Plus she's been sipping away on a chocolate Up&Go.

12.42pm, Vicky

Kelsey is a little champion! Just wondering how her dressing changes went yesterday, and are the skin grafts starting to take that they were worried about? 🫣 💕

Dad

From a kick in the guts after Monday's dressing change to the opposite for Friday's, a lot of the fragile-looking grafts have taken. She will still need to have areas redone but nothing like what they first thought.

Mum

Kels just sat up again. It sounds so much simpler than it actually is. She's in a lot of pain and it takes four people to help her and support her. But she sat up for about twenty minutes on the side of the bed. Lots of mindful breathing[113] but she did it!

---

112 It was *hideously* painful. I was lightheaded and nauseous, and I got cold sweats and my limbs went black with the blood rushing into them, but I did it! As I did it, my catheter tube seemed to always be in the way too, pulling on my bladder.

113 Following that turtle!

Red Book

3.42pm, Mum

What a little battler you are. After all of your meds being fed down your tube, you were sick. Tom and I had a great little bucket-passing system going on and you were so brave about it all. Then, after all that, the physio and nurses came in to help you to sit up on the side of the bed! You did it, too! It took everything you had and more, but you persevered and managed to do it.

A few hours later, at midday, they came back and you did it again!! This time off the other side of the bed and you sat about twenty minutes!! Tom was keeping your focus both times and did an incredible job. Go, you!!

The focus and strength you showed today was phenomenal. I am so bloody proud of you. Just wow! I have so much love and respect for you, my awesome girl xxxx

Sunday, 5 January 2020
Family Messenger Chat

8.04am, Mum

Kels isn't keen to see anyone outside of family just yet. She's been vomiting after her meds for the last three days so not sure what's going on there. She's been asleep since we got here this morning – feeling sick again.

Red Book

2.43pm, Mum

Another great day as far as progress is concerned. This morning you sat on the side of the bed with your feet on the floor for 45 minutes!! You did great!!

Your tummy is very rumbly so we're taking it easy on you when it comes to shovelling in your meds. Nice and slow over an hour or so seems to be helping a bit.

Physio is kicking in with a vengeance. Your sessions are rough on you, but even sleep-deprived and at the limit of your pain, you keep pushing through.

You are awesome, sweetheart, and I love you so very much!! Mumma xx

Monday, 6 January 2020
Red Book

10am, Mum

Nanna [Jenny] and [Aunt] Kath have come to visit this morning, which is nice. The usual cheeky banter between you and Kath has us all smiling.

Great progress today as you stood up! Your pain levels seem to be much more under control and your mobility has increased massively. You are doing the most incredible job of pushing yourself and trying everything you can to progress your recovery.

Family Messenger Chat

5.01pm, Mum

Kels didn't go into theatre until 12.30 today, and she's due out in half an hour or so. But the plastic surgeon just phoned me to say how well she's doing. Back, thighs and butt (donor sites) completely healed so no dressings there anymore. Lower back, arms and hands all good now, and just light dressings on lower back and upper right arm. Legs looking good. Just three sites on each leg that will need re-grafting, but much smaller than anticipated. Catheter out! She requested Ribena and homemade fried rice for tea, so I have made that and am waiting in her room for her to come back. A decision about a move to Waikato burns unit will be made within the next two weeks.[114] This will mean she's

---

114 There are four burns units in New Zealand: Middlemore Hospital in Auckland, Waikato Hospital in Hamilton, Hutt Hospital and Christchurch Hospital. Those of us who made it off White Island were initially dispersed according to the severity of our burns, with the worst going to the National Burns Unit at Middlemore and the rest of us split between the other three. Those not from New Zealand (the bulk) were repatriated back to their countries once it was safe for them to travel. I was to be moved to my regional burns unit, Waikato, once I was well enough, and once there was room for me.

closer to home and will get to become familiar with the burns unit for when she eventually becomes an outpatient and has to go over for regular appointments etc over the next two to three years or so.

Me

Funny story about the catheter: they *had* to take it out.

If you've ever had a catheter, you'll know that there is no sensation or 'need' to wee, your bladder just empties itself straight into the bag – like leaving the tap on. When you've had prolonged catheterisation, the ideal way to become 'de-catheterised' is to retrain your bladder. The tap gets turned off. Your bladder fills. Your body re-learns the sensation of needing to wee. You turn on the tap. Gradually the holding capacity of your bladder is increased until they are able to remove the catheter altogether and you're a normal-wee-functioning human.

In *my* case, my body started bypassing the catheter. This is not normal – and not usually possible. There was no swelling. There was no blockage (a brand-new one had been placed not long before removal). Randomly, I started having the sensation to wee, which was new to me after almost a month of not 'needing' to.

I told the nurses. They told me that was fine: 'Relax. The catheter will get it.' The catheter did not get it. I wet the bed. This happened a couple of times, until they decided that I just had to use a bedpan instead. With my untrained bladder. With my raw backside. Awful.

Tuesday, 7 January 2020
Family Messenger Chat

9.15am, Mum

I'm with Kels. She's a bit teary this morning realising she will be in hospital for so much longer. I had a talk with her and she seemed a bit better. The psych liaison guy just walked in so I have left them to have a chat. She has a blood clot in her neck/chest area so is off for a scan to see the extent and make a plan for treatment. They all seem quite calm about it so I'm trying to be calm too.

12.11pm, Mum

So the *Herald* just phoned me. I told them we want to thank all of the services and people who have helped, plus I said the Givealittle page has been incredible and Kels was overwhelmed by the love and support. I told them she has a long way to go but has an incredible attitude and is doing the absolute best she can. I was careful not to get too personal, and they asked what hospital she was at so I said we weren't prepared to say. I hope you're all okay with that? I just felt it was a good way to say thanks and give a subtle update. I hope they get it right.

Tom

Good work 👍 That sounds like enough to keep the horde fed.

12.52pm, Mum

Kels has had a scan today to confirm that she has a couple of blood clots in her neck/chest. It was always a possibility that this could happen and unfortunately it has.[115] We are waiting to hear the plan

---

[115] The combination of my body being in 'active coagulation' (trying to heal and seal itself back up), being stationary for so long, and not able to 'flush my pipes' properly meant this was always a high possibility.

from the doctors shortly, but it has meant that her rehab/physio will be put on hold until this latest hurdle has been conquered. She's feeling a bit overwhelmed today[116] and is currently sleeping.

Tori

Oh no, that's terrible. Will it require surgery to remove them? Thinking of you guys – it must be overwhelming for you too. Xxx

Mum

At this stage I think they're going to use a more potent blood thinner but I'm really not sure. Will let you know once the doctors have come up with a plan.

Red Book

5.23pm, Mum

So yesterday you went for a dressing change at about 12.30pm. You are healing really well and everyone was stoked about how well everything is coming along. Yahoo!!

But they had trouble feeding the wire through your artery to try to set up your new line, so suspected a blood clot. You went for a scan this morning which confirmed you had a couple of clots.[117] Bummer. Anyway, they are going to swap out your dreaded belly injection for an oral, more potent blood thinner. This should do the trick with dissolving those poxy clots.[118]

---

[116] When you're told you have a blood clot in your neck, it does tend to be pretty overwhelming.

[117] The clots had actually collapsed one of my jugular veins – which, to me, sound *very* important. Turns out, your other veins can just pick up the slack and it was a bit of a non-event.

[118] The poor junior doctor who was tasked with telling me the number of injections I was getting into my stomach was about to double copped a full breakdown from me about it. I've never liked needles, and I liked them a hell of

When I came back from lunch today, I walked in on you standing up! It was awesome. Not only did you stand up *straight* with relative ease, you took a couple of steps/shuffles. And you did all of that *TWICE!! PLUS* you looked good doing it (no pale sweaty face or dizziness). Once again, you are amazing and wowing everyone around you. Yasmin, your physio, then went through most of your physio exercises with you, once you were lying back down. Your range of movement is improving really quickly. Excellent effort, kiddo.

You are currently sound asleep after yet another full-on, exhausting day. To say that I am proud of you is such an understatement! You are incredible and I love you so much. Mumma xxx

Family Messenger Chat

7.14pm, Donna
How are you all tonight? How is Kelsey now? Could she eat her nice homemade fried rice and Ribena last night?

10.23pm, Mum
She's a bit distraught. As I was leaving tonight she started coughing. Not a good sign, as chest infection is also a common complication.[119] Will know more tomorrow. She enjoyed the Ribena and a wee bit of the rice, but as she's fed 20 hours via a tube she

a lot less right then. He left the room, apologising to me as I sobbed. A while later, he came back and told me he'd spoken to the doctor and was going to give me the medication orally instead, due to my 'strong preference'. I have not forgotten that act of kindness.

119 A lot of phlegm was starting to accumulate in my lungs, and once I started coughing I found it hard to take a breath. It began to feel like I was drowning in my own body.

doesn't have much of an appetite. Plus her throat is sore due to having a breathing tube in every second day when she goes to theatre. On the up side, she did manage to stand up twice today and shuffle her feet. A very special moment getting to stand face to face with her for the first time in a month.[120]

Me

I had an NJ tube[121] (or 'fish tube', as I 'affectionately' named it) that kept me topped up on all the goodness I needed to heal, so there was no real need for me to eat. It also meant I could go into theatre whenever they wanted me because my stomach was always empty – no starving required. But, boy, was I *thirsty*.

When my doctors decided it was time to start weaning me off the NJ tube, they would leave me 'unplugged' for periods of time to try to encourage some sort of feeling of hunger in me. Unfortunately, that didn't seem to work – I was never hungry, and all I did feel like eating was fruit, for its juiciness and sugars.

---

120 I still remember the look on Mum's face when I finally managed to raise my gaze from my black limbs to her.
121 A nasojejunal (NJ) tube is a thin, soft tube that is put in through the nose, goes through the stomach and ends in the jejunum (je-joo-num), a part of the small intestine. (Thanks, Google.)

Wednesday, 8 January 2020
Family Messenger Chat

9.22am, Mum

Kels good today. Doing physio now. No more Clexane [blood thinner] injections. They're giving her a strong blood-thinner tablet instead. Her theatre trip tomorrow will be in the afternoon. Not exactly sure of the time yet.

Tom

Yay to no more tummy jabs! Does that mean her clots are sorted/sorting themselves out?

Mum

Not really. She'll have to take the tablet for six weeks and then be checked again to see if they've dissolved or not. It should prevent any more, plus start dissolving them now.

Holly

Are they worried about the clot? Is it a dangerous one?

Mum

It can be serious if not treated, but hers have been found so she'll be fine. A big morning. She's been on her feet again and is doing amazing. She can't wait to have you three back!![122]

---

[122] Dad, Holly and Tom all had businesses to run, so would periodically pop home to Whakatāne to make sure things were running smoothly in their absence.

Red Book

2.53pm, Mum

Another big morning!! Today you managed to walk from your bed to a chair, aided by a frame. You sat in the chair for two hours and had your hair washed and armpits tended to[123] by Kath, Nanna and myself. Then you walked all around the bed with the frame. It tires you out, but you do it and I hope you feel proud of yourself afterwards, because we sure were!

Yasmin is currently taking you through your 'in-bed' physio for your hands, arms and legs. You are pushing through the pain and fatigue, which is great! You got this, girl!!

---

123 One thing I wasn't told is that when your body is in overdrive trying to heal, your nail and body hair growth also go into overdrive. The funniest part about this was my ankles. I have a straight line around my ankles, below which my socks and boots saved my feet from being burnt, but it was high enough to leave a ring of hair on my ankles, which went mental! Mum referred to me as 'Mr Tumnus' (the half-goat man from the Narnia books) for a couple of weeks until one day she walked in and said, 'I can't do this anymore,' and pulled a razor out of her bag and shaved my ankles for me.

Thursday, 9 January 2020
Red Book

Mum

Tom came back nice and early today. You got to surprise him with how good you are looking and feeling, as well as show him how you can shuffle off the bed, stand and walk around the room aided by the physio and walking frame. Super cool to watch. Yours and Tom's smiling faces are just the best part of my day!!

Theatre again today. You went in at 1pm and another good result. Grafts are healing so well and your mobility is improving at an impressive pace.[124] It's wonderful to see you laughing, smiling and chatting. Love you, sweety xx

Family Messenger Chat

10.55pm, Mum

Another really good day. Theatre again this afternoon (fourteenth time) and all is well. She's in good spirits and physio has resumed and going incredibly well.

Me

A lot of people talk about how dehumanising it is when others have to do everything for you because you can't do it for yourself. Cleaning up your messes in bed. Enemas to try to get you to do

---

124 One morning, during the doctors' rounds, my surgeon asked me to make a fist with one of my hands. I made more of a claw than a fist, then he told me I *could* do it, because he's had me doing it in theatre. 'You mean when I'm unconscious and can't feel pain?' I retorted.

After a few days of practising, at my physio-terrorist's insistence, I was asked again by the same surgeon. I turned my hand as I closed all but one finger, flipping him the bird. All four of those fingers were in a near-fist. He laughed and was satisfied.

the mess in the first place. Wiping your butt once you finally get going. But honestly, all I felt was gratitude. I couldn't do these things myself, and I had all of these people around me who were willing to step up and help. Even though it was their job – and quite a grim part of the job at that – my nurses were always respectful, fast and professional. Mum never made it a 'thing' when she helped me, too. In those moments when I was receiving all of this help for such intimate things, I actually felt *more* human. More loved. More seen. More respected. I would gush with thank yous after every messy or painful bit of help I received.

Friday, 10 January 2020
Red Book

10.56am, Mum

Another great start to the day with a beautiful, smiley and chatty girl.

Physio this morning was still a little painful for you, but you are persevering and getting it done with such a great attitude. Once again you stood up and walked around. Today, you even ventured out into the corridor and got a wave from your next-door neighbour!

Yasmin was impressed when we told her that you held a pen and signed your name yesterday! Even though it was super tiny!

Tom has been having fun playing with your bed while you watch from the chair. Now he's playing hairdresser by brushing your hair very patiently and trying to get all the knots out.

2.37pm, Holly

Holy hecka, Kezzels! Being away from you for one week was hard but *oh my gosh* you have made so much progress and you're looking so good! I can't believe how well you are doing.

My favourite part of getting back today was playing volleyball with the balloon with you.[125] I'm so proud of you and admire your attitude and positivity. Can't wait to spend more time with you. Watching you progress and wow me every day. Love you so much xxx

---

125 A family-favourite physio task, and quite creative! Yasmin also stole Jenga from the children's ward to help my hand–eye coordination, as well as improve my dexterity. I won every game! Another favourite of mine was strangling one of the little soft-toy teddies I'd been given … to increase my strength.

Family Messenger Chat

6.31pm, Donna

How is Kelsey? Are you all back with Kelsey now? xx

Mum

Yes, all here now and it's awesome! Kels has been able to show off her progress and completely wow everyone. With the aid of her walking frame, she walked out of her room and into the corridor. Her arm and hand mobility has improved so much in a week. It's painful and she still has a very long road ahead but she has most definitely turned a corner. We are so happy and unbelievably proud of her strength and determination.

Soraya

Go, Kelsey, go!! Soooooo happy to hear this and I bet there were tears of joy from all in her new audience 🙏

Donna

That is wonderful. I can feel the excitement in your message. We are so happy for Kelsey and so happy for you all. Love to you all ♡♡

Mum

It was so cool having her walk out of her room! Some of the doctors and nurses came out of their offices to watch. A very special moment. And Kels had the most beautiful smile on her face the whole time. Oh and she did that all *twice* today!!!!

Donna

Teamwork has certainly made the dream work. You can all be proud of yourselves. The past month has been a long, hard haul and you have all been so strong.

Mum

Still a very long way to go and there are still plenty of hurdles, operations and risks – but we will enjoy this awesome moment for all that it is and for all that it has taken to get here.

Kath

Go, Kels. Hope her gown was 'closed' at the back 😳

Saturday, 11 January 2020
Family Messenger Chat

5.37pm, Mum

She's doing great again today. Just done a lap of the ward with her walker frame. Third time today. Graham and I are actually going out for dinner tonight with an old friend.

Me

I wasn't allowed flowers in my room or on the ward, due to the risk of infection. I guess soft toys were the next best thing to bring a twenty-five-year-old burns patient, and there were SO. MANY. People still sent flowers, and they filled my family's motel room. My family started bringing in photos of them and sticking them on the wall at the foot of my bed, so I could see them. There were tons of cards and letters and photographs of my dogs and favourite photos of me, too.

I kept getting those awful hot flushes (often!). My family would go and raid the ward freezer every time, and come back to my room bearing a container filled with ice, add a bit of water, soak some cloths, then place them over my forehead, chest and neck to try to cool me down. I reckon there was probably steam coming off those cloths, I felt so unbelievably hot.

I also remember coughing and coughing and coughing. Fluid would build up in my chest and throat, so it felt as though my airways were full of mucus, and at times it was hard to breathe. I would cough and cough but never clear it. At one point I came close to developing pneumonia, so I was given this hilarious contraption for doing breathing exercises. It had three blue balls in three separate tubes, and I had to breathe in, then breathe out into a small hose, making the balls rise. The harder you blew, the more balls you could get to move. The goal was to get all three balls floating, and to hold the exhale for a ridiculously long time, to really get my lungs working to shift the fluids.

Sunday, 12 January 2020
Family Messenger Chat

6.55pm, Donna

Hello, how is everything today?

Monday, 13 January 2020
Family Messenger Chat

12.31pm, Mum

Last couple of days have been up and down. Because of the blood clots, she's on blood thinners that have slowed the healing process. She's been really sore on her donor sites (mainly her back).[126] She's been in getting her dressings changed since 10am. She's heavily sedated. Hopefully done soon.

Donna

That sounds hard for Kelsey. Is it the first dressing change with strong painkillers? A shame the blood thinners have slowed the healing process. Hoping they at least get rid of the blood clots. Have been thinking about you, and feel for Kelsey every day.

Mum

Yes, it's Kels's first time having dressings changed on the ward. It's a huge procedure and takes several hours.

Me

I was terrified of having my first dressing change on the ward. There was a special 'burns bathroom' across the hall from my room, which enabled the patient to have their dressings removed,

---

126 The worst itch I've ever had in my life was on the donor site on my back. I remember sitting on the side of my bed, bawling my eyes out because I was *soooooo* itchy and nothing was helping. I couldn't scratch it myself, no one else was allowed to touch my freshly healed donor sites, and the antihistamine that got poked in my mouth was going to take about twenty minutes before it offered any relief. I was beside myself. Holly took off, and my first thought was that I had driven *another* person out of my room with my pain. But moments later she calmly reappeared with something in her hands. *Ice.* She wrapped it in a cloth and pressed it to my back. Instant relief!

wounds cleaned and redressed on a waterproof bed. I was loaded up on a lot of medication (again), and then wheeled across the hall. I don't remember the first two-thirds of what happened, but during the last third, when I was being prepped to have dressings reapplied, I came to. For some reason, seeing my legs as damaged as they were was a truly horrifying experience for me – they were blackened and bloody, like my arms had been when I first saw them, but somehow, they looked like those purple salami sticks you can find in the deli at the supermarket. While I bawled my eyes out, one of my nurses, calmly, firmly talked me through the final part of the dressing change, while the others hurried to wrap me back up. Despite being told by nurse after nurse, doctor after doctor, that they wouldn't always look like this, I never believed them. How could something that looked *that* bad possibly ever look normal?

Red Book

2.40pm, Tom

Special K[127] is actually such a fitting nickname, 'cause somehow you just keep on improving at such a special rate, regardless of the shit that you're continuously put through. You keep looking at me weird 'cause I can't stop smiling and my jaw is just constantly dropped open now.

Today feels like such a milestone day. Your legs are actually healing much better than anticipated (with the potential that they won't even need extra grafts), your range of movement is just

---

[127] I hated this nickname 😄 I don't remember who gave it to me in hospital, but it was widely used among the nurses and my family. A play on the cereal name, or perhaps the drug. Maybe both.

rocketing forward, you even pushed your walker aside for a few steps, and after everything, you just continue to fight and power on. It's really the best thing in the world to see you at this point. Even though there's gonna be plenty of tough times ahead, you can easily do it and I'll be here with all your family. I'm already way ahead in terms of excitement, but I know it's not far off now.

Tuesday, 14 January 2020
Family Messenger Chat

1.37pm, Mum

Kels has had a couple of great days. Most of her grafts have healed now and there is even a possibility that the ones that haven't quite still will. That could potentially mean no more major surgeries!!! Her healing is still a little slower due to the blood thinners but on the whole she's progressing really well.

She's managing to do a lap or two of the ward each day with her Zimmer frame. She's completely exhausted afterwards but it's awesome!!! Can't wait until she can walk unassisted and we can take her outside!! Her nasal feeding tube got blocked yesterday so they removed it, and Kels was thrilled to see one more tube go. Her dressing change went well yesterday. She got to see her legs for the first time, which upset her quite a bit, but she knows they are still healing and have a long way to go, and will look better and better as time goes on. She's also been measured up for all of her compression garments that she will have to wear 24/7 for the next 18–24 months. Lots happening!! I hope everything is good with all of you.

Carol

Wow, Shelley, that's all great news. So excited to hear her grafts are healing well. I guess her legs are the largest body-mass area left, which would account for a longer healing period. Please tell her she is a star and we are all so proud of her. Big hugs and loads of love to you both xxx

Mum

She kind of leans into it [the zimmer frame] and steers with her forearms! Legs are a bit behind due to being grafted first with cadaver skin while waiting for Kels's back to heal enough to take a second graft. Then delays due to infection. Apparently the skin behind both knees was not burnt[128] so that's going to help heaps when it comes to physio. At the moment a lot of her limited mobility in her legs is more due to the massive wads of tightly wound bandages.

Donna

Wonderful news, Shelley. Is she able to eat and drink all right? Still early days for Kelsey, and her little legs will look beautiful once again when they heal. Keep up the good work, Kelsey, and you are being the best mum and dad. Love to you all xxxxx

Mum

Thank you, Donna. She really doesn't have much of an appetite, but knows how important it is to be cramming in as many nutrients as possible to help her heal. She's basically been told that she has to have four to six bottles a day of her Fortisip milk,[129] along with at least some of her meals, or they will have to put the tube back in! So far she's hitting the targets.

Red Book

4.07pm, Taz [friend]

Hey, my darling girl. I finally made it to see you! It felt like both the longest and quickest flights and taxi rides of my life to visit you. I don't know if I can put into words how good it was to see you in that chair when I walked in. You are so beautiful, Kels ♡ I got to see some of your physio session too. It was hard for me to see you

---

128 Kudos to me for staying crouched for the entire duration of the pyroclastic surge.
129 Oh god, even the *name* of this stuff makes me want to vomit now.

in pain, but good you are pushing through that pain to do what Yasmin asked of you. By the sounds of it you have come so far and you even walked for me, my dear. You are freaking doing great! I couldn't be more proud. I always knew you would surpass your own strengths, babe. I've tried to keep my tears from you, but I don't think I'll be able to when I say goodbye soon. I'll miss you like crazy! But I will see you again soon. I love you long time, Kelsey. Taz xxx

Me

My friend Taz 'abandoned' her two kids to fly down and spend the whole day with me. At the time, I couldn't actually stay awake all day, plus I had a lot of 'medical visitors' (physio, nurses, doctors etc), so she ended up spending a lot of time with Mum and Tom. It meant a lot to me that my best friend from uni made the trip down, despite the fact that I was initially really apprehensive about seeing her. I hadn't seen many people other than medical staff and family members (which depended solely on how I was feeling on the day), so I was scared. Regardless, my sweet Taz was there for me when I needed her, and I'll never forget that.

As for taking out the feeding tube when it clogged, the nurse kept telling me that it wouldn't hurt: 'Just a little tickle in the back of your throat.' But I had become so accustomed to pain every time someone touched or did something to me that I expected – and dreaded – it.

I was in tears before she even came near me with the razor blade to cut the stitch in my septum that kept the tube in place. My snout was already sore from being knocked and pulled and tugged over the last few weeks, and it hurt a *lot* more than I thought it would. Now the tears were really flowing. The nurse ignored my protests and tears – which had to be done – and she quickly grabbed the end of the tube, and started pulling as fast as she could. At least a metre of tubing was now in my nurse's hands.

Once it was all over – and once I'd calmed down – I was infinitely happier to have it gone. No more nose-stitch pain whenever I breathed. No more tape on my face. No more beeping every time my food bag ran out. No more getting the tube caught on my pillow every time I was moved.

Wednesday, 15 January 2020
Family Messenger Chat

9.47am, Mum

Dressing change went well. Just spoke to the surgeon and he says the knee graft is very slowly healing itself so they will continue to monitor. They've made the call to keep her until after anniversary weekend, before she'll go to Waikato, where she will most likely only stay for a week before being able to go home!!! That's if all keeps going to plan!!![130]

Vicky

Yippeee!! Brilliant news to wake up to this morning!! You must all be over the moon.

Red Book

11.37am, Mum

So this morning you went in for your second dressing change on the ward. Before you came out, Tom and I got to have a wee chat with Aaron, your doctor, and Angela, the nurse manager. They told us how amazingly you are doing and that you will most likely be ready to go to Waikato within the next couple of weeks! It's great because it means you are doing so well, but it's also really sad because we have all become so attached to everyone here.

Susan from ICU came up to see you yesterday and was so happy to see how far you have come. She has made you promise not to leave without going down to say goodbye to them all. She's going to be working at Homegrown in March, so has asked that you go and visit her.[131] You are a celebrity patient here, for sure!

130 Narrator: *It was not going to go to plan ...*
131 *Boldly*, I assumed I would still be going to the music festival Homegrown

Getting to tell Dad and Holly the great news about you being just weeks away from coming home was so good. They are so excited! Dad had to phone me straight away and his voice was so high-pitched and excited he sounded like he'd been sucking on helium!!

Tom and I have also been given the okay to take you on excursions! So, for your first outing, we're thinking a wee blatt around the hospital and taking you for a peek outside!!

Me

The first time I went outside was a massive milestone. Wearing my hospital gown for my maiden voyage, I was popped in a wheelchair, propped up with pillows so I was comfortable and nothing was rubbing, covered to protect me from the sun, and wheeled out of the ward and into the elevator. On the ground floor, it was a short roll to the front doors of Hutt Hospital. I'd been in hospital over a month yet I'd never seen these doors, or any of this part of the hospital.

Once outside, it took my breath away. I'd been inside for thirty-six days, and this was the first time I'd seen the blue sky above my head again, instead of through a window. My first time hearing traffic in front of me instead of the distant sounds drifting up from the street below and through the walls. My first time hearing birds sing and the hum of the bees busy in the trees above me. But the highlight was feeling the *wind*. What a blessing it was to be in Wellington! I will never forget the feeling of the warm January wind on my face that first time outside. The

---

one month after leaving hospital. In the end, Covid shut that shit down anyway – which I realised was a *godsend* for me. What a fool I was – an optimistic, can-do fool. Bless.

feeling of my hair gently moving with the breeze. The smell of hot asphalt. I was euphoric.

'Are you okay, honey?' Mum asked, a little worried by my total silence.

I'd been taking it all in, overwhelmed in the most beautiful and new way.

'I'm really good, Mum.'

Thursday, 16 January 2020
Me

I wish I had more photos of my injuries and my body during recovery, especially from the early days. But my family didn't feel right taking photos of me while I was in a coma, without my consent, and while they didn't know whether I was going to make it or not. Then, once I made it up to the burns ward, I was too scared of myself to have any photos or videos taken – especially of my face.

Everyone who came into my room exclaimed how good my face looked. Having never been greeted with this kind of enthusiasm or compliment before, I was *convinced* this meant something awful had happened.[132] Mum kept reassuring me that my face was still my face, and even traced the superficial burns with her finger and described them to me. Yet, as she applied paraffin to my face to moisturise the burns, I remained unconvinced that she was being entirely truthful. I didn't want to see it. I wouldn't even let anyone bring a mirror into my room.

Then on my 'lunch break'[133] one day, not long after I'd started learning to walk again, I suddenly decided I needed to know what my face looked like – and that I wanted to be alone when I first saw it. Still lying down, I tentatively wiggled myself to the edge of the bed, got myself onto my side, then dropped my legs over the side of the bed and slowly raised my torso – thinking *Now would be a really bad time to pass out*, as no one was coming to see me for the next two hours. Once I managed to sit, I stayed still for a

132 What was *really* happening was that the nurses, doctors and everyone else who had seen me at my absolute worst in ICU – swollen, puffy, unconscious – were now seeing someone awake, alert and with significantly less swelling around her face.

133 Actually a two-hour midday nap.

moment to let my body adjust to the unfamiliar pressure of being upright, and to make sure upright was how I was going to remain for the next couple of minutes.

Slowly, I shuffled my backside right to the edge of the bed and placed my bare feet on the blue linoleum, struggling to bend my knees with all the bandages still swathed around my legs. I shifted my weight onto my feet. I waited. *So far, so good.* Up to standing. Waited. *So far, so good.* Slowly, slowly, I headed for my bathroom door. This was happening.

I reached the door and used my new-skinned hands to open it – the biggest and heaviest thing I'd moved with my hands since the eruption. I took a deep breath and inched around to the sink, which had a small mirror above it. And, finally, I saw my face.

'Oh,' I said out loud, standing a little straighter at the sight.

I looked like me. Like me, but with a weird little 'sunburn' around my mouth and nose where my gas mask had been, a burn on my forehead, and some around the outside corners of my eyes, around my jaw and down my neck. *Superficial burns.*

My face was still my face. Just as Mum had said.

Friday, 17 January 2020
Red Book

8.07am, Mum

Good morning, gorgeous girl! You're off for a dressing change at 10am. The doctors have all just been in for their morning rounds. You're doing so well that they don't really even need to discuss anything 'medical' any more. They pretty much just talk café recommendations.

Yesterday was a great day. You were officially told by the doctors that you won't be needing further surgeries![134] Yay!! Plus, you'll be heading to Waikato within the next couple of weeks!

You did physio with Yasmin, and I walked in to find you laughing away as you practised on a staircase with the theme from *Rocky* blasting around the ward!

Tom and I took you for a ride around the hospital in the wheelchair and we went to ICU so you could say 'hi' to everyone. It was so funny how you didn't remember anything about the rooms or recognise any of the nurses – except Monica. They all remember you though, and are so excited for your progress and how good you are looking.

Keep on doing what you're doing, sweetheart. You are incredible and we all love you so much! Mumma xx

---

134 Foreseeable ones, anyway.

Saturday, 18 January 2020
Red Book

10.25am, Holly

Hugging you was the best feeling I have ever felt! I didn't want to let you go and I keep playing that moment over in my head. It made me so happy, I cried. I even cried in the taxi before I saw you yesterday because Mum told me we could hug you.[135] AND YOU HUG BACK!![136] You have made another incredible amount of progress in the four days me and Dad were away. You've always got something new to show us that you can do. I'm so proud of you and you continue to amaze me! I love you so much! Keep doin' what you're doin'. Possum xxx

Family Messenger Chat

10.43am, Mum

So our girl is walking. Unaided. How awesome is that!! She's a bit wobbly but she's managing a lap of the ward a couple of times a day. Normally they would expect that she would go from the big walker frame to a smaller one and then to crutches. But nope – not for Kels.[137] She skipped right up to going it alone. Now she's working on trying to lift her legs high enough for steps. To the *Rocky* theme song, of course!![138] Hands and arms are going to take a lot of painful rehab for a very long time, but she's pushing through despite the pain. We took her across the road to the bar yesterday!!! In her wheelchair.

---

[135] I was not consulted.
[136] Obligated to – I'm not a hugger!
[137] I don't think anyone told me the usual progression of things – oops.
[138] AC/DC and Nirvana also featured!

It was so nice for her to get out and about for an hour.[139] Might take her for a wee drive out Eastbourne way this afternoon. Xxx

Donna

Wow, Kelsey, our hero. She is doing so well. Nice you got to go out yesterday after six weeks inside. Hope you get to go out today for a drive. Love and hugs ♡♡🏆🏆🥇 xx

---

[139] My first proper meal out was a couple of slices of pizza and an ice-cold Coke at the pub across the road from the hospital. It was – and still is, to this day – the best drink I've ever had in my life. I am not typically a Coke drinker, but by god that was the best, most quenching drink of my life.

Sunday, 19 January 2020
Red Book

10.30am, nurse #1

Kelsey, you have done so well in your recovery and have made such great progress in such a short time. Even though for you it probably feels like forever! It has been a pleasure to meet you. Such a strong, determined lady. You have much more to achieve in your life and I know you will be amazing at this too! It's easy to say everything happens for a reason when there is a positive outcome. The positive is that you are still here and you are a survivor. Stay strong and keep surviving – and on the days you can't, lean on your amazing family. They have brought you this far already and are doing a wonderful job.

Nurse #2

I did your very first dressing on the ward and you did really well. We had the pain nurse as a back-up and morphine on standby. You only needed 10mg for the whole change of dressings. You were so worried[140] prior to me taking you into the burns bathroom, but you were a champion and coped really well.

    There was one afternoon I was looking after you after you'd had a really bad morning being turned. After a lot of phone calls and annoying after-hours, we got some fentanyl charted for you. We, the old ducks of the ward (don't tell the others this), turned you no sweat. From that day onwards, it was just improvement after improvement. Now you are getting up and going to the toilet by yourself. You can hold a cup and bend your own arm well enough so you can drink by yourself. You have been going out for the day,

---

140 Rightly so, I might add. If it was necessary to take me to theatre for dressing changes, doing it lucid and conscious was *incredibly* daunting.

walking around and enjoying the time away from the ward. You have made tremendous progress.

Just remember that the end of the tunnel is getting closer and closer. And please don't frown – your face is too pretty to get frown lines.

Your amazing nurse AKA 'the Witch'.[141]

Nurse #3
Kelsey (Special K). This nickname is so fitting as you are a very special girl. It has been wonderful to watch you progress over the last few weeks. You are an inspiration to us all. I love seeing you smile and give me a bit of cheek – then I know you're feeling better.

There were times when I looked at you and thought, *What else can I do to help you?* These were some pretty difficult times for you. I said it would get easier, but I know at times it was hard to believe. And look at you now. You truly are amazing and I have so loved looking after you. You have the most wonderful family. They have been such an amazing support to you. Come back and see us when you are back down this way. You will not be forgotten by us.

Nurse #4
Kels! All I can say is *wow*! You are one incredibly strong person! I have absolutely loved looking after you over the last few weeks. I 'specialled' you the very first night you came up to the ward –

---

141 This nurse scared the shit out of me initially: straight-shooting, no bullshit, kept telling me to stop frowning – she would *physically* smooth out my forehead with her fingers. I came to absolutely love this about her, and she was one of my favourite nurses – especially when she hooked me up with fentanyl for the flipping.

it was just you and me for eight hours! It was one busy night shift with lots of funny conversations. Over the weeks since then, you have improved so much and had so many milestones! From helping you into the chair for the first time, first steps out of the room, first time using the toilet!! Getting to this point we have definitely had our hard days, but with lots of chatting, tears, laughs and distractions we have got through! Two weeks ago we were turning you every two hours with three or four nurses and we told you that you'd be up walking around! At the time you never believed us, but look at you now – you're out escaping on leave! We will always remember you here and I can't wait to keep watching your recovery!

Love, the Devil Nurse – always popping your blisters!

P.S. Your family are AMAZING!

Monday, 20 January 2020
Family Messenger Chat

8.41pm, Donna

How are you all? How is Kelsey doing? Dressing changes go well today? Been thinking of you xxx

Mum

Dressing change went great today, thanks. Still having a few rough times as the pain and reality is setting in. But for the most part she is doing amazingly well and continues to have the most inspiring attitude. So, so proud of our precious girl. Xx

Tuesday, 21 January 2020
Me

It was always in my future that I would have compression garments, but all of my open wounds needed to close before that could even be entertained. Compression garments are made from fabrics such as Lycra, and are worn to flatten the skin and reduce the appearance of scarring. They're custom-made to fit you specifically – measured to the nearest millimetre. They are *not* comfortable, but for the best results they need to be worn as close to 24/7 as possible, to minimise the inevitable scarring. Given burn scars can take anywhere from eighteen months to two years to totally mature and stop changing, most patients wear them for around that amount of time – especially for major scarring.

When my first set of compression garments arrived at the hospital, there was a little bit of me that was excited. It was a definite step forward in my recovery, and I loved the idea of having my grafts covered, because they were so fragile.

The wounds on my legs were still too open for compression garments, but my arms and hands were ready (supposedly). I had opted for long 'gloves', which covered my whole hands (but not my fingertips) and came all the way up to my armpits. A zip on the outer side of the forearms made it a little easier to slide my arms into them.

The sun shone through the window behind me as I sat on the chair in the corner of my room and one of my nurses attempted to put them on for the first time, with my family eagerly waiting behind her. I say attempted because, even though we got one on eventually, I really wasn't mentally prepared for the ordeal. It was akin, I imagine, to being sausage meat squeezed into a tight casing – the meat in this scenario being my hypersensitive arms and hands, which already struggled if more than one person touched them at a time.[142] Now there was pressure on all sides, compressing every single *millimetre* of my skin, plus the horrific sensation of having the tight garment pulled over my hands and arms.

As soon as we got one on, I looked at my nurse, then at my family, and burst into tears. *More pain.* It felt like every step forward was accompanied by a big, painful step back. I was more than over it. Sobbing, I said I wasn't doing that again. 'Get them off.'

When everyone left to give me a break, I didn't notice Holly take the compression garments with her. Unbeknownst to me, she spent most of the next hour with them, trying to figure out the least painful way to put them on. When she came back, garments in hand, she asked if she could try. Reluctantly, I agreed, and she pulled one garment on over my hand and up my arm, then the other. It was almost painless. Thank god for sisters.

I hated those things. Even though it became less painful, and I was eventually able to get them on and off by myself, I hated them. Especially the gloves – they were always wet or dirty, and I was always having to take them on and off.

To this day, despite the fact I still *need* to wear regular gloves for protection – because the grafts are not as tough as normal skin – I often don't.[143] I would rather get cuts and bleed and wear plasters than wear gloves – a fact that anyone who has never *had* to wear gloves for more than a year usually fails to wrap their head around.

Don't tell me to wear gloves.

---

142 I vividly remember one day when I had about three sets of hands on me, all moisturising my grafts, and it was a sensory overload for my nervous system. There were too many points of sensation, all of them feeling weird and off. As politely as I could (before I blew up), I asked everyone to stop touching me, then for only one person to touch me at a time.

143 The fact that my ability to feel the shape, size and texture of objects is greatly diminished when I am *not* wearing gloves is another reason I hate them. I can't feel *anything* that is remotely fine or delicate when I wear gloves.

Wednesday, 22 January 2020
Me

Once someone found out that I love dogs, I was lucky enough to be able to meet a therapy dog, a chocolate Labrador. Unfortunately for me, he didn't give a shit about me – he was more interested in leaving.[144] The worst part, however, was how his fur felt when I patted him. It felt *horrible*, all coarse and spiky, because of my new skin and frazzled nerve endings. I didn't even *want* to pat him, and it made me worry about when I got to see River.

What if I can't even pat my own dog?

---

144 Apparently, I was his last stop of the day, so he was tired and wanted to go home for his dinner. Typical Lab!

Thursday, 23 January 2020
Family Messenger Chat

6.32pm, Mum

Kels will be transferred to Waikato on Tuesday for the next leg of her journey. At the rate she's going, it may very well be a pretty short stay there before she can go home!! Will know more when we get there I guess.

Carol

It is wonderful news. So happy for you all xxxx 😍

Red Book

Nurse #6

You are a real shining star, a sweetheart, and you have a purpose and plan in this life. Stay strong like you are, always believe in yourself and surround yourself with beautiful people like your family and friends.

Nurse #7

Hi, Kelsey girl. What an absolute pleasure it has been to care for you. I have loved listening to your stories and life experiences and hearing your plans for the future. You have come so far in such a short time. You should be *so very proud* of how hard you have been working with your recovery. It has been lovely meeting your family – they clearly love you so much! I am really going to miss you. All the very best for your future!!! I know you are going to do amazing things!

Doctor

Kia ora, Kelsey! Mine is one of the many faces popping in and out with the crowd in the morning. Particularly memorable was earlier this week when we had to do a blood test and I didn't quite have the speed of old mate Liam.[145] We got to talk about Jess and River about four times over, trying to keep your mind busy. You were pretty over it![146]

It's been incredible seeing you go from feeling miserable in bed to up and wandering around with your whānau or surprising me on my way home as you're down by the café. Your sense of humour is gonna get you far – everyone is careful to mention the hard stuff ahead, but I think you've already pushed through most of it. Just the long haul of getting back to a new normal. Your whānau are so incredible for all their support while you have been doing the hard mahi. Hopefully you'll be seeing far fewer doctors in the near future, but I'm sure the team will look after you well up in Waikato. We've also told them to cut right back on the blood tests! Yay!!

I probably won't see you again (for all the right reasons), but it's been so awesome being part of your temporary whānau here at Hutt. Can't wait to hear about your great next steps! Maybe read your memoir?[147]

Me

Today was the day I finally used my phone for the first time since the eruption. I waded past the notifications – the many missed calls and texts from 9 December and the days following, and opened Instagram. All I wanted to do was thank people – thank

---

[145] Baby-doctor Liam, who got me oral blood thinners, was apparently also a whiz at getting my blood. I never knew who was taking my blood – I never looked.

[146] I remember this so clearly. This poor doctor was trying to get blood from one of my very few accessible veins, and he tried *everything*. Tourniquet. Warm water in a glove. Nothing was making a vein surface enough for an easy draw. I think in the end he managed to draw just enough to do whatever tests they needed to do, but I probably wasn't very friendly by that point. Sorry!

[147] Here yah go, Devin!

everyone who had a hand in saving my life – but I was at a loss as to how to do that, other than to put it on Instagram. Knowing that the media was desperately waiting for any news of me (like a gross, jealous ex), I decided to use that to my advantage.

I found a picture of home – my favourite place on the farm – and captioned it:

> Thank you to everyone who has reached out or helped my family since 9 December. And to those who have generously donated to my Givealittle – I've been reading your comments in small batches, as the kindness is overwhelming. It's hard to fathom the amount of love and support from people I met through work, and even people I haven't met.
>
> Thank you so much to the emergency services, doctors, nurses, surgeons that got me from the Whakatāne wharf, through ICU, to the plastics and burns unit. You literally saved my life, and ensured that I will go on to live a long and beautiful life. Here's hoping that fourteen trips to the operating theatre are the only trips I'll take!
>
> Thank you doesn't seem like a big enough word(s) to my family and partner, who have been by my side from day one, through the low-lows, and the 'baby's first step' highs. You've been through hell with me, and I am lost for words in how to thank you all. I'll just keep pushing forward, and hope that that will do for now.
>
> Can't wait to be home.

Sure enough, the media sank its teeth into the post, and pretty soon I had to turn off the notifications on my phone, before it vibrated itself to death.

Friday, 24 January 2020
Me

A couple of days after I met my first therapy dog, I got to meet another – and this one was much better at her job! It was also my first introduction to a Russian terrier. Her coat was less hair-like, so it was much nicer for my hands to get used to ... although it still felt really weird.

Even my own hair felt weird, and it took me a long, long time before I was able to wash it myself – and even longer before I actually enjoyed it.

There were a lot of textures that I hated feeling with my 'new' hands. My friend Taz bought me a beautiful crocheted humpback whale, and I couldn't stand to touch it. Dad's old jeans felt like sandpaper. And I *hated* washing my hands – the feeling of graft on graft, and drying my skin, even on the softest of towels, made me want to vomit. But the only way out of this was through it. I had to desensitise my hands to different textures by touching all of the things all of the time. Thankfully, nowadays there are only a few things that still make me draw my hands back at lightning speed.[148]

---

[148] Which I won't mention, because Dad will read this and cover the house in them!

Sunday, 26 January 2020
Me

I didn't want to leave the hospital. It was my safe place, where everyone was watching out for me – a controlled environment. I felt like I was made of wet crêpe paper. What if something went wrong while I was out? It was a terrifying thought.

When the nurses started telling me I was allowed to spend the night out of hospital, I was petrified. I didn't want to, for a long time. My family had a big motel room – almost an apartment – just a couple of hundred metres down the road from the hospital, and they wanted me to come there. But I was too terrified.

Tom tried convincing me, but he was actually one of the reasons I didn't want to leave. I'd been living with him for most of the year before the eruption, and I knew he wanted me back by his side. I wanted that too – I hated having to watch him leave every night that I stayed in hospital – but I was scared. What if sharing a bed with him hurt me? Or I had nightmares? What if I had an accident in the night? What if? What if? *What if????* I was so scared that somehow I would put him off me, or he'd take it personally if I freaked out or kept him awake if I couldn't sleep from worry or ended up in pain. I didn't want to risk pushing him away. I couldn't get my head to relax into the idea, so I wouldn't let him try to convince me.

Then, on my second-to-last night in Hutt Hospital, while it was just Mum, Dad and Holly with me (Tom had popped back to the farm), I decided to try. I slept in a single bed at the motel, opposite my sister. She was prepared to be my nurse in the night if I needed help, and Mum and Dad were in the room next door, also prepared to help, in whatever way necessary, *if* necessary.

I think it hurt Tom quite a lot that I waited until he wasn't there, and even though I felt a tinge of guilt, I knew it had nothing to do with him. These were *my* fears, and I wanted to deal with them alone.[149]

Of course, nothing bad happened and I was absolutely fine.

---

[149] Unfortunately, this would become a major theme in my future.

Monday, 27 January 2020
Family Messenger Chat

12.11pm, Mum

Hi, all. Sorry it's been a while. Kels is making good physical progress. Her grafts are all looking pretty good and her physio is progressing well. She has the odd rough day/moment, as there is a lot of emotional stuff to work through now. It can be very frustrating and overwhelming for her but she is working so hard.

Off to Waikato tomorrow, which is bittersweet. It will be so hard leaving her Hutt ICU and burns unit family. They helped save her life and brought her this far. But it will be good to be closer to home – both physically and as part of her recovery journey.

Donna

Good to hear Kelsey's progress going well. She has a long, hard road ahead, but she is doing so well and we are very proud of her. Good luck with the move to Waikato. How will Kelsey get there? Much love to you all ♡♡ xxxx

Mum

We will fly via air ambulance. Xx

Tuesday, 28 January 2020
Me

The day had finally come to be transferred from Hutt Hospital to Waikato Hospital. None of us wanted me to move – we felt safe and so well cared for at Hutt, and the thought of a whole new hospital and whole new team was incredibly daunting. But it was inevitable.

On the morning of the move, I had my last wash and dressing change in the burns bathroom – hair included – and wrote some thank-you cards for my incredible medical team. There were a lot of tears, and as I was wheeled out of the burns ward I was treated to a 'guard of honour' from most of the staff who had treated me. Even some of the other patients popped their heads out to say goodbye and good luck.

Mum and I headed to the airport via ambulance, where I was loaded into an air ambulance – a plane the same colour as a tennis ball with only two seats in it, and lots of room in the back for me to be strapped to a bed and monitored – and we took off. We were picked up in another ambulance from Hamilton Airport and finally arrived at the very big Waikato Hospital.

It was incredibly disorientating and overwhelming, going from the quiet and secluded room around the corner from the nurses' station at Hutt to a room on what felt like a main highway. Despite having my own private room, out in the corridor there was noise and foot traffic *constantly*.

Mum was staying in a hotel around the corner, and we asked if I could go and stay with her so I could get a decent sleep. But despite the fact I'd spent two whole nights out of hospital in the lead-up to the move, Waikato wanted to keep me in for the night. They didn't know me, and they wanted to play it safe, which was fair. I didn't sleep *at all* that night. Thankfully, it was the only night I would spend in that hospital – after that, I was allowed to stay with Mum in the motel for the duration of my time as an inpatient.

A couple of days after arriving at Waikato Hospital, I was granted weekend leave. This was a *massive* deal: I hadn't been home since the morning of 9 December. It was going to be a good little taster for getting ready to be discharged, hopefully the following week, so, on Friday, 31 January, I was loaded into the car, and Mum, Tom and I headed for Whakatāne.

As we came around the corner onto the Matata Straights, running along the shore of the Bay of Plenty, I could see White Island sitting on the horizon. The island looked the same as it always had. For some reason I'd expected it to look different, but of course it didn't. Just the same old lump of rock at sea, steaming away happily.

'There's the bitch,' I said out loud.

Part III

Chapter 6

Mayday

Naturally, Mum and Dad strongly wanted me to come and stay with them at home, but I decided to go back to the farm with Tom. That was home to me, so that's where I wanted to go. I wanted to be in the country. I wanted to see the dogs. God, I was *so* excited to see the dogs – especially my boy, River.

I never thought about how hard this must have been for Mum in particular. This was her first time home since the eruption, too, and she'd spent two months barely leaving my side. Now, she was suddenly Kelsey-less. It took a long, long time before it sank in for me what this must have been like for her. Sorry, Mum.

Seeing the dogs again was incredible – though I had to wait in the car for a while before they calmed down enough for it to be safe for me to get out. My grafts were still really delicate and would be for a long while yet, and I was paranoid about wrecking them. I was super-careful about what I did, and how close I was to solid objects like furniture. For a long time, I walked with my elbows tucked into my body, and my arms and hands out in front of me, much like a T. rex.[150] I really didn't want to damage anything or hurt myself. Despite being ecstatic to be home, I was riddled with anxiety about something going wrong.

I tried to revel in the fact that I was home and enjoy everything I'd been missing. I'd missed the country air, and the feeling of wind on my face was still *heaven*. And the peace and quiet of the farm was something else – no constant drone of people talking or machines whirring all night as the ward continued to run. Instead, there were so many other sounds – the trees moving with the wind, birdsong, cars driving past on the road below the house, cows grazing in the paddock, and my favourite sound: Jess and River being lunatics. Taking it all in was a full-body experience and I was filled with a mix of relief, guilt, happiness and fear.

I really wanted to go to the beach that first evening. I wanted to be by the sea more than anything, and smell and feel the salt air on my face. It was the only bit of my body I *could* feel with, since everything else was covered with clothing, compression garments or bandages.

Tom obliged and we took the dogs with us, arriving at Ōhope Beach at sunset. The sky was a beautiful soft pink and the sea was relatively flat. Tom helped me across the soft sand, while also wrangling our two young, wild dogs – then, once we hit the hard sand, he let all three of us go. The dogs ran around, demanding sticks be thrown into the sea, which Tom did. I stood back, taking it all in.

In that moment I was *so* happy. Tom wasn't far away, but I felt like the only one on the beach. I closed my eyes – the smell of the beach, the sound of the waves, the feel of the salt wind on my

---

[150] I fondly remember Tom telling me one day, 'Straighten your arms.'

face. A smile spread across my face as I soaked in every blissful second.

When I opened my eyes, they weren't automatically drawn to Tom and the dogs; instead, they dropped down to the wave that was rapidly approaching.

No matter, I thought, as I began to turn to shuffle away from it.

My legs were still heavily bandaged with Tubigrip, which – true to its name – is indeed grippy. My legs tangled together, and my already poor balance was thrown off entirely – I'd only been self-propelled for about three weeks by this stage, so I was still pretty weak and unsteady. As if in slow motion, I started falling towards the hard, wet sand.

I landed on my knees and tried to break my fall with outstretched hands attached to weakened arms that had no business supporting my full weight just yet. I went down hard, and to add insult to injury, the wave went over the top of me. All of my dressings, all of my clothing, were soaked in salty sea water.

Suddenly, I was being scooped out of the sand. *Tom*. The whole event had unfolded in a couple of seconds, and he had reached me just as I'd hit the ground.

We looked down at my legs. Blood was already coming through the bandages – the blood thinners really working their magic at the least convenient time.

'My grafts …' I said quietly.

'I'm sorry. I know. I'm sorry,' Tom said, already blaming himself.

He called the dogs in and we started making our way up the beach as fast as we could. After loading the dogs on the back of the ute, Tom loaded me in the passenger seat, then we took off. As we drove, he called my mum: 'Kels has had a fall. We're on our way to the hospital.'

'Okay, we're on our way.'

When Tom and I arrived at Whakatāne Hospital A&E, we walked up to the nurse behind the desk and were sent immediately through to a cubicle, where some other nurses began talking to us about what had happened. News that an eruption survivor was back at the hospital spread quickly around the staff, and I had nurses and doctors popping their heads in the whole time I was there. They were all so happy to see someone from the eruption who had made it home. Some of them even remembered working on me when I'd come in (not that I remembered them). I'd always wanted to come back to say thank you to the hospital staff for everything they'd done on the day of the eruption – I knew a lot of them had no idea what had happened to their patients[151] – but this was *not* how I'd imagined my return.

Then the doctor *actually* treating me arrived, and after a brief Q&A session, she headed off to call Waikato to ask what they wanted us to do. They wanted to know what was going on under the bandages before deciding whether or not I needed to head back to Waikato immediately, possibly for surgery. That meant that, unfortunately, I needed my dressings removed.

We all knew this was going to hurt, so I was loaded up with meds, then a nurse, Mum and I headed off to one of the showers for undressing and wound flushing, while Tom raced off to drop

---

151 This is the norm for most patients who get transferred from their initial hospital, but our case was unique because a lot of White Island patients still hadn't been confidently IDed when they arrived at Whakatāne, so the hospital staff had no idea whether or not their patients had survived.

the dogs at a friend's house – after apologising profusely to my parents.

I felt awful. Not only had I retraumatised Tom – he was taking it pretty hard – but my parents were ashen-faced, seeing me back here at Whakatāne Hospital. I might not have remembered much about being here last time, but they did – vividly. But I was about to feel much worse.

While I sucked on Entonox gas,[152] the medical team took off my dress, then slowly peeled off my bandages, revealing the damage. I'd shunted a lot of my shin and knee grafts out of place and the sand – as it has a knack for doing – had managed to make its way under my bandages and into my new wounds. They'd need cleaning before anything else. I huffed the Entonox deeply.

Once I was back in my cubicle, donned in a hospital gown, they were able to have a closer look at my legs. The nurse called Waikato again after sending some photos, describing how the graft had been moved, and explaining that most of the grafts on my knees and a bit of my shins had been damaged. Somehow, my hands and arms were relatively unscathed.

'Do you want us to get her on a heli or in an ambulance now?' I heard the nurse ask. *Oh god* …

In the end, it was neither. It was about 9.30 on a Friday night, and there was no point in us trekking back to Waikato at this hour because they wouldn't be able to make a call on surgery till Monday morning, when the surgical team did their rounds.

---

152 If you've ever had the pleasure of huffing this gas, you might relate to what I'm about to explain. This shit made my pain *echo*. That's the only way I can think of to explain how it made me feel. In Hutt, whenever they were 'flipping' me I would bite the regulator as hard as I could, inhaling the gas until I was dizzy. The nurses would stop touching me, but the pain kept coming in waves – like an echo, slowly getting less intense and feeling further away. The same happened here in Whakatāne Hospital.

'Just put back as much as you can,' they told the nurse – in other words, clean my wounds, remove the sand, and put the grafts back in place as much as possible. So out came the tweezers and saline, and the nurse got to work. I huffed the Entonox *deeply*, re-entering the pain echo.

Once the nurse had done everything she could, she re-mummified my limbs and sent me home. Thankfully, once it was 'hands off', I was in no pain, but I was deeply aware of my new open wounds. On the way home, Tom and I swung past our friend's place to pick up the dogs, then went to get the pizza I had been promised much earlier in the evening.

Come Monday, back in Waikato Hospital, word had got out about my little mishap, and a team of nurses, doctors and surgeons all came to have a look at my legs. All was quiet as my dressings were removed, and as they looked over my legs the room was *silent*. You know it's bad when your medical team says nothing at all. Mum and I stared at each other blankly.

One of the doctors said, just before she left the room, 'I think it's fair to say you won't be getting weekend leave for a while.'

It was absolutely *devastating*. I felt so shit for ruining all the hard work everyone had done to put me back together, and for scaring the crap out of my family yet again. The original plan had been for me to return to Waikato for just a few nights after my weekend leave before being discharged, but my little whoopsie scuppered that. Instead, it landed me as an inpatient for another two and a bit weeks.

Thankfully, I didn't require any more surgery or grafting, but hospital life was still full on while we waited for everything to heal enough for me to be discharged. Every day, first thing in the morning, there were doctors' rounds, which I would pop over for from the motel. There were dressing changes, physio, occupational therapy, and adjustments to my splints and compression garments. Without ever meaning to, I managed to somehow never cross paths with a member of the psych team in Waikato, as after my physical check-ups were done, Mum and I would go and sight-see around Hamilton.

It was while in Waikato that I got to take my first shower standing up, and the whole time I giggled so much that the nurse with me started laughing, too. 'I'll give you a few minutes,' she said, and left me alone to have my moment (a brave move, given recent history). It felt *so good* to be standing under the water, feeling it fall on my head, run through my hair and then down my face and back – sensations you just don't get when you're lying on a bed with four nurses washing you down like a fish on a filleting bench.

My grafts and donor sites were still super-fragile, and the smallest knock could be damaging. When they got wet – and especially after they'd soaked for a while – they'd get even more fragile. One day, a 'baby nurse' was tasked with covering my leg wounds to protect them while I was in the shower, and taped a plastic sheet around my legs. When it was time to remove the plastic after the shower, we discovered that where the tape was coming off, my skin graft was coming too. I ended up losing quite a bit of skin graft, and the head nurse was furious. More holes to heal. *My poor legs.*

My burns and donor sites still needed moisturising at least twice a day, and any infected sites also had to be soaked in a Betadine antiseptic solution twice a day. By this time, I'd started becoming marginally more independent as the dexterity in my hands increased, but blood blisters kept forming on them – especially on my left thumb and left index finger.[153] These blisters would become so big and painful they had to be 'deroofed', meaning the outer layer of skin was removed so the fluid could drain and my grafts would continue to heal.

For months, I wouldn't touch anything with my hands if I could avoid it – I would suck my hands into my sleeves. Everything felt horrible and made my skin crawl. Tom and my family would open doors for me, and even something as basic as washing my hands was a whole ordeal. I hated the feeling of graft-on-graft (or lack of feeling, in some cases),[154] and fabric may as well have been made of bark. I didn't want *anything* touching my skin, and the only thing I wanted to wear was my hospital gown, even after I was told I could wear normal clothes again. As well as everything feeling awful against my skin, I think the gown was a bit like a safety blanket.

At night, I elected to sleep either at my family's hotel around the corner or back home in Whakatāne, rather than in my designated hospital bed. One evening in the hotel room, I was in the middle of brushing my teeth when Tom looked down. 'Where's all that blood coming from?' he said, in a bit of an alarmed tone. I looked down to discover the bathroom floor was scattered with a *lot* of blood, and it was pouring out of one of my knees through the bandages.

---

153 We would find out later on that these weren't blood blisters but trapped fluid stuck under the skin grafts where normal skin had survived/regenerated and been grafted over.

154 This was a weird one. Touching my hands against one another, or touching my other grafted areas with my grafted hands, is like if you were trying to touch your skin through plastic film – there is *some* feeling, but not much. It took me a long time to get used to it, and even now I still find it odd.

Mum, Tom and I all panicked, naturally – it looked really serious, even though we knew that it was probably not as bad as it seemed because I was still on blood thinners. So it was straight into the car and round to the hospital, navigating the labyrinth of white hallways, then up to my room on the plastics ward, where a nurse unwrapped my leg to find the source of the bleeding – but it had stopped. No one could figure out where it had come from. There was no majorly open area, no injury, no bleeding. It was really weird, especially given how much blood was on the bathroom floor back at the hotel.

I was wrapped back up and sent on my way. 'Come back straight away if it happens again,' the nurse said as we left.

It never happened again.

On 13 February – a total of sixty-six days after the eruption – I was, at last, officially discharged from hospital. All in all, this was a rather short stint, considering the initial prognosis had been so grim, then amended to 'at least six months in hospital'.

I had mixed feelings. I was well and truly ready to leave this time round, but I was worried about not having 24/7 access to help if I needed it. Rationally, I knew this wasn't the case, as I would technically still have access to round-the-clock help – the only change, really, was that I would be considered an outpatient rather than an inpatient, and I always had Whakatāne Hospital nearby, plus Tom and my parents were basically nurse-grade bandage-wrappers now, having seen and done so many of my dressing changes! Even so, it felt like I was the member of the wolf pack who had been cast out into the big wide, dangerous world and had to learn to fend for herself, with her crêpe-paper skin.

Before leaving, I took one last shower in the hospital bathroom (less giggling this time, but still many closed-eye moments of watery bliss), then there were some final appointments to adjust my splints and check my compression garments were fitting snugly, a bunch of paperwork, and I was cleared for departure. I said goodbye to the lovely nurses, knowing that at some point I'd be back for more surgery to tidy things up or if my scars began retracting and affecting my range of motion. Then we left.

I arrived back at the farm to find all of my family, and all of Tom's, waiting for me. Together, we celebrated with a barbecue out on the deck, looking over the farm and the harbour entrance. It was bliss. I still needed a lot of help and care, but I was home.

Sink or swim, baby.

Chapter 7

The teething period

The day after I was discharged (a Friday), Tom reluctantly went away for the weekend for a much-needed break from being a full-time farmer and carer. I went and stayed with my parents, much to Mum's delight. The weekend was very low key and quiet, as you might imagine. I was doing pretty well, and gaining some confidence – so much so that I didn't bring my shower chair or any other bits of assistance equipment that ACC had provided for me on discharge.

On the Monday, I was due to meet one of the district nurses for the first time. She was going to come and check my grafts – on my legs, especially – to make sure things were healing after both the beach incident and the tape incident, then redo my dressings. We Waghorns are a helpful bunch, so Mum and I decided to save her a job by getting the dressings off in the shower before she arrived.

The shower was still a novelty for me, and I spent most of the time revelling in the feeling of the water cascading over my head and face. I was never going to take washed hair for granted again! Mum, meanwhile, was kneeling in the bottom of the shower, gently removing the bandages as the water lifted the edges, making them easier to remove.

At some point, towards the end of my shower, I started feeling a bit weird. I waited a moment before saying anything, but the weird was just getting weirder. 'I feel ... weird ...' I finally said aloud.

Mum looked up at me, bandage in hand, and her face instantly changed. I think she started to stand up, telling me to step towards her as she turned the water off, but the next thing I knew I was crumpled in the bottom of the shower, blood swirling all around me.

My grafts ...

Mum was yelling for Dad. He'd just popped home from work to say goodbye to his sister and her daughter (my aunt Donna and cousin Tori), who were heading back to Australia that day, but next thing he knew he was lifting his naked, bleeding twenty-five-year-old daughter out of the bottom of the shower. He got me upright, with minimal assistance from me ... and I passed out again, requiring him to *drag* me to the nearby bed with Mum looking on, horrified.

I came to on my back, wrapped in a towel, with my parents' faces hovering over me.[155] I could hear my sister on the phone.

'Who's Holly talking to?' I enquired.

'*She's calling an ambulance!*' Mother informed me.

Suddenly three paramedics were also in the bedroom, inspecting my shins, which had opened *again* when I'd managed to slide down the edge of the glass door. With Whakatāne being such a small place, it turned out that one of the paramedics had

---

155 Much like that scene in *Friends* where they're all looking down at baby Ben while he goes to sleep, and it looks like they all have floating heads.

also driven me and Mum to the airport from Whakatāne Hospital after the eruption. She'd also just been talking about me with her colleagues, wondering how I was doing. Now she knew.

They took my blood pressure while I was sitting down, then standing up, lying down, sitting up again, lying down again and standing up again, and determined that I was dehydrated and still adjusting to all of this upright nonsense. This, combined with the heat of the shower, had caused my blood pressure to tank, and that's why I had passed out. They gave me IV fluids and opted not to take me to hospital – but instructed me that, if it happened again, I was to go straight to A&E. My district nurse arrived to an ambulance in the driveway and fresh wounds to dress.

When Tom came to collect me, we all had to sheepishly tell him what had happened, and that there were now even more bandages on my salami legs.

On a whim one day the following week, Tom decided to take me for a driving lesson. For obvious reasons, I hadn't driven myself anywhere since the morning of the eruption, but I had a new car in the garage – I had bought it just a couple of months before the eruption – and we both wanted me to get back behind the wheel and regain some of my freedom and independence.

I wasn't able to grip things very well with my stiff and weird-feeling hands – it was both a physical restriction and a big mental one – but we decided today was the day. The street we lived on was short and quiet, so it was the perfect place to have a crack. Tom snapped a picture of me in the driver's seat, in my pyjamas and compression garments, covered in bandages, ready to rumble.

I had the *loosest* grip on that steering wheel, but we made it down the gravel driveway and down the road, turned around and came back. *Perfection.* Even though I was still a *long* way off driving on the 100km/hr road back to town it felt nice to try my 'new' hands at something I used to be so confident doing. I love driving, and even just this little taster of my old life and something I enjoyed doing felt good. The heel of my left hand hadn't been burnt thanks to the bandage that Hayden had put on me, so I could use that to apply pressure to the wheel to keep the car straight. As long as I didn't need to do any evasive manoeuvring, I was golden.[156]

One thing that *never* crossed my mind about the effect major trauma has on a woman's body is how your menstrual cycle reacts. Turns out, when you're fighting for your life, your body decides now might not be the best time to be fertile.

Sorry, lads. We're going there.

Early on — it must have been while I was in ICU — I did have a hallucination that I got my period. There was blood all through my bed, but I couldn't move to do anything about it, and *no one* was helping me. Of course, the reason no one was helping me was because there was nothing to help with — I didn't have my period at all, as the hospital staff patiently tried to explain to me.

When I finally did get my period again, it was right before I was discharged from Waikato Hospital. I woke up in my hotel bed, and the sheets were red. Thankfully, Tom wasn't around this particular morning.[157] Before stripping the sheets off the bed, Mum helped me get to the bathroom to clean myself up.

---

156 All you law-abiding citizens, please know that I didn't drive myself anywhere or alone until I was properly able to grip the steering wheel. It was all above board.

157 And suddenly those fears I'd had about sharing a bed with him again felt justified.

My hand dexterity was still very limited, and we all know how I felt about textures during this time, so this was a disaster. I was so deeply worried about any kind of risk of infection, and didn't want to do anything that would mean I'd have to wash my hands.

Despite having always hated sanitary pads, I had to use them until I had better control of my hands – and my mind. After a few months of battling with it, constantly resenting my hands and grafts and being a woman, I finally spoke to my GP about getting an IUD implanted, to stop this rubbish for the foreseeable future.

Western medicine for the win once more!

My extreme reluctance to do anything that would mean I had to wash my hands meant I ended up in a bit of a bind with my compression garments. I had to wear them, and they did protect my hands somewhat if I bumped them – but touching anything while wearing them had me keenly aware that whatever ended up on them (dirt, dog slobber, food, any kind of germy stuff etc) couldn't just be washed off under the tap because they would stay wet. So I would have to take the garments off to handle things, then I would need to wash my hands. But I didn't *want* to wash my hands … Do you see my dilemma?

Regularly, I pulled my shirt-sleeves down over my hands so that neither compression garments nor skin grafts touched anything. Until the sensation in my hands settled down, I became a bit of a germophobe and texture-phobe.

The nerve pain I experienced, especially in my legs, made me want to rip my skin off. Sometimes it was numb and achy, sometimes like sharp needles, and sometimes it wasn't even pain but something else entirely. It might feel like bugs running across my legs – even under the compression garments (literally not possible – which my brain knew, but my body didn't). Or warm water flowing over me. Or cold water dripping on me. Or maybe a gush of what felt like warm blood leaking down my arms, hands or legs. Sometimes my shins would get so hot that I'd have to try to cool them with cold towels.[158] Other times it was itchy – but, because the nerve endings weren't in the new, grafted skin, I'd feel the itch *beneath* the graft, meaning that trying to scratch the itch often resulted in me trying to get my nails under the graft itself.

To help with the nerve pain – and in an effort to save my sanity and my grafts – I went through four different medications over the course of four years. After a while of taking the first one, I started having breakthrough pain, so I had to switch to another. That one lasted a couple of years before, once again, I started getting breakthrough pain.

The third and worst of them all made me think that perhaps I *had* been hit on the head on the island, because all of a sudden my vision went really blurry and I thought I had 'delayed blindness' from the knock on the noggin that never happened. I went to see an optometrist who worked out that it was a side effect of the medication, and I was sent to a pain-medication specialist who found me a new drug that didn't make me question my sanity.

Before the eruption, I'd rarely taken even paracetamol, and suddenly over the course of a few months I'd been pumped full of every kind of pain medication imaginable. Then I went home

---

158 I even have a photo of my best mate sitting on the floor, wrapping cold, wet towels around my legs, as I stood by a window on New Year's Eve, trying to get a breeze.

and had to carry on taking this medication every day. It was a lot to get my head around – not least because of the horrifying list of possible side-effects, which included (but weren't limited to) crushing chest pain, yellowing of the skin or eyes, uncontrollable body spasms, seizures, hallucinations, changes in sex drive, excessive sweating, changes in appetite and weight, confusion, unsteadiness, shuffling walk, changes in eyesight, swelling of various body parts (eyes, face, throat, mouth, lips, gums, tongue, head, neck, arms, hands, feet, ankles, lower legs) and bluish-tinged skin, lips or fingernails.

In the end I had only a few of these side-effects, but you can probably see why I was hesitant to take any more medication than I had to.

Around the same time that I was discharged from hospital, cases of Covid had started to pop up close to New Zealand. I was told in no uncertain terms that I had a high risk of complications if I caught it, so I kept my return home very quiet. No one knew I'd been discharged, and I kept it that way for over a month. I didn't want to see people yet.

It wasn't until the eventual lockdown late in March that I finally revealed to everyone that I was home. A lot of people hated that lockdown period, but I *loved* it. It was the safety net I needed and allowed me to adjust to my new normal and figure things out for a while before having to 'entertain guests'. I was on the farm. I had my dogs. I had my partner. I had all the space and quiet in the world to heal.

But then my birthday rolled around in mid-April. I'd never dreaded my birthday before, but for some reason I found myself dreading this one. I don't know if it was survivor's guilt or something else, but just the idea of it made me feel physically sick.

It didn't help that three-quarters of my support crew (Mum, Dad and Holly) was cut off from me in another household, and 'bubbles' weren't allowed to mix. Right before the lockdown came into force, my sister had flown back to Whakatāne on a plane with a confirmed Covid case, so I knew I definitely couldn't see my family. And, before someone jumps down my throat about this, know that I'd had the fear of god put in me by my district nurses, and social media didn't help, either. When you've just dodged a bullet and someone tells you there's another one in the chamber, you tend to listen and obey.

In order to reduce my exposure, I wasn't even seeing my nurses. They would come to the letterbox, drop off my dressings, and Tom would then do all of the dressing changes.

On that first 'bonus birthday', Tom took me for a walk around the farm, as far as I could manage. He was trying so hard to cheer me up, but I just felt hollow. I cried. A lot.

The only thing that cheered me up a bit was a gift from his dad. He'd made me a papier-mâché White Island that was incredibly accurate in its geological landmarks – so that I could burn it.

It was only once I was out of hospital that I started to understand the scale of the legal stuff that was unfolding around the eruption. And I started to get scared. *Really* scared. What if I got blamed for something? What if I hadn't done enough? What if I'd done something *wrong*?

White Island Tours had their own lawyers, who I could use for free, but that didn't feel like enough. I decided, with the help of my family, to get my own lawyer – at least initially. Doing so turned out to be a great soother for my nerves. It meant I always had someone to troubleshoot with, someone who had my back completely, without any risk of conflict of interest (should it ever arise).

In *Surviving Galeras*, the book that helped save my life by telling me what to do in a pyroclastic surge, Stanley Williams writes about how some of his colleagues criticised him for not requiring everyone in his party to don helmets and fire-resistant clothing. After White Island erupted, the media and public made similar comments. But, as Williams writes, 'It's a good idea – in theory and in hindsight.' A helmet would never have stopped most of the projectiles that White Island was flinging around. And if a pyroclastic surge can shunt a something-tonne helicopter off its base, your plastic hat isn't going to do shit. Perhaps if we had made all our guides and visitors wear fire-resistant clothing (or even full-body coverings) that *may* have reduced the extensiveness of *some* of our burns that day, but overall the effectiveness of this policy would depend heavily on the type of eruption. Would it have stopped the projectiles? No. Would we have had much higher rates of heat stroke on every single other day we ran tours during summer? Yes.

Williams also writes about facing allegations that he'd missed subtle warnings and therefore recklessly led his colleagues to their deaths. 'How easy it is to snipe after the fact,' he notes. 'To apply knowledge we have now to the events of [the past]'. Similarly, White Island Tours was alleged to have 'known' that White Island was going to erupt but went anyway – driven by money. Now, I'm not good at maths (ask anyone who knows me), but even *I* know that risking your entire operation for a day's ticket sales makes no sense when the alternative is calling off the tour for one day so you can resume activities the next – and not have your entire company shut down due to major injury and loss of life.

I did my police interview voluntarily in June 2020 – six months after the eruption. I knew it was unavoidable: I could either do my witness statement in my own time, in a controlled manner, or I could get called into court to deliver it on the stand for the chief coroner. In an attempt to feel as though I had some kind of control, I went for option one. It took four hours, and by the end, I was absolutely shattered. It was the first time I had gone over *everything* that had happened that day from start to finish in minute detail. As I sat there, in the stark interview room the police were using for their investigation on behalf of the coroner, I was grateful to have my lawyer and Tom by my side.

It took me a couple of days to recover.

For that whole first year after the eruption, my stamina was pretty low. I would run out of steam quickly, and it was quite the learning curve, trying to figure out when to push myself and when to conserve my energy. Usually, I only found the line when I pushed it too far and ended up laid out for a couple days. But there were also times when I was hesitant to push it at all.

For months, I didn't straighten my arms. At first, it was just because it was the most neutral, comfortable position for my arms, in which I couldn't feel any of my new skin being stretched and pulled. But even as moving my arms became easier I still kept them close to my body because I was terrified of bumping them and damaging my new skin, or touching something bad and getting yet another infection.

The skin on all four of my limbs needed to be stretched to make movement easier. A lot of my physiotherapy was around stretching out my grafts and scars so my movement could be fluid once again, and so that I wasn't intensely aware of my own skin every time I moved. The bunchy bits of skin over knuckles and over knees suddenly revealed their importance!

The only stretch I could manage comfortably was a giant yawn – and these yawns would come at the most random times, sometimes mid-conversation. I guess my body was desperate to release all its tension and stress, and this was the only way it could do it without feeling like I was going to burst a seam. I'd never thought about how good it feels to have a good, proper stretch until I couldn't do it anymore.[159] As the year progressed, I slowly started regaining movement. But, for a couple of years – and even now, if I move in a particular way – I would feel my skin when I moved: a pull here, restriction there, an almost-tearing feeling if I pushed it too hard.

Everyone, from Hutt to home, kept telling me how important massage was for keeping my scars under control, increasing blood flow, desensitising my fried nerve-endings, and encouraging the grafts to be smooth and supple. I asked my ACC case manager for a proper scar massage therapist. Initially, there was a bit of pushback, as this wasn't typically funded by ACC, but my team of therapists sent a long, wordy email about its importance and it was approved.

Within about four sessions, I was already noticing the difference, particularly in my right hand. My fingers were straightening, and the web-space between my thumb and index

159 But boyyyyyyy, did that first real stretch feel gooooood!

finger was slowly opening up. The massage even helped to 'free' the grafts from the muscle below so they moved a bit more like normal skin. Even now, the muscles directly under my grafts get sore more frequently than any of my other muscles, and massage helps immensely with my pain levels.

In September – seven months after being discharged – I found myself back in hospital for my fifteenth surgery for some 'excess graft removal'. It was my first at Waikato, and compared to the others it was pretty straightforward – just tidying up some grafting on my hands. I'd known when I was discharged that there would be more surgeries in my future, I just didn't know how many, as that all depended on how my scars healed.

I went into this surgery positive, and woke up with bandage boxing gloves on both hands. Sitting in recovery, I lifted my weighty bandages and realised I should have done one hand at a time.

For the first couple of days, I coped fairly well. But I had to rely heavily on other people again, and not being able to perform basic tasks by myself quickly became frustrating, especially since I'd only just started regaining some freedom.

Thankfully, a little more than a week later, I went back to the hospital for the unveiling, and a big reduction in the size of the bandages. Once again, I looked at my black and bloodied hands and wished this wasn't real, but I was grateful that my days of fluid build-up under my grafts was over.

I swore I would *never* get both hands done at the same time again.

*

Before the eruption, my biggest fear was getting cancer; being in hospital subjected to constant needles and injections, and the possibility of losing my hair if I needed chemo.[160]

Now, though? My biggest fear was getting burnt again. At night, I'd lie awake in bed while Tom and the dogs slept soundly nearby, and I'd be certain I could hear the crackle and rush of flames from the other room.[161] It wasn't actual nightmares that plagued me – it was in that moment right before I fell asleep, when my mind would wander into darkness, into a loop I couldn't get myself out of. Some nights, I'd be back on the island, reliving what actually happened – noticing the pyroclastic surge, then screaming into my gas mask as the dark cloud burnt my skin. Other nights, I would be taking my family on a tour of the island and, as we approached the crater, it would start erupting, and I would helplessly watch on as they suffered the same fate I had. Sometimes I'd be back in Hutt Hospital, screaming into the regulator and sucking the Entonox gas while being turned in my hospital bed. Occasionally, there would be no accompanying images but my body would just flood with pure fear.

160 Funnily enough, I came very close to losing my hair when I was in hospital after the eruption. For women, they try to avoid using the front of the torso as a skin donor site, in case they decide to have kids down the line – the significant stretching of the donor site scars on a pregnant belly would cause a lot of extra scarring. If the doctors ran out of viable skin on my thighs, back and butt, they were going to shave my head and use the skin on my scalp. Mum was horrified – she's always tried to preserve my long, curly, ginger hair. Dad was ecstatic – he is bald, and the idea of a bald daughter was a fun thought for him! Thankfully, they were able to get enough viable donor skin, so my head and front avoided shaving.

161 This still happens sometimes. Not that long ago, more than five and a half years after the eruption, I was away for the weekend with River. I leapt out of bed and tore down the hallway towards the fire to figure out what was going on, only to find it was all in my head.

Nights were rarely restful. Tom would find sleep easily but, as I lay next to him, trying desperately to rest, the cogs of fear would start turning in my head, my breathing would speed up so I was unable to take in a lungful of air, my body would shake, and I'd be overwhelmed with both fear and a deep, *deep* sadness.

I never woke Tom during these 'episodes'. I never asked for help, company or comfort. I was embarrassed to be feeling this way, and painfully aware of how much I had already asked of him (most times without actually even asking), so I would slink out of bed, creep into the lounge and sit in the dark and sob silently on the couch. Alone. For hours.

Only once my body had run out of tears and I had no more energy left to be terrified would I make my way back to bed, utterly exhausted. Even then, it would take a while for sleep to find me.

In the morning, a gross emotional hangover would linger. A feeling of numbness, which I now know to be dissociation – when you disconnect from your thoughts, feelings, emotions and sense of identity, in response to stress or trauma – would stay with me for at least the morning, sometimes longer. My mind would be totally vacant, and all I longed for was peace and sleep.

Not long after I'd been discharged, I got a cryptic message from my friend Liam.

I have a few people who want to have a chat with you lol any chance you'd be keen on a phone convo on Monday?

Er, no.

What people …? I replied.

After a brief back and forth, he finally confessed. He'd been in touch with The Rock radio station.

I said there's probably a few subjects you wouldn't want to talk about so they said they would prerecord it and edit out whatever you don't want to air, Liam explained, already laying the groundwork for me. I finally agreed to answer the phone – and that's how I ended up doing my very first radio interview.

The guys at the station were *incredible* – not pushy, they didn't sensationalise anything, and they respected my no-go topics.[162] Right before the interview, I was incredibly nervous, worried that I had made the wrong call by agreeing to talk to them, but hosts Jay and Dunc made it a breeze. Liam must have told them I was a big fan of Blindspott, because they surprised me with backstage tickets to Blindspott's next gig at the end of our chat. Given the band had been broken up for many years and were re-forming for some concerts, I was elated. What an absolute treat! Thanks, Liam.[163]

I was really nervous about the first anniversary of the eruption. I'd been fairly well sheltered in my own little physical healing bubble, but as December drew nearer, the outside world got louder about the eruption,[164] and I couldn't block it out so easily. It started creeping its way in.

I'd heard from a couple of the other survivors over the last eight or so months. Initially we'd talked a lot, and compared many stories and scars. But, as both a guide and a survivor, I had a foot in both camps. I had been warned by the police and my lawyer that given my unique position, I had to be careful about what I said, as it could be taken out of context to suggest

---

162 Which mostly surrounded anyone else involved, laying blame or anything legal.

163 The Rock ended up being the only mainstream media outlet I would speak to for a very long time.

164 Bitches love an anniversary.

things I did or didn't do, or did or didn't know, on the day of the eruption. So while I wanted to have some kind of relationship with some of the very few people who knew what it was like to be swallowed whole by a volcano and spat out, I also felt like I couldn't get too close. It was an awful, isolating position to be in.

On 4 December 2020, a golf tournament was held in memory of Hayden by his brother, and while I was there I got talking to one of the paramedics who had been dropped on the boat to help us on the way back to Whakatāne. While we were chatting, a man came up to me and asked whether I was Kelsey. When I said yes, he began to tear up and tried to say something to me but couldn't get it out.

I took him by the hand and led him to the back of the clubrooms, where it was quieter, and he broke down. I had no idea who he was, or what was going on. Feeling very confused, I held him as he cried. Eventually, he was able to tell me: he had been the officer assigned to watch and be there for my family in the Whakatāne Hospital waiting room. Once he was calmer, I took him over to Tom – and, for Tom, that brought everything back. A year's worth of pain, stress and worry began to release through a barrage of tears. It was a very emotional day; at the end of the prizegiving, a majority of the people in the room stood up and performed the most gut-wrenching haka I have ever witnessed. There wasn't a dry eye in the room.

In the lead-up to the anniversary, Mum approached our local airline, Air Chathams, about possibly doing a flight over the island, and they were super keen to take us out there – generously, at no charge. So, on 7 December, we rustled up a few people closest to what had happened, jumped on a little plane, and headed north towards the steaming rock in the Pacific.

It was a beautiful, clear, still day. As we approached the island, I was expecting something to be stirred up. I thought I'd cry, or panic, but there was nothing. Instead I found I was simply interested in seeing how the island had changed in the year since I'd last seen it up close. The crater looked different – but it always looked different after time had passed, with vents moving and the mineral composition changing the colours of the landscape. The ash that had blanketed us almost a year ago had turned to a drab grey.

I pulled out my camera to get some photos. As we circled the steaming crater, I took in the sight of the volcano that had almost killed me. No thoughts of the fear or pain I'd experienced, no intrusive sounds of screaming crept into my head. No new memories of the bits my brain had let go of. It was a really weird experience, knowing what had happened there and yet feeling *nothing*, only thinking about it because I was *making* myself think about it, because I thought I *should* be thinking about it and, at the very least, feeling *something*. The brain – *my* brain – works in mysterious ways.

For the day of 9 December 2020, several things were planned, but all I can remember is driving over to the beach, sobbing.

For the 'official' memorial, we (the survivors and the families of those who didn't make it) were all given the opportunity to write something, to either read out ourselves or have read out by someone else at the service. I started writing my message about a million times, but I just couldn't find the words to say sorry deeply enough. I tried. And I tried. And I cried. And, in the end, I didn't submit anything at all.

It broke my heart. I felt as though I needed to apologise to the families for not doing more on the day, especially the families of Group Two – Hayden and Tipene's group. I wanted to say sorry for not going back for them. I wanted to apologise for losing my radio. For not being able to give anyone first aid.[165] I also wanted to thank the people who saved us – my colleagues, the passengers of *Phoenix*, everyone who dropped everything to be at the wharf for us, the countless traumatised medical staff who were tasked with trying to save us and put us back together in the hours, days, weeks, months, years that followed. But I just couldn't string the sentences together. My words felt so small. I felt responsible for so much that had happened on that day, and facing everyone and apologising for it all was just too much.

If I didn't say anything at all, I couldn't fuck it up.

I decided to not even go to the service. Instead, my family and I headed over the hill to Ōhope Beach, and down to the chair that had been erected in the dunes in Hayden's name.

On the way over the hill, I tapped into the live stream of the service on my phone. When the other survivors began reading out their messages, I lost it entirely. I cried for over an hour, and it took me a long time to pull myself back together. I felt hollow for days.

After Christmas, my family and I decided to charter a fishing boat and head out to White Island as part of a fishing trip.

It wasn't my first time on a boat since the eruption; over winter, Paul had messaged to ask whether I'd been back out to sea yet, and when I'd said no, he'd replied, *Do you want to go today?* Tom and I

---

165 The realistic part of my brain *knows* that these are my emotions talking – and are not what my reality was. I *know* I physically could not have done more on the day. I *know* I did my absolute best in the shittiest of situations, with very little time to react.

met him at the wharf, a place where I'd once spent so much time loading other people onto boats. It felt strange to be the passenger.

Rather than feeling something negative, I just felt excited – excited to be going out to sea, even if only to do a loop around Whale Island. It was so incredible to smell, feel and taste the salt air and water on my face again. The sea was flat enough that the outing wasn't a hazard to my new skin, but Tom barely took his hand off my arm the whole time, just in case I tried to repeat history and take a tumble that would land me back in hospital. There wasn't a cloud in the sky, and despite the horrors that had unfolded for me last time I had been to Whale Island, I was grateful to be there. I hadn't realised until that moment how much I had missed – and needed – this feeling of being at sea. Thank you, Paul.

Now, after a morning of fishing, as we headed out towards White Island, I waited to see what I was going to feel as we got closer. Surely I'd feel something, being at eye-level with the island – especially if I caught a whiff of the gases being constantly ejected from the fumaroles. But, just like when we'd done the flyover, I felt nothing.

Well, nothing besides confusion about not landing. All up, I'd made almost nine hundred trips to the island. I guess old habits die hard – I felt like I should be starting to look for my island gear and telling people to get their shit together, ready to go ashore. But as we pulled into the southeastern bay, I locked eyes on the munted helicopter and remembered where I was in the timeline.

No tour today.

Chapter 8

You thought that was bad?

A full year after I had foolishly thought I'd be able to make it to Homegrown, I finally got there. And within all of about two hours I realised just how lucky I'd been that Covid had shut it down the year before. What had I been thinking? Heading to an all-day music festival just a month after being discharged from hospital with full-thickness burns to 45 per cent of my body? I'm sure I would have been well looked after, but still …

Even a year on, it was a massive day – especially since all of my favourite bands were on later in the evening. Struggling through nerve pain and needing to sit down regularly, being intolerant of (and, quite frankly, rather scared of) all the drunk people, I got to see my beloved Blindspott for a second time. I returned to my hotel room absolutely shattered, but very happy.

A month later, it was time for another 'bonus birthday', and again I cried and felt awful.[166] Shortly after that, my family and I

---

[166] At the time of writing this book, the only two birthdays since the eruption that I haven't felt like that were my thirtieth and thirty-first, and for both I wasn't home. On my thirtieth I was away doing a tour of the South Island with my parents, and I spent my thirty-first in transit between Borneo and Kuala Lumpur. I didn't reshare anything on social media about my birthday until it was almost over and I was away from the group I had been travelling with.

took a trip to the lower North Island, and we decided to pop into Hutt Hospital on the way to say hello and see 'my' old rooms.

In ICU, we went to the room where I'd spent the most time. My family had vivid memories of it – the tubes and lines sticking out of me, the constant beeping and monitors, the incessant tests, the fear of not knowing whether I was going to make it – but as far as I was concerned, I had never been there. (On the contrary, I had been *many* other places in my mind while my body was there!) Next, we headed up to the burns ward, and *this* was the room I remembered vividly: the good, the bad and the ugly. It looked bland and drab without all of the photos of flowers, the dogs and my life highlights on the wall, without all the cards and letters from friends, family and strangers, and especially without the windowsill covered in a billion soft toys.

Initially, I believed that the physical part of my recovery was going to be the hardest. My brain had coped remarkably well for the first five months after the eruption. It had compartmentalised the mental turmoil in my mind into a dark corner, so I could focus solely on my physical recovery. However, as time went on, the 'bedtime panic' started and the flashbacks popped up more and more frequently, but I was incredibly good at never letting on that I was struggling. Whenever those small horrors poked their head through the stage curtain, I gave them a little nod and not-so-politely asked them to fuck right off and never come back. Since day dot I'd had no issue speaking about the eruption, I'd been seeing a psych ever since leaving hospital, and I had the greatest support system in my family that a gal could ask for. I thought that meant I was on the home stretch. I was *not* expecting what was to come.

It turned out the physical part was the *easy* part. Just as I had been warned by many people who knew a hell of a lot more than me, the black dog slowly crept into the front room and made himself comfortable.

Initially, I would just feel a bit flat or sad 'for no reason'.[167] Or something small would set me off – like, I'd bawl my eyes out over dropping a teaspoon.

Then, one evening while we were up at Tom's parents' place, I got a call from an unknown number. Normally I wouldn't have answered, but for some reason, this time I did. It was Waikato Hospital. They had a cancellation, and could bump me up the list for surgery on my right hand, aka my claw hand.[168] Was I interested?

'Absolutely! When?'

'Monday.'

It was Thursday.

I wanted them to have a crack at releasing some scar tissue that was stopping me from flattening my hand or straightening my fingers. It had become a running joke in my family that, if I pointed at something, everyone would look in the opposite direction (despite the fact my fingers weren't *that* bent). It was funny, but I had fallen in love with doing Reformer Pilates and found not being able to flatten my hand frustrating. And, really, I just wanted to be as normal as possible.

The plan was to remove a 'cord' of scar tissue from the webspace between my thumb and index finger, in the hope of letting

---

167 It's funny how, at the time, I thought these feelings came up 'for no reason'. Of course there was a pretty big reason.

168 My right hand had been burnt more than my left, and the scarring on it prevented me from entirely flattening it, hence the nickname.

the area open up more. Additionally, I would have some releases done at the base of my ring finger on the same hand. Just before I went into surgery, my surgeon popped in to see me, and she mentioned to the nurse at my bedside to prep my hip as a possible donor site. A new graft in that first web-space, she explained, would be the best way to open that area up.

Mentally, things had really started going downhill for me in the months leading up to this surgery. The moment the surgeon left the room, I started bawling, and I kept bawling all the way to theatre. The rational part of my brain knew the surgeon was right – this was definitely the best way to achieve what I wanted – but the idea that I was about to go through *more* grafting was a shock. Vivid recollections of the pain I'd felt in Hutt with my donor sites overwhelmed me as I remembered what I went through after my legs were grafted – the intense tightness and swelling of the grafted site, the itch of the healing donor sites, all the horrors of rehabbing, stretching and care of the new grafts. I couldn't bear the thought of going through all that again, and I couldn't hide my anguish.

The anaesthetist and the nurses with me that day were incredible. As I was wheeled from pre-op into the operating theatre – still bawling – they held my hand, talked me through everything and tried to comfort me. Then they glanced at each other, that awful look in their eyes of not knowing what to do to help me. One of the nurses kept holding my hand as the anaesthetist placed the mask over my nose and mouth and put me to sleep, still sobbing.

What I was about to learn is that your state of mind when you're put under anaesthetic tends to be the state of mind you come out of it with – I woke up just as distressed as I had been going under. After a couple of hours in recovery post-op, they had to call my mum in to help. Poor Mum. To add insult to injury, I'd agreed to some touch-ups on my left hand, too, so I was back in my bandage boxing gloves *on both hands.* The only good news? Either the nurses had told my surgeon about my meltdown or she'd managed to release my web-space without needing to graft, and I woke up with my hip intact and no skin graft taken.[169]

Things didn't improve once I got home. By now, I was deep in the throes of PTSD, and I felt like I was drowning. I'd been diagnosed with PTSD in late 2020, so at a surface level I knew what was happening, but that didn't mean I actually *understood* it. My psych thought that the various traumatic experiences I'd been through over the years – the boat fire, Lionel's accident on Whale Island, the eruption, and even all the shit that happened in hospital – had compounded, and it was only once my body felt 'safe' that my brain let go. In other words, I'd healed enough physically, and now it was my brain's turn to start demanding some help.

I don't think I've ever admitted this before, but I believe the PTSD actually started creeping in after the accident on Whale Island, and the eruption just kicked everything into overdrive, so that I couldn't control it or hide it anymore.

Before the eruption, I'd never had surgery or even anaesthetic. I'd certainly never had debilitating flashbacks or intense emotional survival responses, like fight, flight or freeze reactions.

---

[169] While I was relieved about this at the time and for a while afterwards, I learnt pretty quickly that my emotions had inadvertently made it necessary for me to have another surgery down the line. The claw hand lived on.

This was all new to me. I was doing my best to use the tools my psych was teaching me to help me manage and get through this, but there isn't a one size fits all response to trauma.

I was an anomaly in the sense that a lot of people with PTSD find that they can't talk about their trauma. I can – in vivid detail, and don't so much as bat an eyelid. I thought perhaps being able to let it all out verbally was how I would heal myself – or maybe I wouldn't even need to do anything special because nothing would be suppressed. Unfortunately, that was not the case.

I was constantly in a state of intense fear and hypervigilance. I was overly sensitive to sound, especially, and certain noises would rile me up *so* fast. The dogs grooming themselves. Cars going past. Bangs or booms that sounded similar to any kind of noise White Island had made in the five years I'd worked there. Chickens around the house.[170]

I was always on the lookout for danger. Any unusual sound. Any weird movement, especially from a stranger. I was constantly looking out for threats, always facing the door whenever I wasn't at home, always had a way out planned. I used any excuse not to go out on my own, and I didn't want to talk to anyone about what was going on – which is difficult when you live in a small town where everyone knows who you are and what happened to you. So many people would come up to me to ask how I was doing and tell me I looked good. I knew they meant well but it made me feel really gross every time. To make matters worse, I'd put on 25 kilograms since being discharged, so I also felt incredibly self-conscious about my weight – even more than I was about my scars.

---

170 If you've ever owned chickens you might still relate to this one, even if you don't have PTSD.

Any kind of inconvenience sent me into a fit of uncontrollable rage. I remember having a conversation with my dad around this time, while we walked River. Dad, bless him, said, 'When you feel it coming on, you should either warn someone, or walk away and cool off rather than blowing up.'

'Dad, I don't feel it coming.'

'What do you mean?'

'There's no build-up. No warning signs. It's like my brain hits the panic button, and in a split second I lose my ability to think rationally, or even see or hear myself in the moment. It's not until after I've reacted that I realise what I've done or said – and then it's too late. That's the problem. I can't stop it. I don't feel it coming.'[171]

Soon, I stopped trusting even the small group of people I kept around me, other than my close family – both because of what my nervous system was telling me, and because every time I had an 'episode', I would see the looks on their faces. Embarrassment. Annoyance. Frustration. Judgement. Most significantly, misunderstanding – on both sides. None of us knew how to navigate this. This was new, it was fucking terrifying, and even though I was trying my hardest to stop it, nothing seemed to be helping. In fact, shit was getting worse.

One day in June, when Tom had gone to town, I left the house with the dogs and we set off for my favourite spot on the farm. It wasn't quite the highest point, but you could see the flats down through a gully, and down the river to the Ōhiwa Harbour

---

[171] This actually makes sense, from a survival perspective. You can't be loading or buffering a reaction in the face of an immediate threat. The response needs to be instant if you're going to survive.

entrance. If you found the right spot, you could see White Island above one of the points, too.

I sat there in the grass, the dogs sniffing around me, and I cried. The kind of crying where you can't catch your breath and it makes your whole body shake.

It was one of those days where just existing was hard. Nothing seemed to help the feeling or lift the weight. Not crying. Not fresh air or walking to a favourite spot. Not love.

The feeling sat in my bones, and in my cells. It was one of those days where the PTSD symptoms were winning, despite me trying to hold that door firmly closed. The anxiety, stress, hyperarousal, rage, crying and flashbacks were all pushing hard and leaking through more quickly and more frequently.

I thought it on that day, I'd thought it during the year before, and I still think it now: *I would rather be burnt again than have PTSD.*

Now, I could see – feel – why some people with PTSD take their own lives. I understood why that was all you ever saw of it portrayed in the movies.

I have got to the point now where I am actively avoiding anything to do with the eruption, I wrote in my journal a few days later. *It triggers me too much, and I live in that state enough as it is.*

I would rather be burnt again than have PTSD.

I soon lost count of how many times I said that during my second year after the eruption. With a physical injury, there are so many questions, but they have answers and timeframes.

How long will I be in hospital?

'Six months.'

How long will this take to heal?

'You can't move for five days, and after that, you'll need physical therapy to regain movement and strength. You'll wear compression garments for swelling and scars for eighteen to twenty-four months.'

I'm in a lot of pain.

'Here are some drugs to help until you heal. You'll feel relief pretty quickly.'

My back is so itchy, I want to tear the skin off to scratch the nerve endings with my nails.

'Here is an antihistamine and some ice.'

With PTSD, it is so much more complicated. Nothing has a clear answer. The time periods are non-existent. Even things that would set me off one day wouldn't the next, and vice versa, so it felt incredibly unpredictable.

How long will this hang around for?

'We don't know. It depends. Could be years.'

I can't stop crying and I don't know why.

'We can give you antidepressants – but you're not depressed. This is just a depressive episode. A symptom of PTSD. The drugs will help mask it. But they might also numb you.'

I can't control my anger or outbursts.

'Try.'

As the end of 2021 neared, my occurrences of 'bedtime panic' became more frequent. One night, alone on the couch after Tom had gone to bed early, my newly adjusted splint for my right hand was causing me quite a lot of pain[172] and I started having flashbacks. I began crying and shaking. I felt so scared, and tired, and sad. I kept thinking about being burnt, about how

---

172 Think: crushed in a vice kind of pain.

Hayden and the others must have died. I felt trapped, terrified. The tears flowed for over three hours before I felt calm enough – or exhausted enough – to go to bed.

Another night not long after that, I went to bed feeling fine, but once I got under the covers I couldn't sleep or relax. So I got up and went into the lounge, as usual not wanting to disturb Tom. My breathing seemed to be getting faster, so I tried to slow it down. I tried reading to distract myself, but I became so overwhelmed with thoughts and sounds and feelings that I cried for two hours.[173] I went outside with River, but the cold air didn't help.

When I went back into the lounge, Tom was there. He'd come out to find me after waking up and seeing my side of the bed empty. He managed to help calm me down and got me back to bed, confused as to why I didn't tell him what was happening so he could help. I don't know if he knew there had been many other nights like this. By hiding these things from him, from my family, I was trying to save my loved ones from more hurt. From seeing how broken I still was. From me.

One symptom which I'm glad only reared its head a few times was nightmares. I didn't have many, but all the ones I did have were about the island.

In one, I was at the fumarole stop with Mum and Dad. We were all wearing our masks and helmets. One of my parents asked me whether or not it was safe to be there, and I replied, as I always had when I was guiding: 'If I didn't think it was safe, I wouldn't be here.' Then I added, 'And I certainly wouldn't have brought you!'

Then we started heading round the corner to the sulphur chimneys, and the island started erupting, just like it did on

---

173 Not just a few tears, either – the whole gross, panicking ugly-cry.

9 December. We ran, but we didn't get far. Then I was lying face down in a foetal position, covering my face, and my body was getting hotter and hotter and hotter until it was burning. I started screaming. I was sure I was going to burn to death …

Then Tom was waking me up and I was crying.

I went to see a cardiologist. My resting heart rate before the eruption had been around 64 beats per minute (bpm), but now it was around 120bpm. Apparently, a rate of 110bpm is where permanent damage can start to occur. Basic exercise was spiking my heart rate up to 190bpm[174], and my physio was getting concerned (naturally).

My cardiologist admitted that he had not personally dealt with a major burns survivor, and wasn't sure if the tachycardia (raised heart rate) was due to the actual burns or to my mental state – or both. Regardless, he wanted to get it down. He got me hooked up to a heart-rate monitor, which I was to wear for twenty-four hours while I logged all of my activity, so he could get an idea of what was happening.

I felt pretty dejected on my drive home. *Another professional who has no answers for me …* But as I walked into the house he called me.

'I've been doing some research since you left,' he said. Turned out he'd deep-dived *hard*. He'd read a few research papers on burns patients, and apparently what I was experiencing was fairly normal. 'Many major burns survivors end up with persistent tachycardia, which is managed, and in some cases reset, with beta blockers,' he explained.

He spoke to me about beta blocker medication, and while he was confident it would do the trick to lower my heart rate, he did

---

174 A speed I'd only ever reached before when I was in a coma.

mention that the side-effects could include lowered metabolism and mood. I needed that like a hole in the head.

I managed to convince him to let me put it off until after the second anniversary of the eruption, and he agreed. I got off the phone feeling rather well cared for after all.

Around this time, I wrote the following quote in my journal from *The Body Keeps the Score: Brain, mind, and body in the healing of trauma* by psychiatrist Bessel van der Kolk:

> Patients may also dislike the parts that are out: the parts that are angry, destructive or critical … Recognising that each part is stuck with burdens from the past and respecting its function in the overall system makes it feel less threatening or overwhelming.

This quote stuck with me because I *did* have parts of me coming out which I disliked — angry, controlling, fearful parts. Despite realising that these parts were just holding on to past trauma — that they were my survival tools — rather than feel less crazy, I decided to use that as my crutch. I blamed all of my shitty behaviour on PTSD, and for a while it worked. But the while was short and tensions became frayed. I knew I was hard to be around. Hell, *I* didn't even want to be around me.

I was also learning that the world doesn't actually stop turning, even when, for you, it feels like it has. And that's awful. It makes you feel so small. So insignificant. My psychologist and my ACC case manager were busy trying to get me to think about what I might like to do for work, going forward — it had been almost two years, after all. But honestly, the whole idea of getting a job scared the shit out of me. It was terrifying. I knew I wasn't ready for that. Not by a *long* shot.

A couple of friends had mentioned that they'd had success in reducing their PTSD symptoms with something called EMDR (Eye Movement Desensitisation and Reprocessing), and my psych also suggested it might be worth a shot. To me, *anything* was worth a shot if it meant I might not feel or act like this anymore.

EMDR is a mental-health therapy that involves you moving your eyes in a specific way while you process traumatic memories, with the goal of helping you heal from trauma or distressing life experiences. It sounds very woo-woo, and in fairness it *feels* very woo-woo while you're doing it. But I was desperate, and willing to give anything a go.

The therapist who performed it was incredibly patient, kind and caring, and explained things to me really well. He really wanted this to help me.

We started with my memories of the boat fire, even though as far as I was concerned it was a non-event. 'I want us to start small and work our way up,' my therapist explained. *Smart.* It felt weird, my eyes following a light on a little T-shaped bar (it reminded me of a hammerhead shark) while thinking about the boat's deck warping underneath my feet, but here we were. Trying. Desperate.

Eventually, we worked our way up to the Whale Island accident. This one was harder. I knew I hadn't really worked through what had happened in any capacity, beyond just keeping myself busy and away from that island. I cried a lot, and I started to feel a slight sense of dread as my appointments approached.

After each session, I would feel completely wrung out, and it would take me a day or two to come right afterwards. But we made it through that trauma, then it was on to the big one: the eruption. That small amount of dread ballooned into a huge feeling of apprehension that would start *days* before my appointment. Afterwards, it would take days for me to recover. I was seeing this therapist weekly, and there are only seven days in a week, so you can see how this was starting to present a rather large problem.

After just a few sessions of trying to scratch the surface of the eruption, my brain went into lockdown. I'd already established that my brain was hella good at compartmentalising in a crisis, and now it had registered this man sitting across from me – who was doing all the right things to try to help me – as a threat.

In hindsight, it's actually quite incredible knowing my brain can do that. In the moment, however, it was *awful*. I couldn't answer simple questions. I could barely tell the therapist my own name. I was numb, and I couldn't stop crying. My brain was entirely silent, giving nothing away – not even to me.[175]

We tried for a few months, into the new year, 2022. Tom wanted me to keep trying, and I get it – I wanted to keep trying, too. But I wanted to keep trying something that didn't feel like it was fucking me up even more.

And that's what this was starting to do. The emotions I was experiencing in my therapist's office lingered longer and longer, and I was more on edge at home than ever. I cried almost daily. I snapped at everything and everyone. I would have moments of full-on, uncontrollable rage that would leave me feeling vacant

---

175 There were *many* times when I was asked what was going through my head by Tom and my family, and I answered with 'Nothing.' And it was the truth. Not a single thought, sound or tumbleweed in there. But no one ever believed me, and I could always tell by the looks on their faces that they thought I was hiding something from them.

for days, then desperately trying to wheedle my way back into the good books. I leant heavily on my diagnosis, as though it gave me an excuse – a right – to act like this. I knew that wasn't right in my gut. It *explained* my behaviour, but it didn't *excuse* it.

Eventually I pulled the pin on EMDR. I still believe this was the right call for me at the time. While many people have said not to rule it out entirely, I have no desire to try again. Unfortunately, it was not the silver bullet I was hoping for.

Dad turned sixty in November 2021, and we all went to Queenstown to celebrate. On a bit of a whim, Tom and I decided to climb Roys Peak, a steep, 18-kilometre zig-zag straight up the side of one of the mountains that looms over Lake Wānaka. I managed to make it to what's become known as 'Instagram Point', thanks to the hikers queuing to get a snap for their feeds that shows them perched on a dramatic outcrop with the lake below and surrounding mountains unfurling around them, and it was stunning. The actual summit of Roys Peak was another kilometre uphill, but by that point I was done.

I had been jovial the majority of the way up, but in that moment the idea of climbing another kilometre was soul-destroying. Tom gently encouraged me to trudge on. 'You'll regret it if you don't make it to the actual top,' he said.

Eventually I caved in, but I had well and truly reached my limit. I barely spoke, and soon I started crying. Every little slip on ice or trip on a rock fuelled more tears, and I ended up a wreck. I'm pretty sure Tom was starting to think he was wrong for not letting me stop sooner. But at last, we rounded a corner and hiked the last stretch to the summit. Sitting down felt great. Knowing there was no more uphill felt greater.

But of course going downhill turned out to be its own beast. I'd had a similar issue coming down from the Tongariro Crossing a few years before the eruption, when my IT band (a tendon running along the outside of the thigh from the hip to the knee) had got so tight it started feeling like my knee-cap was being lifted by a knife. The same thing happened coming down from Roys Peak, and once again I ended up feeling it for the following week.

Once we got back to our rental car, I *was* grateful we'd made it to the true summit. Grateful Tom had known I needed that push (despite all the crying). And even more grateful that we were done with Roy.

By the end of 2021, I was exhausted. Utterly, totally exhausted. If you've ever had a major physical trauma followed by years of rehab, you'll know what I mean. When everything takes more effort, when you have to try harder for basic shit, when you're always having to heal and start again, and be strong, and try and try and try … it wears you down to nothing.[176]

After ending EMDR therapy, I continued with my regular psych appointments. I was trying so hard to fix myself, but I knew I was getting worse. Even as I struggled desperately to keep my head above water, I could tell I was alienating everyone around me. I could see the looks Tom had started to give me when he thought I didn't notice – and he wasn't alone. I saw it in the couple of friends I'd kept at arm's-length. I saw their need for distance. I heard the tone-of-voice change in my family. Just like with my EMDR therapist, my hypervigilant brain was registering new threats, and it was becoming increasingly

---

176 I actually learned that there is a term for this: rehab fatigue.

difficult to be calm. To feel safe. To be happy. My grip tightened in an effort not to lose anyone, but tensions were growing as that very same grip I was using to keep people close became a chokehold. On me. On them.

One day, when things were notably low, as I cried on my psych's couch, I asked, 'Is this what the rest of my life is going to look like?' I don't remember verbatim what she said, but the gist of it was: Yes, this is it.

I didn't want to hear that. I wanted her to tell me there was something I could do to stop feeling like this, not that I would feel like this forever. That this was just something I had to live with. In hindsight, I know I misunderstood what she was saying – she probably meant that I would have to *manage* this indefinitely. But at the time I took it as: 'This is your life. It is going to be hard, and it is going to continue to have these incredibly dark moments.'

It broke me.

I didn't think there was anything left to break, but I reckon you could have heard my heart and soul shatter in that room at that moment, as my head dropped and tears streamed down my face.

I was done. I didn't want to keep trying to heal a wound I thought would never heal. I didn't want to keep having therapies not work for me. I was so fucking tired. Wrecked. Done. I decided I wanted – *needed* – a break from psychological rehab. So I stopped everything.

What was the point in fighting something that couldn't be beaten?

Chapter 9

Ameliorate

Despite how my brain was dealing with life (or not dealing with it, as the case might have been), and despite the growing tension between me and Tom and everyone else in my orbit, I kept trying to push on.

I'd been doing Reformer Pilates for about a year, and it had helped me to regain a full range of motion in my knees and elbows. I absolutely loved it. So I thought, *Maybe this could be my new career?* With my instructor's support, I enrolled in a training course and headed off to Auckland in February 2022. What did I have to lose? If I became an instructor and loved it, great. If I didn't, I would have a whole lot more knowledge that would improve my own practice.

I really enjoyed the first half of the course, but the night before the second half was due to start I woke up in the middle of the night, sick as a dog. I messaged the trainer to explain that I definitely wouldn't be able to attend the rest of the course. Thankfully, there was another one being held a few months later in Hawke's Bay, so I could finish off my training down there.

On my way back to Whakatāne, I picked up a dog we'd agreed to foster. For some reason, despite everything that was going on with me, Tom and I decided this would be a good idea. Maybe we were that couple who thought bringing a 'baby' into our lives would solve all of our problems.

Spot was a cute little thing – a skinny white bully-mix with big, bat-like ears. True to his name, he had one big brown spot across his hips. He was incredibly sweet, had no idea about anything, bounced like a rabbit when he was happy, and if you tried to move him by grabbing his collar, he would scream like you were trying to kill him.

Spot settled into farm life pretty quickly, running next to the motorbikes on a leash and then off leash. He got along well with River and Jess, which was a good thing because it ended up being three months before he got adopted and left for his new home down in Gore (where he is thriving!).

Having Spot in our lives illuminated a lot of my weaknesses. He'd been an abandoned 'chain dog' most of his life with no training whatsoever under his belt, so when he came to us, this clashed with my need to control everything around me in order to feel some semblance of safety.[177] My patience was pretty thin, and caring for another being who was also in the throes of relearning how to live was tough to say the least. I loved him and his soft little head, but I also found him incredibly difficult – through no fault of his own – until we got some basic training sorted. But, boy, was I sad to see that little bouncy fool go. I still miss him now, as I go through videos of him bounding merrily through the paddocks.

---

177 I didn't realise this at the time, but it made sense further down the track.

I felt like I was losing everything around me, including myself – though, in reality I had been lost for a long time before this. Between the different court cases surrounding the eruption, my increasingly frequent bouts of rage, sadness and numbness, and my own withdrawal into myself, things were pretty bleak, and I felt more isolated than ever. In an attempt to make connections with other people, I decided to go to a retreat on the North Island's west coast for women who were burn survivors. Turns out I wasn't ready for that, either.

The whole time, I felt an overwhelming panic in every fibre of my body. My beautiful roommate, who I met for the first time when I arrived for the weekend, did her best to coach me through it – she was my anchor and my protector, and I am so grateful to her – but not once did I relax. I was stuck in fear, and I just couldn't pull myself out.

At one stage, I called Tom and all but begged him to say it would be okay if I came home. But he encouraged me to stay on, so I did. Looking back now, he was probably enjoying the weekend without me and, quite frankly, I don't blame him. Whether I chose to admit it or not, I was one very sick puppy.

After a weekend with plenty of opportunities for connection and a feeling of safety, I drove away from the retreat relieved to be leaving. And even more rattled and lonely than I had been when I'd arrived.

In May of 2022, I headed down to Hawke's Bay to complete the second half of my Pilates-instructor course. The day the course finished, Tom and a friend flew to Wellington, and I drove down to pick them up. We'd decided we'd catch the ferry across to the

South Island the next day, and spend a week or so down there – a great idea. A little holiday. A little break from life.

But, as I drove into Wellington through Transmission Gully, my vision started to go all weird. It was as though all of the headlights of the oncoming traffic were on high beam and shining right into my car. I had one hell of a time keeping my eyes focused on the road. As I got closer and closer to the city, the lights got brighter and brighter – and by the time I got to the airport, I was frustrated, tired and fighting back tears and rage. Why was this happening now?[178]

When I saw Tom and our friend – welcoming them to Wellington with an onslaught of negative energy, angry words and a bit of hysteria – there was no missing the look on both of their faces, or the eye-rolls. Another bit of me died inside, despite the arms around me.

God, I wanted this shit to stop happening so bad. *Hopefully the rest of the week will go more smoothly*, I thought. But honestly, I don't remember much of that week. I was so over the threshold, I was barely there mentally. I know there were a lot of lovely moments, but I was so on edge. I just didn't feel safe.

The absolute low point came on the way home, when we stopped for the night in Taupō to break up the long drive. We arrived at the hotel after dark, and Tom ran inside to check in. When he came out, he pointed to the park in front of us. 'That one's ours.'

'Is that a joke?' I said.

The park would have fitted the car, but only just – and I doubt we could have got out without hitting the vehicles parked on

[178] Maybe because I'd topped off an intensive, week-long course with a four-hour drive? Just a thought …

either side. (To be clear, it was the size of the park that was the problem, not shitty parking from our neighbours.)

I'll be fucking damned if I'm going to put my car in there, I thought.

I lost my shit and totally exploded. It was an absurdly out-of-proportion meltdown, but I was out of control – in all senses. The poor man showing us to our room copped it, along with Tom and our friend. I'll *never* forget the looks on their faces. Even thinking about it now makes my stomach turn.

By the time I'd been shown another park with marginally more space, Tom and our friend had gone into the room. I'd returned to myself, and I sat in the car shaking. *What the fuck was that?*

When I finally went in, I was met with awkward silence and the avoidance of eye contact. I didn't realise it yet, but that Chernobyl-scale meltdown was probably the straw that broke the camel's back.

June came, and one Sunday night Tom and I went with the same friend to a movie in town. Afterwards, we all went back to the farm for a few hands of Rummy. Some gnarly weather was rolling in, so Tom walked the friend home, five minutes round the corner. And, as the wind got windier, I waited … and waited. No Tom. I waited some more. Two hours passed, and he still wasn't home.

I lay in bed, shaking, crying, paralysed with fear. I was so worried. *He's hurt. Something has happened. Something is wrong.*

Then, just as I managed to convince my terrified body to get out of bed to go and find him, I heard his voice outside, talking to the dogs. He was home. And he was fine.

When he came in, he got into bed and saw my eyes red from crying. I realised that he had continued drinking at our friend's place. Eyes locked, he turned out the light. Neither of us said a word.

The rest of the week was weird. Tom was distant, and I tried desperately to act normal and fix things.[179]

Friday came. Tom went into town. I stayed home.

When he came back later, I could tell just from the way he approached the house that something was wrong. I walked out to meet him. We hugged. Then he said, 'We need to talk.'

My gut dropped.

'I can't do this anymore,' he said, as we sat on the porch of the sleepout.

I sat in silence as he talked. Not that he said much. Not that I heard much. I was so fucking done with fighting. First I'd fought to get off that flaming boat, then fought to keep my shit together to get Lionel off Whale Island, then fought to survive the eruption, then I'd fought to recover physically, and now I was stuck fighting. Fighting my own brain. Fighting to have any semblance of my old self. Fighting to stop fighting. I wanted it to stop. That fight that everyone raved about and commended me for in the early days was now destroying everything and everyone around me.

Eventually, I muttered numbly, 'I'm going to pack,' then stood and went inside to do just that. My response, or lack thereof, must have caught Tom off guard, because he tried to sit me down again. Tried to get me to talk, but I didn't have anything to say. My head was silent. No noise, no thoughts, no tumbleweeds.

'You don't have to leave right now,' he said.

'Well, I can't fucking stay here.'

---

179 I now know this is a 'fawn' response, also a product of PTSD. That bitch is *everywhere*.

There was a brief mention of River. 'He's coming with me,' I said. I pulled a suitcase out, and began trying to figure out where the hell to start. *What do I take? What do I need? What the fuck …?*

As I sat on the chair in our bedroom, it hit me, and I started crying uncontrollably. I shoved random items of clothing into the bag, threw the bag in the car, grabbed some things for River, then got in my car.

'You can't drive like this,' said Tom.

'What? But *you* can?'

He was crying, too – both of us bawling our eyes out in the driveway, arguing about who would drive. Tom won.

He drove me to my parents' place. I'd later learn that he'd sent a message to warn them about what was happening and what was about to arrive on their doorstep.

Mum welcomed me in with a warm hug, and sat with me on the couch as I sobbed, broken, confused and tired. Holly came around. Then Dad came in the door from work, and the first thing he said was, 'What a bastard.' Classic Dad.

At the time all of this felt like a huge blindside, but in hindsight it had been a long time coming. Hell, while I've been writing a lot of it down for this book, I've realised *you* probably saw it coming. Things would have needed to change drastically for both of us to save that relationship.

I vividly remember, sometime during the year beforehand, Tom saying offhandedly to me one evening, 'You love River more than you love me.' And that voice in my head – the one that had told me to keep my shit together through the Whale Island accident, and reminded me of Stanley Williams's words about pyroclastic surges during the eruption – piped up: *Yeah, River would never leave me.* Perhaps that was the first of many alarm bells that I chose to ignore.

I would like to say that moment in June was the end of it. That it was a clean break. That Tom and I broke up and we each moved on and healed, but that's not what happened. We kept ourselves in limbo for three months. Three months of me desperately searching for ways to fix myself. Three months of me being so stressed I couldn't eat or sleep.[180] Three months of me begging. Three months of my mum gently telling me to let go. Three months of Dad bluntly telling me Tom wasn't worth *this*. Three months of me holding on to the hope that we would figure things out and get back together.

Once again, I felt as though the world had stopped. Or that it should have. But it stubbornly kept spinning. Life carried on, undeterred by everything melting down around me.

A month after I moved off the farm, my sister had her first baby. My very first nephew. My godson, Will. And the first time I met him, I took one look at him from the end of Holly's hospital bed and started sobbing – and they weren't happy tears. They were selfish, sad tears. It broke my heart seeing my sister and her little family so happy and healthy when my own little family had fallen apart, and it felt as though I had torn it down with my own hands. Seeing everything they had only reminded me of all that I had lost.

In all of this, and entirely by chance, Mum found someone who finally kickstarted my healing – and, probably most importantly,

---

180 In the space of less than a couple of weeks, I lost 16 of the 25 kilograms I'd put on since leaving hospital.

made me realise it was even possible. Mum was down in Queenstown for a conference when she bumped into an old friend. They got chatting, and he mentioned that his wife worked with people with trauma.

Enter Sam.

This trauma-informed wellbeing coach and wizard of the brain lived in Wellington, so the first time we met was online. Then I started making a weekly trek to Wellington from Whakatāne so we could meet in person. I love driving, and it gave me plenty of time to think, listen to music and podcasts and, most importantly, decompress alone – a habit of mine I keep to this day.

Initially, I was sceptical that Sam's way of doing things was actually going to work, but I was desperate. What else did I have to lose? She taught me breathwork, yoga, meditation and how to practise gratitude. And she taught me about what my brain was actually going through – helping me to understand *why* it was doing what it was and how it thought it was helping me. All it took was a few sessions of seeing her for the weight to start lifting from my shoulders.

As I've said, other professionals had thrown the term PTSD around to describe what I was going through – always in the sense that 'this isn't right and we need to fix you', which made me feel like an absolute freak, especially when those professional judgements were coupled with the looks I saw on the faces of the people I trusted whenever shit kicked off. I figured I was broken and everyone had been through enough with me, so I just stopped talking about what was going on in my head – not that I really knew how to put it into words. I didn't want to add to everyone's burdens. But we all know what happens when you put the lid on emotions and trauma.

Sam was the first person since the eruption to tell me that what I was experiencing, and how I was acting, was actually fucking *normal*. Stock-standard PTSD. Not weird or left field. There was nothing unique or special about the way that my brain was responding to an incredibly specific trio of traumas.

This changed my life. For the first time, I understood that I wasn't going insane, I wasn't crazy – I was just someone experiencing classic PTSD. It's amazing how comforting it was to be told I wasn't special or unique when, for the past two and a half years, all I'd felt was ostracised for what I thought was unusual. Up until that point, no one – not even me – properly understood what was going on with me. I felt like a three-headed beast, because that's how everyone was treating me. My belief in myself had taken a monumental hit. There were 'You're losing your mind, hun' vibes all over the place. So to hear someone who *understood* how trauma manifests in the brain and the body say she thought I was a textbook case was an incredible feeling. That alone calmed my nervous system significantly.

As Sam explained, I was locked in fight mode. The various traumas I'd been through had taught my brain that fight worked, and so it had rewired itself accordingly. And it *had* worked, to get me through some incredibly shit times. But staying in 'fight mode' meant that any time something didn't go my way or was an inconvenience of any kind: *Boom*! No build-up, just an instant, knee-jerk reaction of pure, unbridled fight for survival.

Comprehension was key for me. The big learning was that you can quash your fears pretty quick when you get curious about finding answers for *why* things are the way they are, instead of just accepting that this is how things are now, which is what I'd been doing for a couple of long years by this point.

This is something I heard ultra-athlete, author, and all-round badass David Goggins talk to Jay Shetty about on the podcast *On Purpose*. Goggins says to learn from yourself, from life; from your failures, your insecurities, your self-doubt. 'Don't just say, "I'm afraid to jump out of the airplane." What makes you afraid of it? Study it.' Sam taught me the same thing: 'Be curious. You can't be afraid if you're curious.'

Together with Sam, I worked out the following causes and explanations for the symptoms (or traits) that were spilling out of me.

Trait	Cause	Explanation
Outbursts of anger	Fear of losing control of a situation	Pretty fair enough, considering I had no control during the boat fire, Whale Island, the eruption and my time in hospital
Anxiety and stress	Trying to foresee every possible outcome so I can be prepared	Multiple traumas = tendency for the ol' brain to stay in overdrive so it's prepared for whatever new fuckery is around the corner
Lazy, unmotivated and/or unable to move forward (physically and mentally)	Fear of physical and/or mental suffering	Everything in hospital hurt before it helped, so I started avoiding any possibility of hurt or discomfort
	Freeze response	When I was exhausted and couldn't muster fight or flight, freeze was activated
Critical and judgemental	Loss of control, triggered by seeing undesirable traits in others that are actually the traits that I don't like about myself	They say you see the world the way you see yourself … and boyyyy did I not like myself. My tolerance for myself and others was at an all-time low

Deflect and defence	Fear of making a mistake or being wrong	My brain was stuck thinking everything was a life-or-death situation, so in my mind being wrong or making a mistake was catastrophic
	You/Me mentality, not Us/We	'I will fix this/save you' because I know I can do it. God forbid I let anyone else have a turn!
Adopting unhealthy long-term traits	Using a shitty, weak foundation to build anything on	Given my self-worth kept taking a hit, and I thought everything and everyone was a threat, it's really no surprise that my diet was shit, my outlook was shit, and my relationships turned to shit
Catastrophising	I had some major unexpected shit happen that was literally the worst-case scenario	My brain got so used to the worst-case scenario that it became my default setting

Sam also helped me learn what to do whenever I started to feel 'strong feelings' – anger, anxiousness, sadness, and so on. Once I'd managed to soothe my nervous system a bit and got to a point where I could start to feel things bubbling up, rather than just exploding, I'd sit down with my feet firmly planted on the ground, fingertips together or hands in fists. I'd focus deeply on my feet on the ground, on my back and butt pressing into the chair. Then I'd breathe in through my nose and out through my mouth, then notice: *three* things I could see, *two* things I could hear, and *one* thing I could smell. Repeat as needed.

We worked on improving my self-worth. My feelings of safety. Calming down my nervous system.

Around the same time, I also switched to working with a new psychologist. I needed someone with more trauma experience, someone who was going to complement the work I was doing with Sam. Thankfully, ACC helped find me someone who I really gelled with.

Another thing Sam did was listen to me talk about Tom endlessly. About how I was going to fix this – fix me – and it was all going to be okay. But by the end of August, Tom and I were still stuck in limbo. One day, when he wavered again on whether or not he wanted to fix things, I called it. 'I can't do this anymore,' I said. 'This is cruel. I'm done.'

Within three days, I was fully moved out of his house. For good.

In an effort to put some space between myself and Tom, I 'ran away' to the South Island – my favourite island. I drove from Whakatāne to Te Anau and back over the space of a few weeks, and on a couple of occasions wondered whether I would actually go back home at all.

Just outside of Kurow, out the back of some cattle or sheep station, I was dropped off by ute at a little cabin, and left there alone for just over forty-eight hours. *Alone with my thoughts for forty-eight hours … right …* I had a fire to keep me warm, an outdoor bath under unobstructed dark skies, a couple of books, and no phone coverage. I practised yoga, did my meditations religiously, and realised I hadn't packed enough food. But I had packed enough wine and cheese.

On the final morning, I woke up and thought something was wrong with my eyes. The cabin had those sheer wind-down blinds and they were glowing weirdly. *It certainly didn't look like that yesterday morning*, I thought, still lying in bed, peeking up over the duvet. Then it clicked. *That's fucking snow!*

I leapt out of bed and galloped down the tiny hallway into the lounge, where I hadn't closed the curtains – there was no time to wind up a blind in the bedroom. And, sure enough, it had snowed. Not just a little bit, either – the whole valley was thickly blanketed in cold, white snow.

I bloody love snow! I put the kettle on, then stepped outside in my way-too-flimsy-for-this pyjamas. The crisp air woke me up completely, and I smiled at the vista and thought, *I don't want to leave.*

That trip was one of major ups and downs. I would feel okay, like I was getting through everything, then I would have a big depressive episode where I didn't want to keep trying or feeling or healing or living.

As I turned my car north, the darker feelings became more prevalent. Driving from Christchurch to Kaikōura, I remember thinking, *If I don't turn the wheel, I can go through that barrier and just end it now.* My new green Subaru Outback[181] neared the outer white line of the road, then reminded me that it was smarter than I was as the steering wheel vibrated and it pulled itself back into the lane; I remembered that it would slam on its brakes if I tried any funny business. I made it to Kaikōura, but the dark feelings remained.

I stayed in Wellington a couple of nights after that drive, and was lying in bed listening to The Rock when a new Blindspott song came on: 'Tonight'. I messaged Damian, the lead singer, on Instagram to tell him that it was beautiful and resonated deeply with the struggles I was going through. He replied:

181 I'd given my sister my older car earlier in the year before she had Will, and replaced it with a vehicle better suited to farm life. Ha …

Mate, I wrote that song when I had absolutely nothing left in the tank. I was on my knees just hoping I'd wake up tomorrow ... the darkest place I'd ever been in my life. My struggles are nothing compared to yours ... the pain, the hospital visits, the bandages, and the emotional and mental torment in between. I can't even imagine. Life is a fucking asshole to the ones that deserve it less than anyone. All you have to do (as hard as it might be) is wake up tomorrow and punch it square in the fucking face.

Be you ... be strong ... and cry if you have to. Mate, you're a fucking trooper, and we/I think you're an absolute weapon!!

Shelton[182] gave me a piece of advice once, and as much as it pains me, I hear it every day in my head: 'Just keep showing up, bro.' No matter how prepared or unprepared you are ... just turn up and do your best.

That's all we can do. Just keep turning up, Kelsey.

I saved that reply as the background on my phone for months.

As I left Wellington the next day, en route for Taranaki, I had a short and heartbreaking message exchange with someone I'd considered a no-matter-what friend, and realised that even that relationship had its limit. And then, as I reached the outskirts of Palmerston North, I discovered that Tom had removed me from our shared phone plan, without warning. My phone was now just a glorified camera. The simultaneous finality of two relationships I'd held so dear ending together in that moment felt too much.

I can't do this anymore.

182 Blindspott's drummer, Shelton Woolwright.

I managed to keep my shit mostly together as I entered The Plaza shopping mall to get my phone working again. The man in the shop assured me he'd done it – 'Just give it twenty-four hours.'[183]

I managed to connect to the McDonald's wifi on my way out and send a message to Mum: *Call me.* She did, just as I got back to the car. At this point I came completely undone, and kept saying over and over, 'I don't want to do this anymore.' Because I didn't. I was done. Done with trying. Done with people leaving. Done with hurting all the time. Done with crying. Done with done with done with done. *Done.*

Imagine the absolute fear Mum must have felt in that moment. She'd already come so close to losing me, more than once, and I'd survived all those terrible things – but now there I was wanting to take my own life, and she was five hours' drive away. Thankfully, she still had some incredible friends and family in Palmy, and she panic-called all of them. Within half an hour, one was in my car, sitting beside me as I sobbed over my steering wheel. From there, I was taken to Mum's uncle's (empty) house and given some space to calm down.[184]

I'm really privileged that my family and I have always been close. No matter what, they have always been there for me. They always show up. Most people take that for granted when things are going well, or when they're young. But I can honestly say my family are the only reason I am still here today.

I know that others aren't so lucky, and I hear it all the time when people reach out to me on Instagram: *I can't talk to my*

---

183 He had, in fact, not done it, and I had to go back the next day to get it sorted.

184 Mum's friend was still there, and kept popping in to check on me, but I'd calmed down enough that I wasn't a danger to myself.

family. What do I do? I have made sure there is contact information for professionals in the back of this book so that it's always easy to find. There is *always* help for you. Just as there was help for me.

My old life was gone. I had shed it – or, more accurately, it had shed me right off. My options were suddenly the same as back when I'd been in hospital: give up, or keep trying.

I wanted so badly to go with Option A. But I realised I'd been trying to do that for the past two years, and all it had got me was this lousy, empty, broken, exhausted feeling. It only seemed to cause more problems. Also, I was beginning to realise that I couldn't do that to my parents.

Keep turning up then, I guess.

The rest of the year was a slow and steady slog to try to right the ship. I didn't know it then, and wouldn't realise it for months yet, but the last couple of months of loss were the earth-shattering jolts I needed to bring me back to myself. Despite my broken heart and shattered soul, the beauty of finding rock bottom was that I also found solid ground. Gradually, I started confiding in people outside of my immediate family. Tentatively, I trusted myself to make new friends – ones who knew of my past, knew of my demons, but pushed me to always be better and to keep trying. I came to understand – the hard way – that I had to remove all access to my past life, especially online. It was only breaking my already broken heart, so I muted, archived, unfriended, removed tags – the whole nine yards – in an effort to create some space to let my heart heal. Anything that wasn't adding positively to my life had to go.

Speaking of my heart, I caught up with my cardiologist towards the end of 2022 and he asked me how everything was going.

'Okay,' I said.

'What dose of beta blockers are you on now?'

'I've been reducing them because my heart rate has come down.'

He was thrilled to hear that. He was less thrilled when he put his heart-rate monitor on me and discovered that I was, in fact, *not* doing so well, and my resting heart rate was actually back up to around 100bpm.

I confessed to what had been going on, and he was sympathetic. 'I think you should go back on the original dose until things settle down,' he said.

I didn't want to, but I agreed.

Then I found out, also the hard way,[185] that the beta blockers were *so* good at their job that, during any exercise that raised my heart rate, they'd cap me out at about 120bpm. My physio and I eventually worked out that the beta blockers were creating a kind of glass ceiling, stopping my heart rate from going any higher. As a result, if I tried to exert myself – which I was trying to do more of – I would all of a sudden get extremely fatigued, my body would feel heavy, and I would drop into a depressive episode that involved a lot of crying. This was all because I was actually *running out of oxygen*: my body would go first, then my brain would follow. It had been happening for months, but I just thought that I had gone backwards with my fitness, or it was just me and my low tolerance for anything uncomfortable.

Once we worked out my ceiling, exercise became a breeze again – all we had to do was keep my heart rate below 120bpm. Knowledge is power, as they say, and we moved on better equipped.

---

185 A common theme, and perhaps an alternate title for this memoir?

In mid-November, I wrote a note in my journal:

> There's been a shift in me these last few days. My mind is quieter and clearer than I think it's ever been. I am putting myself first, and prioritising my mental health and people around me who are genuine, real and loyal. I have been focusing on my values. I have been ensuring I keep up my physical movement. I feel <u>good</u> despite these last ~~five~~ twelve months. I am finally healing.

Around the same time, when I went down to see Sam in Wellington, I decided to pop in to Hutt Hospital and ask to see one of my original surgeons. The surgery I'd had to try to open up my right hand (the claw) had ultimately failed, so I wanted this surgeon to have another crack at it.[186]

After he'd given me a thorough once over – checking all my scars, the texture of my grafts and the range of motion of every joint – I asked him why he'd given me a gloss and not a matte finish on my legs,[187] then what he thought about my hand.

'I'd recommend taking a full-thickness graft from your hip to place on it,' he said – exactly the same plan that had been sprung on me and had sent me into panic mode just before my last surgery. This time, though, I was prepared. I was of a sounder mind. And I was on board with the idea.

My surgeon then explained that he couldn't promise a flatter hand,[188] but that grafting was unlikely to make it worse. 'It will

---

186 This was my own fault for not allowing the skin graft when it was suggested. It hadn't been a complete failure – I had gained *some* range of motion – but I knew we could do better.

187 The skin grafts on my legs are genuinely much shinier (gloss finish-esque) than my arms, but this is just the way that they have healed.

188 They never promise anything. Wise!

leave a scar, though,' he added, as though it might be a deal-breaker.

I laughed. 'Add it to the collection.'

He said his people would get in touch with my people when he had some space.

The third anniversary of the eruption crept up on me. The good thing about this one was that some of the Australian survivors and the families of those who hadn't survived were coming over. Despite having technically met some of these people on the day of the eruption, I didn't know them. It was my first opportunity to put faces to names – and compare scars. Despite the court cases still dragging on, I felt significantly more confident and safe to start having some kind of relationship with the other survivors.

As a group, we went to Whakatāne Hospital to see and speak to some of the A&E staff who had been on duty when we had filled their hospital with the smell of sulphur and screams of pain. As we survivors and family members of those lost sat before them, medical staff from all areas of the hospital took turns telling us about their experiences that day. They spoke of their fear, their prayers, and the amount of medication we'd sped through. One of the A&E staff had written and read to us a story in the style of *The Lord of the Rings* about her experience, and it was even published in a book.[189] By the time all those who wanted to speak had had their turn, there was not a dry eye in the whole room.

---

189 *When Minutes Matter: Emergency Care Across the Globe*, a collection of stories written by frontline healthcare workers and their connection with patients and communities in times of crisis.

A group of survivors and family members then stood and thanked the staff for their incredible speed, efficiency, knowledge and preparedness.

Without every single action they had taken that day, more of us would have been lost.

A small group of us survivors ended up spending a few days together, and we did some of the touristy stuff they'd missed out on three years ago. Finally, I felt like I had someone to relate to – something I had spent three years searching for.

A few days later, the Netflix documentary *The Volcano: Rescue from Whakaari* came out on the streaming platform. I had been interviewed for it at the start of the year, but my involvement had been complicated. I didn't really want to do it, but I *did* want to make sure it was balanced, by having the voice of at least one guide represented, so I'd ended up agreeing, with quite a few terms and conditions. It was (and still is) wild to watch myself on screen, knowing how much I was struggling with life at the time of the interview.

Even before the documentary was released, I'd had some weird messages online. So many people try to attach themselves to tragedies they're not a part of, and the eruption was no different. Suddenly, every man and his dog had a tie to White Island. People I hadn't heard from in years were trying to contact me or make out like they hadn't been assholes to me at uni or work. *I'm always here if you want to talk X*. Yeah, I'm sure you are. People made posts on social media about how much they loved and missed and cared about me when they had made my life hell. Even strangers got in touch, trying to suggest they were closer to the eruption than they were: *I was on the island [insert number of months/years] ago. It was so close*. You know who was closer? Me and forty-six others. It was as though the eruption had been a party they'd been out of town for.

The messages that came in after the documentary were on a whole other level. I was inundated with the most bizarre messages – some lost in translation, and some just downright odd. I have a whole album of screenshots on my phone dedicated to these brilliantly amusing messages. Messages such as:

Have you tried moisturiser?

Zelensky is working as agent for USA.

HEAL.

Damn.

This is why I like wearing high-waisted jeans!

So glad I have a boring winter cold life in Sweden.

Was it really that awful?

👍 2 of em

People also started recognising me in public. A friend organised a New Year's event and I helped her out by putting arm bands on the punters as they came in. I'm not much of a hugger, but probably 60 per cent of the people who came in (drunk) that night wanted to hug me. Some cried and got really emotional. It was a very weird experience for sober me.

Chapter 10

Taking off the training wheels

In early 2023, on a bit of a whim, to test where I was in myself, I decided to go on another trip to the South Island – a trip with twenty Americans I'd never met before. What better way to find out how healed you are after all that work you've done over the last nine months than going all-in with a bunch of strangers for a week? At least it was relatively close to home if I needed to abandon ship.

Initially, I was actually pretty good. But as I got tired and became conversationally exhausted, the cracks began to appear. Somewhere around the middle of the trip, while we were in Queenstown, I opted for a day off to rest and try to pull myself together. I was walking the familiar streets, enjoying the solitude, when a maintenance worker dropped a manhole cover behind me. Remember how I mentioned earlier that, on one occasion, White Island had been making a sound like a metal gate slamming shut? Turns out that sound was incredibly similar to the sound a manhole makes being dropped into place.

My body registered the noise immediately and I jolted. It took every single fibre of my being to stop myself from ducking behind the nearest lump on the ground. I felt as though I was trying to walk underwater. My body wanted to curl into a ball and wait for everything to blow over, despite there being nothing to take cover from.

In an effort to ground myself, I counted each step as I walked back to the motel, and once I made it back to the room I lay on my bed and had a full-blown meltdown. Needless to say, I was no better rested by the time the group came back at the end of the day.

From Queenstown, we headed over to the West Coast, where we went kayaking. I was a good and confident kayaker, but we were in double kayaks with spray skirts. I'd never used a spray skirt, let alone double-kayaked with a total stranger. But when one of the women asked whether I wanted to be her partner, I said yes and kept my worries to myself.

It was raining and cold, so I was wearing six layers of clothing, and my mind instantly began preparing for the worst. *What if we tip up and I forget to release myself from my spray skirt? How am I going to swim in all this gear?*

I was already feeling a bit off after Queenstown, not helped by the fact I was also sleep-deprived, and as soon as we pulled away from shore onto the lake I felt worse. My partner was sitting in the back, in control of the steering, and she clearly had very little experience. She kept leading us off course and crashing into the other kayaks, and I barked at her a couple of times. This poor, poor woman – she had no idea that the way she kept wobbling the kayak and weaving about wildly was about to trigger my first outburst of PTSD since leaving the farm seven months ago.

Halfway across the lake, I really wanted to pull out, but my ego wouldn't let me. Perhaps I should have, but I was reluctant to quit, despite how I was feeling – and despite how far behind we were, a fact only reinforced by the guide calling to us to catch up.

We made it to the other side of the lake, and that's when I had a panic attack: short, sharp breaths catching high in my chest, and *so* much fear. My paddling partner remained none the wiser, however. This was not my biggest panic attack by a long shot, so I was able to keep it hidden, as I kept facing forward and down in my little kayak of hell.

We followed the rest of the group down some narrow river channels, and I had to keep counter-steering so we wouldn't get caught in the grasses and branches lining the edge, or hit the other kayaks. By now, I was getting really exhausted. Then, as we went to head back across the lake, my partner managed to turn us in a circle, and that set me off again.

I couldn't keep *this* panic attack quiet – I shouted at her, and started hyperventilating and bawling my eyes out. It took me several minutes to get my shit together (trying desperately to channel *anything* that Sam had taught me) and start paddling back to our starting point, miles behind the others. My paddle partner didn't say a word. She felt *awful*.

Apart from this outburst, I did enjoy the trip and the new friends I made, but the experience brought back a lot of shitty feelings and memories of people's faces when I'd reacted this way before (though no one on this trip – not once – looked at me the way people had in my past). For the rest of the trip, I retreated into myself. I told myself I'd pushed it too far, too early. I'd regressed.

In hindsight, I can see my reaction in the kayak was a result of feeling a lack of control in a situation that, to my mind, had the potential to become life-or-death. I had to share responsibility for our wee watercraft – and, most importantly, keep it from capsizing – with a person I barely knew, who seemed incapable of the task. *Of course* this situation brought back bad feelings and flashbacks for me.

Logically, I know there was probably only the most *minute* chance that I was going to capsize and drown because I couldn't remove my spray skirt. But there had also been only the most *minute* chance I'd find myself facing down a pyroclastic surge, and yet look how that panned out. My brain was working on past experience. It wasn't wrong – it was just doing what it thought it should to keep me safe.

When I got back home to Whakatāne, I told Sam and my psych about what had happened, and how I was disappointed in myself for pushing too hard and making myself worse. They both gave me the exact same look: the slightly cocked head, the gentle smile.

'You haven't regressed at all,' they both told me separately.

'Things will pop up, and sometimes you might react,' Sam explained. 'Honestly, I'd probably have had the same reaction if my kayak was going round in a circle in a lake while the rest of my group paddled off into the wind.'

That was some comfort, but the message was clear. The trip had been a good way to test the waters (so to speak), but I still had a lot of work to do.

In April, I turned twenty-nine. This, my fourth bonus birthday, felt even worse than the other post-eruption ones. As well as that gross, empty, sad feeling about my birthday in general, I'd held on to the hope that Tom and I might have found some sort of reconciliation by now. This was not how I had expected or hoped that my future birthdays (or any other days) would look.

I spent a lot of the day alone while everyone was at work, but my family (being my family) came and wrapped me in their deep love. Despite the fact I was crying into my sushi, I *felt* loved, which took away a bit of the sting. But I hoped more than anything that all of my future birthdays weren't going to feel like this.

Despite a tumultuous couple of months, I was actually starting to feel lighter, brighter, spunkier, healthier – more like myself. Like pre-eruption Kelsey. But ... better.

Dad must have sensed this – or was just gently trying to push me in the right direction – because one day he messaged me on Facebook (a rare occurrence) while I was out of town: *You should apply for this.*

I took a quick glance. There was a link to something called the Inspiring Explorers Programme offered by the Antarctic Heritage Trust. I promptly forgot about it.

A couple of days later, when I saw Dad, he asked me, 'Did you apply for that trip yet?'

'What trip?'

'The one I sent you.'

Oh yeah.

I took out my phone and clicked on the link, quickly skimming the webpage Dad had sent. Something about an opportunity 'for young people to experience and challenge themselves in Antarctica and the polar regions'. The Antarctic Heritage Trust was offering a group of twenty-two young 'explorers' the chance to travel to South Georgia Island, the croissant-shaped sub-Antarctic island off the east coast of the bottom tip of Argentina, to follow in the footsteps of Sir Ernest Shackleton and the pioneer explorers of old. *Well, why not? I've always wanted to go to Antarctica, and I haven't had enough challenges.*

I quickly filled out the written questionnaire, then realised I had to answer some video questions, too – right then and there, in my oversized pink Metallica shirt. I started responding to the question prompts as they popped up. *Showtime?!* I remember one of the questions being something along the lines of 'What can you contribute to the trip if you are selected?' Part of my answer included 'a banger playlist'.

There's no way they'll take me, I thought. *Not with PTSD. What a liability.*

But they got in touch to arrange an online interview, and suddenly things started to feel like they might actually happen. Enter Mike, the manager of the Inspiring Explorers Programme. He wasn't fazed by the fact I had PTSD – as I'd come to learn, he had actually had some dealings with it in other people in the past. He knew how to handle it if it reared its ugly head. He certainly had more faith in me than I did, and for that – and the friendship that quickly grew between us – I will forever be grateful.

And then I got the nod. I was going to South Georgia Island!

Was I ready for a trip of this magnitude? The memory of the South Island experience was still raw. But I'd learnt from that trip, and done more work, so maybe ... *Right?* I told my psych team, and they were so excited for me. We got to work hatching a plan of what we needed to do between now (May) and the trip (September). We discussed things that were likely to catch me out, and how I could prepare and manage on my own on the other side of the world.

Who should be my safe place on the ship, in case shit hit the fan? Mike, of course. I pulled him into a chat with Sam and my psych, and we went over what would be my likely triggers,[190] and what tended to work for me in terms of coping and management. Then we made a spreadsheet. Mike had a copy. I had a copy. He could be my external brain if my internal one began malfunctioning.

'But we won't need it,' he assured me.

Shortly after I was accepted for the South Georgia trip, the phone rang. It was Hutt Hospital: 'We have you booked in for your hand surgery on July thirteenth.' Eleven whole weeks before South Georgia. *Yeah, that'll be enough time to heal.*

It was not. Well, it was – but only just. As it turned out, the damage to my muscle tissue underneath the grafts was still pretty extensive, which was going to majorly slow my recovery. It was only once I was in surgery (when it was too late to turn back) that my surgeon realised the new grafts might not heal very well – or at all. In the end, I had open wounds for *eight weeks* before they all started closing up.

Then, since everything else was ramping up in my life, I decided I might as well book in that tattoo I'd been wanting to get on my left hand for a couple of years.[191] I'd always talked about getting something in the space on that hand that Hayden had inadvertently saved with his bandaging, and I was finally brave enough to make it happen. I scheduled the tattoo for 17 August and, together with my brilliant tattooist, designed a piece that encompassed the smart, brave and wily octopus – for Hayden,

---

190 I hate this word so much, by the way.
191 I'd very much expected the 'surgery hand' to be closed by then!

one of the greatest lovers of the sea that I have ever had the privilege of knowing. *A new hand and a new hand tattoo.*

Six weeks before South Georgia, I was invited to go and speak at a conference in Brisbane for the company that had been doing some laser work on my scars and grafts.[192] *Might as well …*

I was about to go on stage to speak when I found out a friend of mine had died suddenly, from a brain tumour that had been found only a couple of days beforehand. George was a really good friend of mine in high school, and everyone who knew him was devastated at the sudden loss of such a light. Unbelievably, I managed to compartmentalise enough to do my bit on stage, despite my heart being back home.

Three weeks before South Georgia, and back in New Zealand, Mum, Dad and I shot down to Hutt Hospital for my final check-in with my surgeon. 'How did it heal?' he asked, looking it over.

'Terribly. It took eight weeks to close.'

That was when he told us that he was not surprised, based on what he'd found when he removed the graft. We drove back to Whakatāne that afternoon, and I grabbed my car and headed to Hamilton for George's funeral.

Despite the mildly chaotic, head-spinning lead-up, I did manage to make it to South Georgia Island with a calm and excited mind. That trip was pivotal for me. It proved that I wasn't made of glass (even though while washing my clothing in the bathroom sink,

---

192 A trial to see whether we could reduce the purple pigment in my leg grafts and soften some of my thicker scars.

I managed to rub off the graft on the palm of my hand; thankfully, not badly enough to need another trip to the surgeon!). It proved I could go to the middle of nowhere and thrive, even in freezing temperatures.

All the work I had done with my psych team paid off, and Mike was right – I didn't need to tap into him or the spreadsheet to try to regain control of my nervous system. The location certainly helped. Being on the high seas lit me up like nothing else. There, every *cell* in my body sang. I don't think there was a moment on that trip when I wasn't beaming, exploring one of the most stunning and biodiverse places on Earth.

Even the 10-metre swells on our ride home didn't manage to wipe the smile from my face. Alone in the Panorama Lounge of the *Magellan Explorer*, lurching in every direction, I could not *stop* smiling. I even laughed, hanging on to the furniture, and I knew in that moment that *this* is where I needed to be. This was my calling. Nothing and no one makes me feel the way being on the open ocean does. I realised I wasn't done with the sea.

I have to come back here, I thought, a huge grin on my face as yet another wave shook the boat.

At the end of the year, I saw another of my favourite bands live: Highly Suspect.[193] I made Holly come with me, because I didn't have any friends who shared my taste in music. Despite thinking that she was going to be surrounded by punks, she actually enjoyed it. They were even better live than I could have hoped.

---

193 I also went and saw another of my favourites, Dayseeker, on Will's second birthday in July, winning no competitions for most devoted aunt and godmother! They were incredible and I have no regrets. Sorry, Will. Sorry, Holly.

Music has always been a massive love of mine. I rarely operate in silence,[194] and listening to music is one of the best ways to give my mind something else to focus on when I am going through bad bouts of PTSD. Music provides predictable background noise that helps drown out anything startling or irksome. That aside, music just makes me feel so much, and has the most beautiful way of helping me never feel alone. I think it's one of my love languages.

After the concert, my family and I 'ran away' for the fourth anniversary of the eruption. My sister's birthday always got overshadowed, no matter how hard I tried to keep 8 December 'White Island free', and she was always a champ about it. But this year I said I didn't want to stay in Whakatāne. 'Instead, let's go and give Holly a birthday.'

So we took off to one of our most favourite places in the North Island – a secret location I shall not divulge. We took River and Beau [Holly and her partner's dog], we took the nephew, and we had the most relaxing, White Island-free week. Bliss.

---

194 Even as I write this, Bob Segar is telling me that we still have tonight.

Chapter 11

Unfuckwithable

It was in 2024 that I fully got my groove back. Thanks to my trip to South Georgia Island, and all the work I'd put in (with the help of my family, friends and psych team), I finally felt like I was living again – not just surviving. Stronger mentally and physically. More confident. More unfuckwithable.[195]

Six months after my hand surgery, I said yes to a job working to socialise packs of dogs. I could even bring River along. It was daunting, but for the first time in four years I didn't feel absolutely petrified at the prospect of entering the workforce again. I started out only working once or twice a week and slowly built my confidence, but eventually I ended up with three set days a week, plus extra shifts in other aspects of the business as needed.

For the first few months, I wore my compression garment on my right hand, as the grafts were still pretty delicate and a leash can do a lot of damage if the dog takes off on you, which I had found out before I'd even left the farm. But, in the end, I think using my hands a lot more actually helped to stretch them out and strengthen them, as well as work down or flatten a couple

---

195 Which, to be honest, is a state everyone should be striving towards.

of the scars on my fingers. Now, I have almost the full range of motion in my right hand.

In April, I decided I wanted to run away for my birthday, too. But this year it was my thirtieth, so there was no way my parents were letting me escape without them. We hatched a plan to tour the South Island for a month, and it was *incredible*. We saw stags fighting on the road during the roar, we found epic hikes, we went to my favourite chocolate factory, I made Mum and Dad go horse-riding with me, and then Holly and her family met us along with some other family in Queenstown for the actual day. And you know what? The weird little gross feeling was still there, but it didn't override the whole day as it had done the previous four birthdays. For the first time in four years, I was actually happy on my birthday.

From mid-2023 and through a lot of 2024, I became brave enough to accept some of the speaking opportunities that came my way. My favourite was in Auckland. I'd received an email asking if I would speak at the twentieth anniversary of the Plastic Surgery Nurses Symposium to a room full of not just nurses but doctors and specialist surgeons, too.

Of course I will, I replied. *You can have whatever you want from me.* What an honour. Multiple times over the years since the eruption, whenever a nurse or doctor had asked anything of me, I'd said that I owed them my life, so I was on board with doing anything I could to help them. You want to use photos of my grafts healing? *Done.* You want to use me as a case study? *Absolutely.* You want me to speak at your event? *I'll clear my calendar.*

What a privilege it was to stand up in front of those incredibly talented men and women and show them what their hard work and sleepless nights had achieved. Many of them had worked on patients from the eruption, and most had no idea what their outcome was once they were repatriated. In the crowd, I spotted many familiar faces – some I'd had the pleasure of meeting in either Hutt or Waikato hospitals, others since I'd been discharged.

Being able to give back to these professionals and tell them how my life had changed and evolved since I was an inpatient was hands-down one of the best things I have been able to give back to them. To be able to thank so many in the same room felt incredible. To get to show them that at least one of us was thriving after surviving the eruption was something I will never adequately be able to put into words. A lot of them thought they were just doing their jobs – but those of us who found ourselves on the table in their operating theatres knew they were miracle workers who had saved our lives. At the end of my talk, which included all of my gory hospital photos (not something I included in any of my other talks), one of them stood and thanked me for sharing, and we all got emotional thanking each other. It was incredibly moving.

Afterwards, they let me stay for the rest of the conference and see – in graphic detail – some of the work they do. There were craniofacial specialists, anaesthetists, paediatric specialists, flap specialists[196] and specialists who literally reattached limbs, and they spoke of some of their more complicated cases – uncensored photographs included. There I was in the room with these wizards, and I was queasy as all hell. Queasy and in awe. I couldn't look away from the screen, and I couldn't have left the room even if I'd wanted to.

196 A real thing where they move your skin around and create 'flaps' that they stick back down in certain ways to reduce scarring.

When Tom and I had first separated, the prospect of dating again scared the absolute shit out of me. *I don't want to date again … who the hell is going to want to date someone covered in so many scars?*

But eventually, as it had started to do, curiosity got the better of me, and I went on a few dates. The overarching theme? There were actually a lot of guys out there who *didn't* care about my scars, and didn't care that I was still a work in progress. At least I *was* progressing.

Another common theme: their perspective on what I was taking on. Between work, seeing friends, spending time with family, ensuring River was kept moving and fulfilled with early-morning hunts and hikes, driving out of town for events and adventures and saying yes to more speaking gigs, I kept hearing the same sort of thing:

'You do too much.'

'You need to rest more.'

'Take the week(end) off.'

'Just chill out for once.'

'Say no to things.'

Coming from a long line of 'active resters', late retirers and early risers, this irked me no end. I felt like I was just starting to make up for a lot of lost time. In the two (almost three) years after the eruption, I'd spent a lot of time first physically recovering, then hiding from the world and from myself. During that time, I had said no to a lot of things I had wanted to say yes to because of fear, because I was exhausted, because I had rehab in one form or another. Now, I was finally reclaiming my life. I was not going to waste *any* of the weird, wild, back-to-back opportunities that were popping up along the way. And here these people were – these strangers – telling me to slow down? I was sucking every last drop out of all of my days and enjoying every second, and now *boys* were trying to clip *my* wings?

After very prematurely bringing some of these boys to meet my parents, because I just wasn't sure what to do and I needed an adult to tell me, I asked Mum what she thought.

'You're too strong for them,' she said. 'You'll walk all over them. You need someone on your level or you are going to eat them alive. Or even worse, shrink. Do not settle. After everything you have been through, *do not settle*.'

Everyone has different ceilings, different thresholds and different expectations. These guys were trying to put their own limits on me. I worked very hard to expand my window of tolerance and push my thresholds – not shrink them. Sometimes, I think, it was just an attempt to get me to spend more time with them. But it felt like someone trying to put me back in a cage – one that I had just managed to claw my way out of – and it bothered me. I wanted to be out living, doing, seeing everything I could.

For a long while, I couldn't decide whether or not I had accumulated a bit more trauma through the break-up. Was that actually what was holding me back from totally falling into another relationship? I discussed it at length with both Sam and my psych, and in the end we came to the conclusion that I'd done so much work on myself, and my life was in such a good place, that that wasn't the case. I was just so sure on my boundaries and values now that these guys weren't the right fit, even though I actually really liked some of them.

So I stopped looking. There's something totally freeing about embracing being alone and not being lonely. Even though there were (and still are) times when I missed being in a relationship,

I realised that I wasn't willing to risk my solitude for 'maybes'. I stopped actively looking for dates, and continued living my life fully. For me.

I realised that I'd created a life that filled me with more happiness and satisfaction than I ever could have imagined. I didn't think it was possible to do it alone, but in the wake of losing everything, I'd built myself to be the happiest, strongest, bravest and most authentic I had ever been in my life.

I now protect the life I have built with very strong boundaries, and I continue to spread myself too thin because it makes me *so damn happy*.

Never forget, darling: your ceiling is not my ceiling. Your limits are not my limits.

In August 2024, I finally weaned myself off the medication I'd been taking since leaving hospital to help with my nerve pain. Over the years I had dialled it back at times, to see whether I was ready to come off it – and, on one occasion, went on holiday and realised that I didn't have enough to last the whole time, so accidentally weaned myself off them. Every time, though, I ended up uncomfortable and wanting to rip holes in my grafts. But I tried again that August, and found that things had settled down with the help of regular movement and intensive massage. I still have odd[197] sensations, but nothing like in the past. To this day, I am still off it.

Right before I came off the nerve blockers, I decided to try to come off the beta blockers, too. After slowly dropping back the dosage, and a little bit of an adjustment period, my heart rate stayed down – and actually ended up slightly *lower* than

---

197 Odd as in occasional, *and* odd as in feels weird.

pre-eruption! The ultimate test was when I went to a friend's wellness retreat. Earlier the year before, I'd been doing one-on-one boxing and kick boxing classes with her, and she'd worked out where my ceiling was on the beta blockers and adjusted my sessions accordingly. But then she had *selfishly* moved away, so this retreat was the first time we'd done anything together since I'd come off the medication.

It was a little daunting for both of us – especially when I discovered the 'retreat' was actually a full-on bootcamp, an intensive weekend of boxing, functional strength training, kayaking, mountain biking, Pilates, ice baths and general tomfoolery. But, despite getting lost in the forest mountain-biking and being a little chicken about jumping in the lake after kayaking, I smashed the whole weekend and totally exceeded my own expectations. It was the best feeling. I loved it more than I thought I possibly could have.

By the end of 2024, I was officially off my meds. In the best way possible.

The end of 2024 went out with a big ol' bang.

Mum, Dad and I went over to Perth for my cousin Ashleigh's wedding, and during set up, one of the groomsmen and I heard that the pub across the way was airing the Mike Tyson versus Jake Paul fight. We looked at each other, and we decided we wouldn't be missed for half an hour. We shot to the pub for a couple of beers and to watch the fight, then slunk back.

The wedding was amazing. And we *did* get caught.

The day we flew out of Perth, I got a message that made me stare at my home screen for about half an hour before I opened it. *There is no way this is who I think this actually is*, I was thinking.

Oh but it was!

Ryan Meyer, the drummer from Highly Suspect, had sent the loveliest message to say he'd seen the Netflix documentary about the eruption, and the band wanted to know if I'd like to come and see them play live while they were in New Zealand that month.

I'm sorry ... did I just get invited to a Highly Suspect gig by Highly Suspect?!

I couldn't bloody believe it. After trying to figure out whether the Wellington or Auckland show was going to be the most convenient with my work schedule, I messaged my bosses to ask if I could get the time off. Unfortunately, everyone else had locked in plans, so there was no way out of work (short of quitting). I was devastated, and had to tell the band I couldn't make it.

But I guess at least I can add 'turning down a major rock band's personal invite' to my bingo card, right?

Sometime in mid-2024, a message was posted in the group chat we had for the South Island trip I went on with the Americans. Ally, who hosted the trips, was going to Borneo, and had sent an early-bird link through to the group. Never in my life have I ever wanted to go to Borneo, yet there I was sitting in a parking lot paying the deposit.

There was a running joke in my family (mostly Dad and Holly) that Borneo was where I was originally from – a really original ginger joke – but when I sent them a screenshot of my booking they were naturally surprised and a bit confused. But the trip was over a year away, so it was fine – plenty of time to back out.

A month or so later, the same thing happened. Ally posted an early-bird link to the South Island group chat, this time for a trip to China. Many of the group said they were going to book it, so – not wanting to miss out – I booked it too. It was quite a while later that I realised that there was only a month between the two trips.

As the trips drew nearer, I paid for the flights, bought an eSIM, and became rather committed to going to both Borneo and China. All the while, the little voice of fear was yelling down the hallway of my mind that this was a mistake.

Even as I sat at Auckland Airport before my flight to Kuala Lumpur I was not excited, I was scared. But I made it to Borneo, I got my transfer to the resort, and I met one of the other group members who had also arrived a day early.

The first thing Ally said to me the next morning, when she saw me again after two years, was that I looked like a totally different person. In fairness, I *am* a totally different person to the shell of a human she met in early 2023, but it was interesting how visible it was to her.

'You look happy,' she said. And I was. I *am*.

That trip was *incredible*. Wild orangutans, sun bears, *two* herds of wild pygmy elephants trumpeting to each other across the river (with us in the middle), and more hornbills than you can shake a stick at. I ate noodles and rice for breakfast; I squared off with a couple of wild male macaques (one of whom was missing an arm); I sweated continuously out the remaining 55 per cent of my skin that *can* sweat in the humidity; I sat on a tiny boat as we hooned down a swollen river in torrential rain; I got bogged in a mud volcano and inadvertently got the poor sod who tried to help me stuck too – and I realised that I was right where I needed to be. Pushing my limits. Feeling scared of the unknown but diving in anyway.

When I landed in Auckland Airport, depressed after leaving the serenity of the jungle and the new friends I'd made, I arrived to the news that I was now an aunty for a second time, and that Holly and baby Rio were happy and healthy. This time, all I felt was pure joy for my sister and her growing family.

The China trip came around *fast*, and this time I was excited. Still a bit nervous, but definitely excited. *The perfect combination.*

After finally making it through Guangzhou Airport thanks to the help of a Chinese-and-English-speaking stranger who took pity on me in the early hours of the morning, I made my transfer to Chengdu and spent the next nine days exploring the countryside with the group. After seeing pandas, exploring markets, ancient monasteries and an ancient kung-fu school, cities full of greenery, tea farms and farmers' houses, the most incredibly mind-blowing statues on mountain tops, and once again making beautiful new friends, I realised I was never going to be the same again – and for all the right reasons.

I'd faced death several times and made it out, only to then have to fight with my own nervous system to stay alive. I'd pulled myself out of the darkness and built a community of safe, loving, adventurous, funny people who never once shamed me for my past or when the devil himself (ol' PTSD) peeked back through the curtain – the people in my life expected me to push myself to be better, not for anyone else's sake or comfort, but for my own personal growth and to meet my own standards. That's how you know you've found your tribe: they will never let you settle for anything less than you deserve or are capable of.

> For the strength of the pack is the wolf,
> And the strength of the wolf is the pack.
>
> – Rudyard Kipling, *The Jungle Book*

I am so lucky, and that fact is rarely lost on me. I am lucky to have the family I have. The friends I have. The life I have. I will not take this time I have left for granted – however long or short it may be.

I will continue to squeeze everything I can out of life, and I encourage you to do the same.

Take the trip to Borneo. Take the trip to China.

Do it scared. Do it alone.

Treat those heart-shattering moments where you lose everything as a clean slate. You have nothing to lose, and everything to gain. From the bottom you can only go up.

You might not have a choice in some of what happens in your life, but you have the choice in how you show up. That's all you can do.

Just keep turning up. And keep fighting like hell.

Acknowledgements

I am bloody lucky to have so many people to be grateful for and I want to acknowledge everything they have done for me and my family, and everything they have contributed to my life – thanking everyone is a *mammoth* task, especially with eyes full of happy tears. It has kept me up at night trying to make this list and ensuring I don't forget anyone!

Mum – for being the most caring, kind-hearted and warm woman I know. What a privilege to call you mum. Thank you for always having my back, for advocating for me when I couldn't do it for myself, for your honesty, and for reliving every horrific moment and every victory with me many times over as I wrote this book. I am grateful for every single piece of me that came from you.

Dad – for your humour in my darkest moments, for always keeping me humble and realistic, for being the only family member that has the ringer turned up on their phone and for answering when I call, for setting the standard on how I should be treated by a man (except for that time you jokingly put me in a dog roll fridge when I was five). Thank you for being my unshakeable rock.

Holly – my fiercest protector and best friend. Thank you for always having my back no matter what and for *always* making me laugh. You regularly put others before yourself, and you are one of the most generous and thoughtful people I know. I am so lucky to call you my sister. I'm glad I have proof of nice things you've said about me immortalised in this book.

River – my soul dog. You can't read, so I won't write much here, and you know it all already. I love you more than I thought I could ever love anything.

My colleagues and the other passengers on 9 December – your bravery ensured we made it back to Whakatāne. Your fast thinking, fast driving, fast action, ensured that we were well set up once we reached the mainland, and that *everyone* was ready to receive us. Thank you for every single thing you did that day. Thank you for every single thing that you have done for me since that day.

The pilots of Kahu and Volcanic Air – what fucking badasses. You guys are truly the most incredibly courageous and humble lads. You didn't have to do what you did, but there are a hell of a lot of people who are grateful you did. You deserve every piece of praise you receive. It's an honour to know you.

First responders (police, fire, ambo, military, etc) – you guys saw (and see) some truly fucked up shit, and I'm sorry that will probably never leave you. You guys show up for people in their darkest hours and put yourselves on the line to help. I'll always be grateful to you for getting us to hospitals all over the country so we could get the help we desperately needed. Thank you for supporting my family through this process – sitting with them in waiting rooms, keeping media away from them, calling and texting to check in. Your kindness toward them will not be forgotten.

My medical teams – I genuinely couldn't name you all if I tried (thanks to the drugs, but also the sheer number of you).

<u>Whakatāne team</u>: you did the grunt work in ensuring we made it to specialised help – and as I've mentioned *many* times before, without every single thing you did that day, our outcomes could have been vastly different. Thank you.

<u>Hutt team</u>: words will never do justice as to what you mean to me and my family. Without all of you and your expertise, care and humour, I wouldn't be here. Thank you for fighting for me, for crying with me, for absolutely everything you did for me *and* my family. You all went above and beyond, and we will carry that kindness forever. You all have a very special place in my heart.

<u>Waikato team</u>: Thank you for getting me home. I'm sorry for all the whoopsies I had on your watch!

My incredible orderlies, cleaning staff and security in Hutt Hospital – to this day, my family and I still speak of you all and everything you did for us. Your professionalism, your attention to detail, your kindness, your humour and your speed and efficiency did not go unnoticed. We are so incredibly grateful for the hard work you put in to keeping us safe and where we needed to be.

My physical rehab teams – from my teams in Hutt ICU, to my teams back home in Whakatāne, you guys *all* ensured that I got the best outcomes after all my surgeries. Thank you for pushing me through my pain – though I probably didn't appreciate it at the time! Thank you for your encouragement to go hard for those first few months so that the rest of it was a breeze – it made a world of difference.

Meg – my most incredible GP. On more than one occasion you pulled stitches from my body, helped adjust my medications, had to figure out how to deal with my grafts doing weird things, helped me find specialised help, and supported me through my darkest moments – including my breast cancer scare. Thank you for everything you do for me.

Ant, Leanne and Simon – you three are so very special. Thank you for protecting me, for making me laugh, for supporting me, and for helping guide me and my family through the worst years of my life. I am *so* grateful for everything you have done for me – except for that time Ant showed up at my house in full uniform.

Kate from ACC and Crystal – my early-day heroes. Thank you both for everything you did for me. You always knew what I needed before I did and read my mind when I was about to contact you about something!

Jake – I'll always be grateful that I was encouraged to seek out my own lawyer, and that it was you who was recommended. Thank you for wading through the ridiculous amount of paperwork on my behalf, for sitting with me through my police interview, and for your advice.

My extended family – for continually checking in on me, Mum, Dad and Holly. For all the love, support, food, cards, hugs, laughs and shared tears. I have the greatest family ever.

Mik – thank you for showing me what real friendship should feel like. For supporting me no matter what. For knowing my worth and ensuring I always know it too. For the three-hour phone calls – when I eventually answer. For your alternate ending for my book – *'and then I woke up, and it was all a dream'*. For still being my best friend even though you told me not to name you in the book. I love you.

Nico and Hayley – you guys were the definition of stepping up and back into my life for all the right reasons after the eruption. Thank you for always checking in, always having my back and always making time for me. You both make me laugh on the regular, and always when I need it.

Laura – thank you for the phone calls, the late-night texts, the check ins, the constant support and help. Thank you for always letting me pick your brain, and for talking me through those 'late night panics' when you somehow guessed I was not okay. I'm so grateful for you.

Mike Barber – for believing in me before I ever did. For taking me to South Georgia Island and literally showing me that I was capable of more than I ever thought. Thank you for your friendship, the banter, the shit-talk, the unwavering support, the pep-talks, and for being the most consistently annoying person I know.

Charlie and Kaitlyn – my high-sea buddies for life. My god. I cannot imagine my life without you two in it now. How lucky am I to have two such close friends who shared South Georgia with me! Thank you for consistently making me laugh and being my most wildly reliable friends.

Lydia Brady – my very own hype woman and one of the most incredible people I have ever had the privilege of knowing. Thank you for your support and belief in me from the second we met. Your outlook on life is one I am consistently aiming to adopt, and your energy is infectious.

Tammie – River's other mother. I tell you all the time how grateful I am for you, and I truly mean it. You always push me to be better, stand for less shit and live more. What a blessing it is to have you in my corner. I love you to bits.

Stanley Williams – for writing *Surviving Galeras* and the information you included in that book on how best to survive an eruption – it saved my life, and all of those with me that day. I will always be grateful to you.

Sam – the very first person to tell me that I was normal and what I was experiencing was normal. Thank you for your guidance, knowledge, experience and, most importantly, your love and friendship. Thank you for being my light and for helping me save myself. I wouldn't be here without you.

Tyla and Nikki – for helping me understand my own brain and nervous system, for helping me rewire it, and for listening to me fall apart and pull myself back up. Thank you for always supporting me through all the wild back-to-back things I take on and helping me find my version of balance!

Tom – you were my rock through the worst time of my life. Thank you for your selflessness, care, kindness and love through ICU, surgeries, hallucinations, dressing changes, the good days, the bad days, the great days. For supporting my family. For standing by me for as long as you did through the heaviest shit. You made the right call, and I hope you have found the lightness and freedom I have.

Tom's family – thank you for taking over the farm and the two wild young dogs while I was in hospital, which allowed Tom to be by my side. Thank you for your support, humour and love every day after. I will always be grateful for everything you gave to help. Especially the papier-mâché White Island.

Haydz – my most annoying and passionate friend who was like a brother to me. Thank you for everything you taught me – both at work and in life. We butted heads, but you were always there for me – crying phone calls after a bad day, road trips, pub trips, full-throttle zodiac trips, banter, laughs, and 5am phone calls when someone was trying to break into my house. I miss you every day.

You lot – my followers on Instagram, my donators to Givealittle, the readers of this book, the brands and companies that have sent me products expecting nothing in return – just that it would make my life easier or more comfortable. Thank you for the unbelievable level of love and support you have sent to my family and me since the eruption. Thank you for the messages of encouragement on my lowest days. For the messages from burn survivors offering their insight, tips, tricks and hacks. Thank you for always showing me how far I have come. You helped more than you will ever know, and I will pay it forward as often as I can.

Kimberley – for helping me compile my screeds of notes and short stories into a coherent tale of my life. If it weren't for you, this wouldn't have come together so smoothly or so fast.

HarperCollins – for your five-year patience. You were all so understanding and never once pushy. Thank you for making this process as easy as possible.

There were a lot of people that reached out and helped my family in the early days that I was unaware of. Mum, Dad and Holly would like to take this opportunity to thank them:

> A huge thank you to our family and friends for their unwavering support. There are so many who stepped in and helped out in ways we didn't even know we needed. They travelled distances and took time out of their lives to be there when we needed them.

ACKNOWLEDGEMENTS

Sam – thank you for saving our girl and helping bring us back to life too. You will forever be family, like it or not.

Wade and Di – for the groceries and keeping us fed and watered daily.

Jen, Tiff, Nessie, Lucille and Paul – for dropping everything on day one to be there.

Patrick and Dani – for arranging flights and transportation to and from Hutt for us.

Amanda – for rallying half of the Wellington district to supply meals, toiletries, coffees and more.

Sam, John and Karmann – for taking such great care of Oska and Harley.

Karl and Megan and the staff at BayFab Ltd – for keeping the business running.

We know there are so many more and are grateful for every single one of you. Thank you all.

Where to get help

1737, Need To Talk?

Support and resources to help with your well-being. Free call or text 1737. 1737.org.nz

Anxiety New Zealand

Mental health support, treatment and education. Call 0800 ANXIETY (0800 269 438). anxiety.org.nz

Depression Helpline

Get immediate help or if you just want to talk. Call 0800 111 757 or free text 4202. depression.org.nz

Healthline

Health advice and information. Call 0800 611 116. healthy.org.nz

Lifeline

Call 0800 543 354 or free text 4357.

Parent Help

Call 0800 568 856. parenthelp.org.nz

Outline Rainbow Youth
Call 0800 OUTLINE (688 5463) or chat online at outline.org.nz

Rural Support Trust
Call 0800 787 254. rural-support.org.nz

Samaritans
Call 0800 72 66 66. samaritans.org.nz

Shine (Domestic Violence)
Call 0508 744 633 or chat online at 2shine.org.nz

Skylight
Helping young people navigate through tough times. Call 0800 299 100. skylight.org.nz

Sparx
SPARX e-therapy equips young people and rangatahi with life skills to power through stressful and negative emotions. Call 0508 4 SPARX or chat online at sparx.org.nz

Suicide Crisis Helpline
Call 0508 828 865.

The Lowdown
Find support for your hauora, identity, culture and mental health. thelowdown.co.nz

What's Up? Kidsline
Call 0800 942 8787 or chat online at whatsup.co.nz

Women's Refuge
Call 09 378 7635.

Yellow Brick Road
Supporting families in mental illness. Call 0800 732 825.

Youthline
Call 0800 37 66 33 or text 234.

INTERNATIONAL

AUSTRALIA
Lifeline 13 11 14
Kidsline 1800 55 1800
Beyond Blue 1300 22 4636

USA
Suicide Prevention Helpline 988
Crisis Text Line Text HOME to 741741

UK
Suicide Prevention Helpline 0800 587 0800
Mind Support Line 0300 102 1234
Shout Crisis Text Line Text 85258

CANADA
Suicide Crisis Helpline Call or text 988
Kids Help Phone Call 1 800 668 6868 or text CONNECT to 686868

Left 25 December 1998. Squishing my little sister, Holly, on Christmas Day. This was the last known time I was taller than her.

Below 10 April 2015. Graduating with my Bachelor of Science, my parents, Shelley and Graham, and my sister by my side.

Above 18 January 2016. *PeeJay V* on fire. David doing a dramatic swan dive. I'm either in the water or in one of those inflatable boats.

Right 28 August 2018. En route to get *PeeJay IV* some new engines. This was the trip where we saw a massive number of blue whales in the Hauraki Gulf.

Top 19 September 2019. A photoshoot we did for White Island Tours. I'm standing with another staff member on one of the many mounds of rock on the inner crater floor. *(Shaun Jeffers)*

Above Hi! Welcome to White Island. My name is Kelsey and I will be your guide!

Above 9 December 2019. White Island in full eruption, taken from the northern side of the island by one of *Phoenix*'s passengers. The pyroclastic surge is just about to roll over the lip of the crater walls. I am with my group somewhere on the crater floor. *(Michael Schade)*

Opposite top 11 December 2019. The confusing burn lines on my left hand, which I would later remember had been wrapped in a bandage.

Right 11 December 2019. My right arm. A section of my elbow crease was spared because I kept my hands over my face for as long as I did. But most of my old-school dive-helmet tattoo was destroyed and removed during debridement. Where they have opened my thumb is the tail end of the cut they made to save my arm – it runs all the way up to my shoulder. All four of my limbs had one or two of these cuts, made to reduce the pressure. The cut on my thumb was pretty much down to the bone, and now I have a spot there that is alternatively numb or oversensitive!

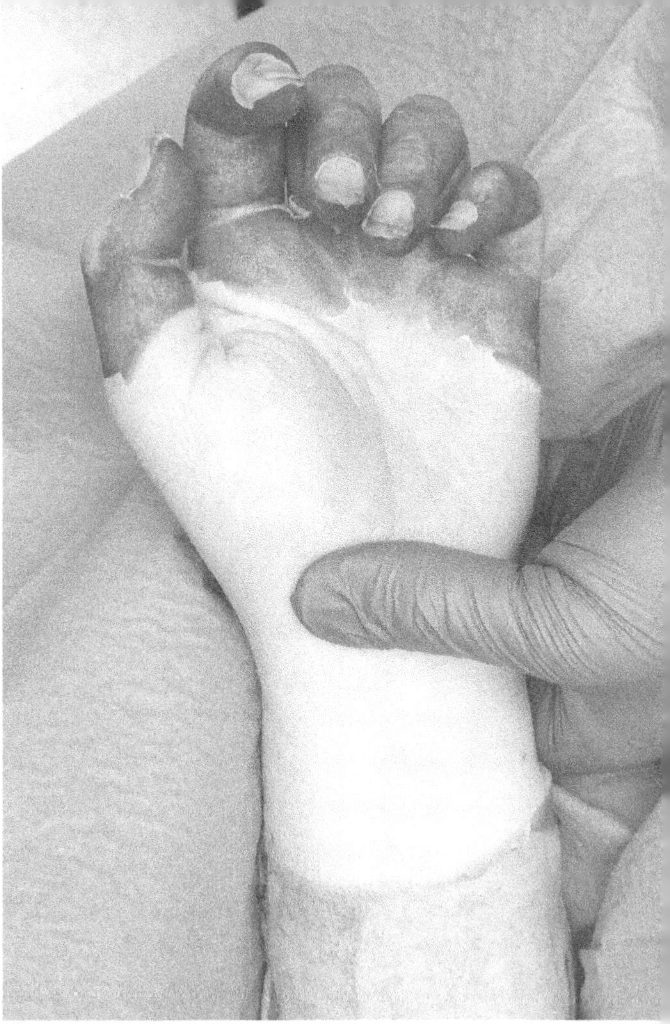

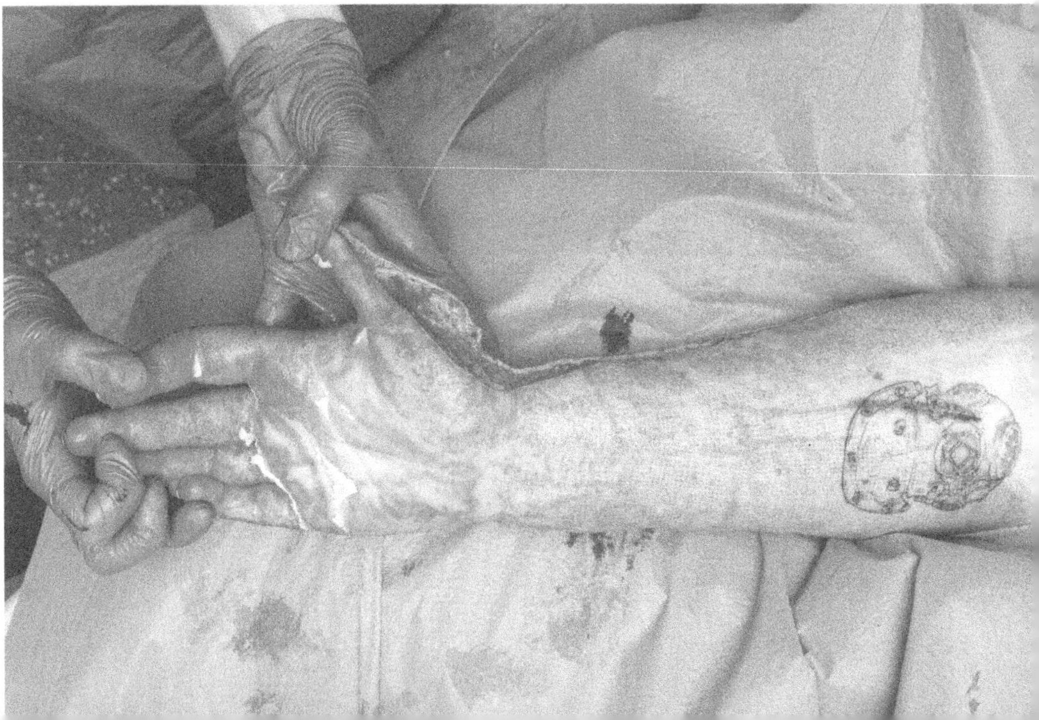

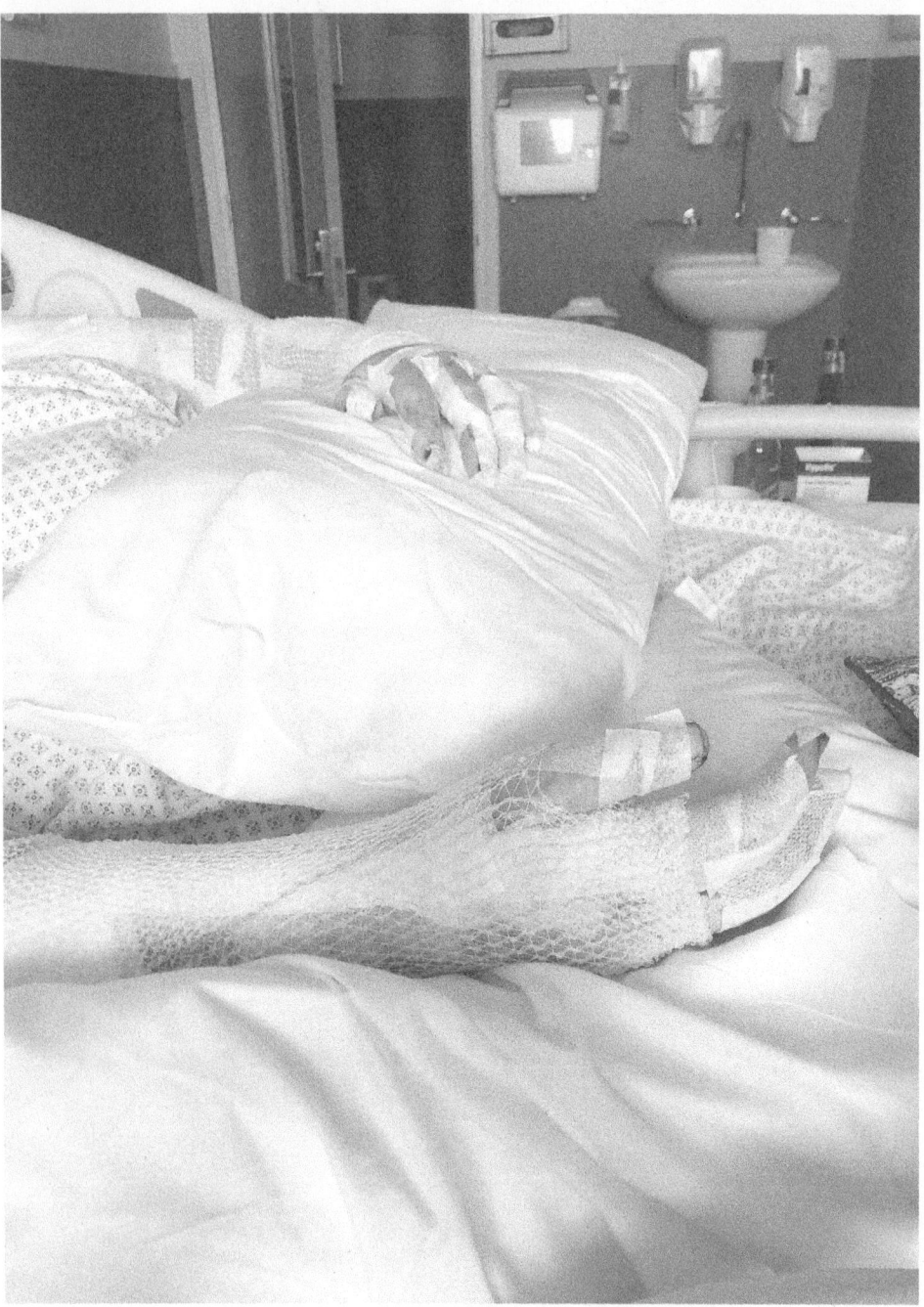

Above 20 December 2019. Arms and hands mostly uncovered here, for the first time since I'd been in hospital. It's hard to tell how much they looked like something that belonged to Frankenstein's monster in this photo, but you could see every bloody (literally) seam between the sheets of grafts, and it freaked me right out.

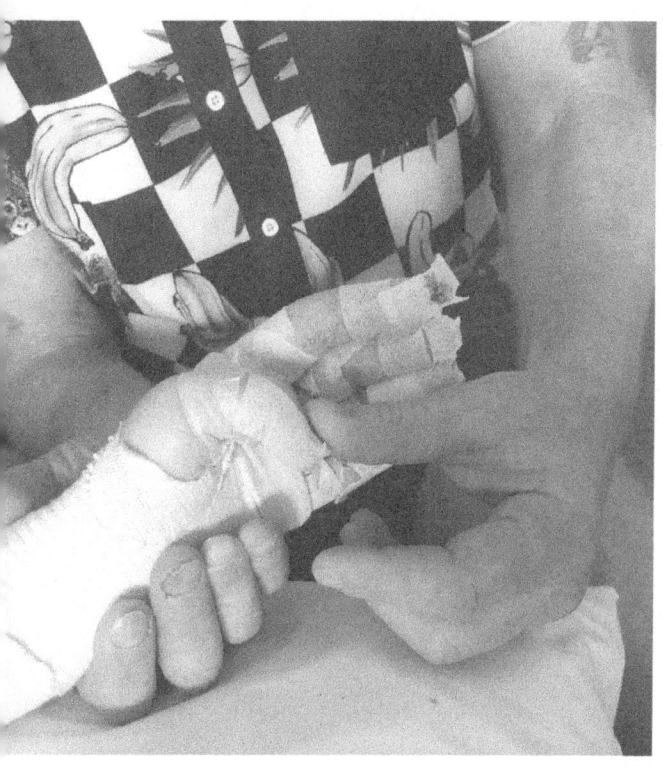

Left 25 December 2019. A very different Christmas to the first picture! Dad doing my hand physio in a shirt of orangutans and bananas that Mum made him wear.

Below 30 December 2019. My wall of goodies. I spent many, many hours staring at this wall, grateful for all the love and well-wishes sent to my family and me.

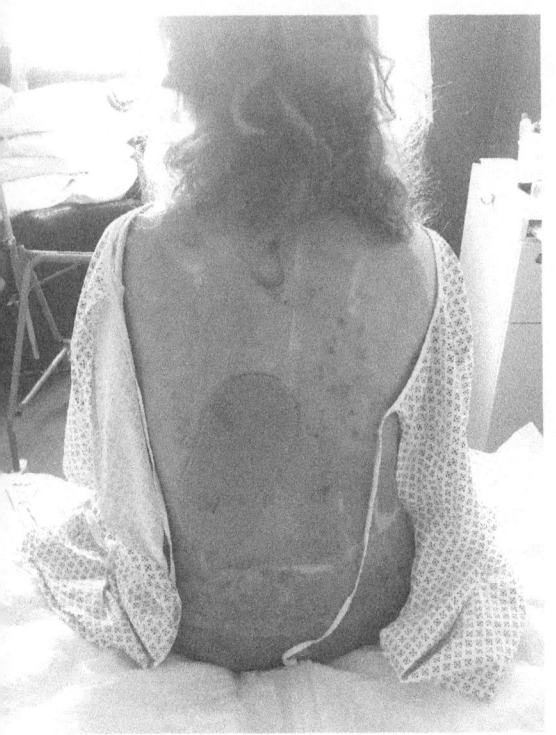
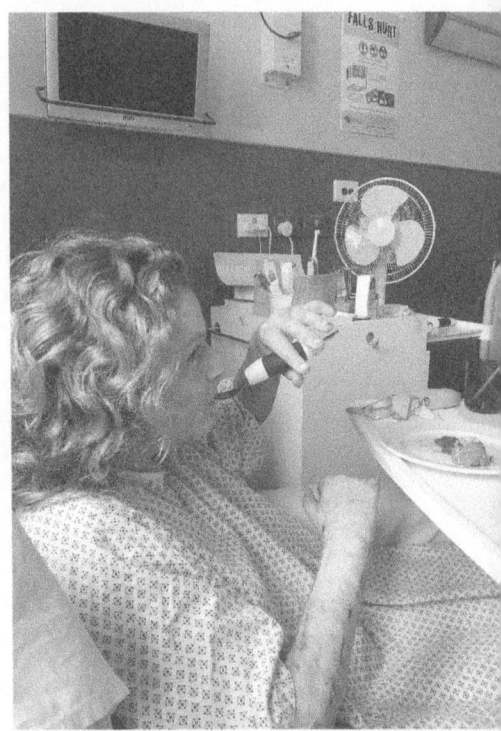
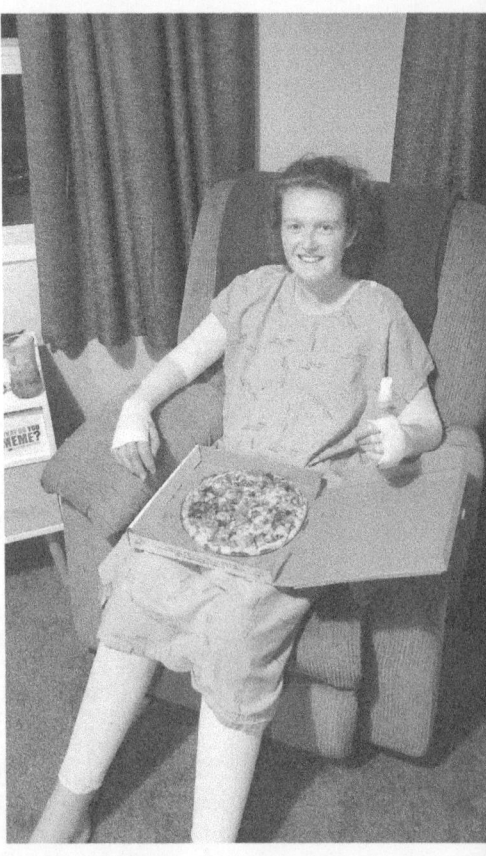

Top left 14 January 2020. I got Tom to take a photo of my back because I wanted to see what was left of it. You can see the horizontal line across my lower back from what was grafted, and the rest of the red is healing donor site.

Top right 16 January 2020. Relearning how to feed myself. It took a long time before I stopped bringing my head to my hand – my family would yell 'TURTLE NECK' at me in an attempt to make me use my arms.

Right 1 February 2020. Back home on the farm after my little whoopsie on the beach, in fresh bandages and a hospital gown.

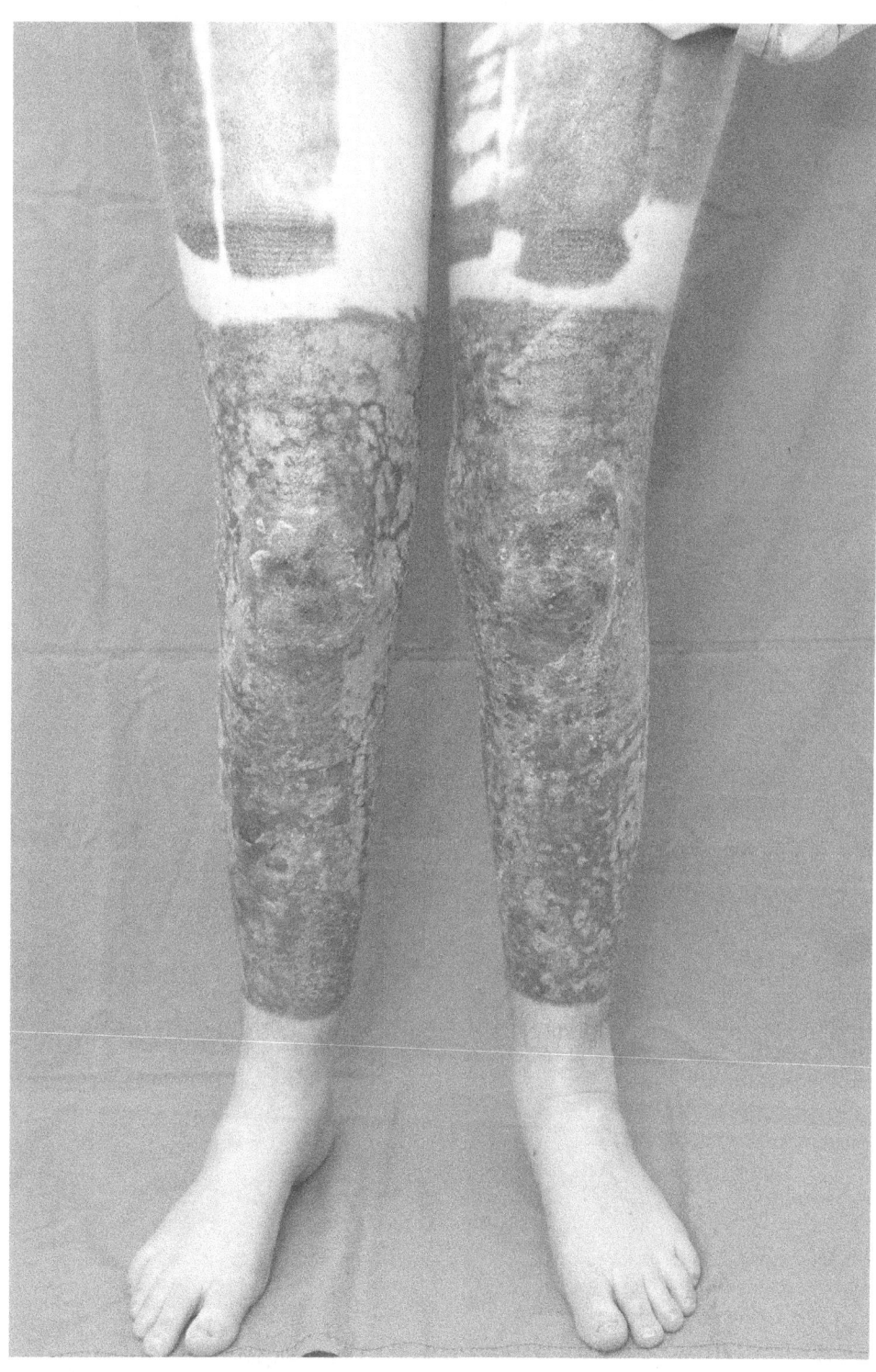

Above 13 February 2020. Discharge day. It's hard to believe that this isn't a post-eruption burns photo instead of a healthy and healing photo. I didn't think I should be going home looking like this!

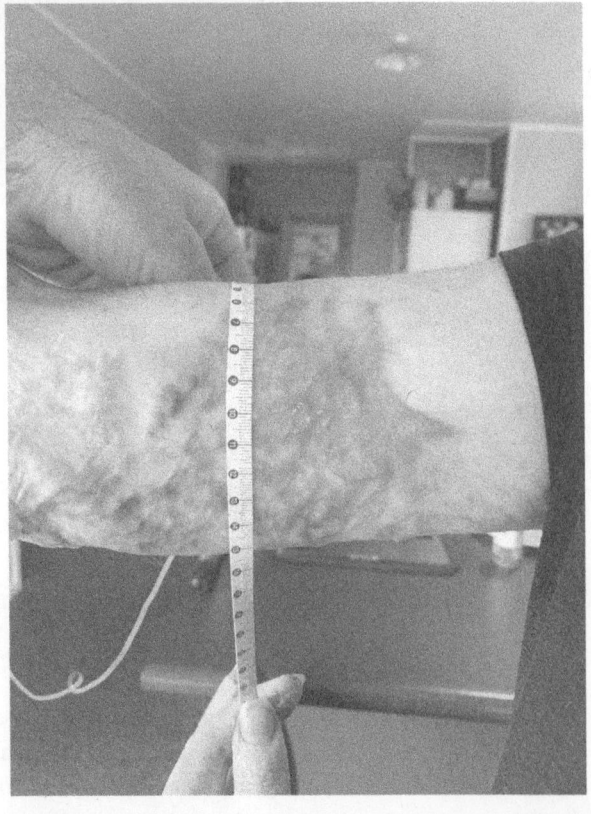

Above 25 February 2020. Baby's first drive! I had missed driving, and this felt like a little taste of freedom, which encouraged me to do more work on recovering to get even more freedom.

right 8 April 2020. Sending measurements of a thicker part of scarring on my inner upper right arm to my scar specialist during the first Covid lockdown. There's a glimpse of the still excessive growth of armpit hair.

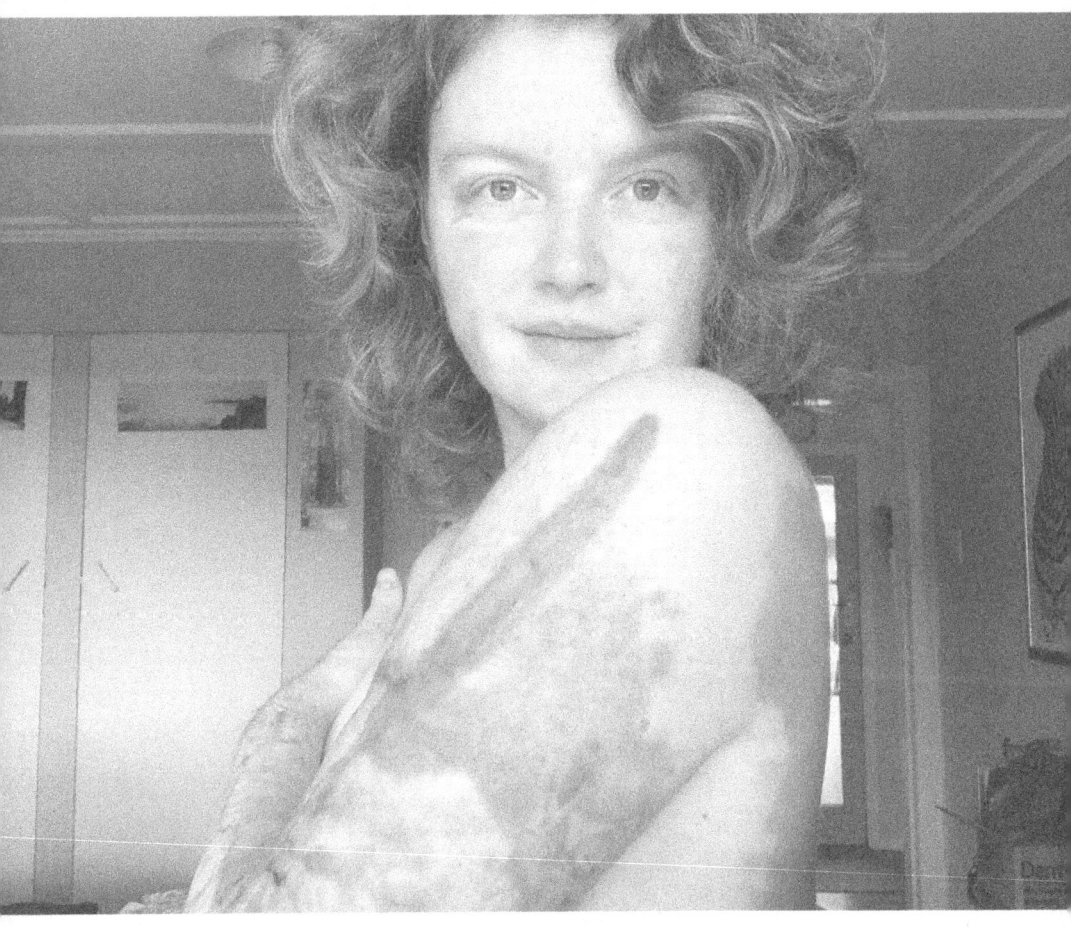

ABOVE 12 April 2020. My first bonus birthday. I posted this photo to Instagram with the caption, 'Somehow, I have made it to 26. I've survived a boat fire, a near-miss car crash, a volcanic eruption, 45 per cent full-thickness burns, fourteen trips to theatre, and, so far, a global pandemic. My body has a million scrapes, scars and burns, which I am learning to love every day. My mind and soul are still catching up and trying to accept what has happened over the last four years. For some reason, it's started to catch up today. But I'm here and that's all that matters. I'm so proud of how far I've come, how resilient my body is, and I couldn't be more thankful for all the love and light I have in my life. Happy birthday to me, and here's to a slightly quieter next four years.'

Right 28 April 2020. My best mate, River, in a headlock of love. Compression garments cover my arms and hands – I opted for subtle colouring, but you can get pretty wild with it.

Below left 2 September 2020. Measuring up for compression garments for my legs and lower back – a tedious process.

Below right 20 July 2023. Absolutely rocking my dressing change – I huffed that gas so hard I passed out several times.

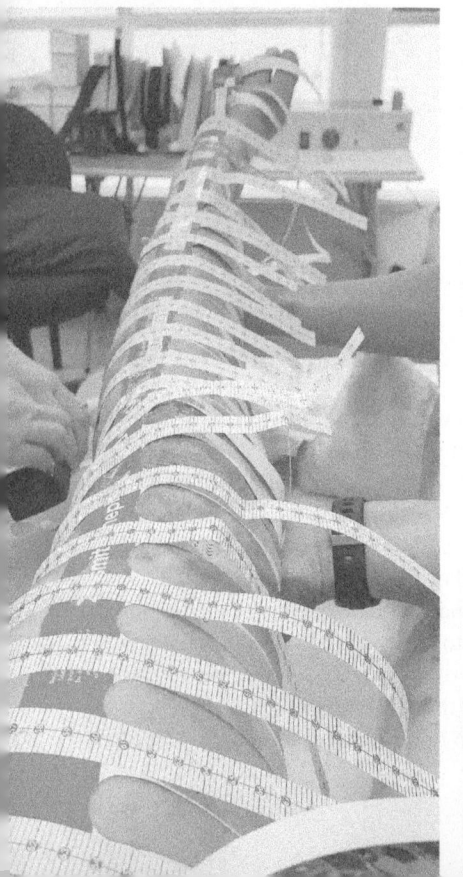

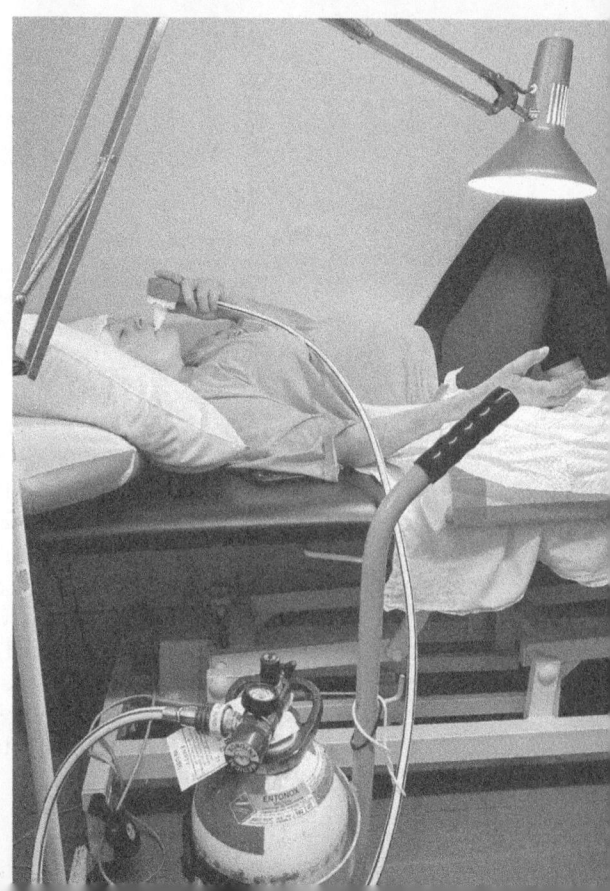

Above 10 October 2023. Saint Andrew's Bay, South Georgia Island. One very happy Kelsey, on the island that changed my outlook on my new life. Who would have thought that another white island could uproot everything again? Not me.

Left 4 December 2023. Teaching River how to get paua – also trying to teach him that he doesn't need to swim out and grab me by the flippers to 'save' me.

Top 29 January 2024. Back out on the beach that tried to take my skin grafts, with my little mate Will.

Right 6 February 2024. Climbing mountains (Mount Maunganui) with friends.

ABOVE 11 January 2025. Little chicken hesitating before diving into Lake Taupō during a 'retreat' (read bootcamp weekend).

Above 26 February 2025. A typical Waghorn family photo.